The Open Mind
and other essays

Donald M. MacKay

Edited by Melvin Tinker

Inter-Varsity Press

INTER-VARSITY PRESS
38 De Montfort Street, Leicester LE1 7GP, England

First published 1988

British Library Cataloguing in Publication Data
Mackay, Donald M. (Donald MacCrimmon), *1922–1987*
The open mind and other essays
1. Christian doctrine – related to science
I. Title II. Tinker, Melvin
261.5'5

ISBN 0-85110-640-4

Set in Linotron Ehrhardt
Typeset in Great Britain by Parker Typesetting Service, Leicester
Printed in Great Britain by
Biddles Ltd, Guildford

Inter-Varsity Press is the book-publishing division of the Universities and Colleges Christain Fellowship (formerly the Inter-Varsity Fellowship), a student movement linking Christian Unions in universities and colleges throughout the United Kingdom and the Republic of Ireland, and a member movement of the International Fellowship of Evangelical Students. For information about local and national activities write to UCCF, 38 De Montfort Street, Leicester LE1 7GP.

Contents

Acknowledgments

The following essays have appeared elsewhere: Chapter 1, in *Science and Faith Today*, Lutterworth Press, 1950; chapters 2 and 16, in *Science, Chance and Providence*, Oxford University Press, 1978; chapter 3, in *Where Science and Faith Meet*, Inter-Varsity Fellowship, 1953; chapter 4, in *Faith and Thought: The Journal of the Victoria Institute*, Vol. 97, No. 1, Spring 1968; chapter 5, in *Christianity in a Mechanistic Universe*, Inter-Varsity Press, 1965; chapter 6, in *Cerebral Correlates of Conscious Experience*, eds. P. H. Buser and A. Rougheul-Buser, North Holland Publishing Co., Amsterdam, 1978; chapter 7, in *Horizons in Science*, ed. Carl Henry, Harper and Row, New York, 1978; chapter 8, in *The Journal of the Institute for Reformational Studies*, 219, 1986; chapter 10, in *Faith and Thought: The Journal of the Victoria Institute*, Vol. 107, No. 3; chapter 11, in *Christian Graduate*; chapter 12, in *Essential Christianity*, 1961; chapter 14, in *Philosophy: The Journal of the Royal Institute of Philosophy*, 47, No. 179, 1–18, Cambridge University Press, 1972; chapter 15, in *Scottish Journal of Theology*, 21, 13–26, Scottish Academic Press, 1968; chapter 17, in *Faith and Thought*, Vol. 113, No. 2, 1987; chapter 18, in *Journal of the American Scientific Affiliation*, Vol. 38, No. 2, 1986.

Foreword: Donald MacCrimmon MacKay 1922–1987

This collection of some of Donald MacKay's best short writings is in the nature of a portrait, but those of us who knew him and owed much to him are conscious of how much more could be said. It is not only that he wrote more books and technical articles; the man himself was a large part of his influence. He showed, as so many great scientists before him have done, a transparent love for his Creator and eager delight in exploring his world. His was a bounding mind that found the clarification of ideas a joy as well as a necessity. Being firmly persuaded that all truth comes from the God of truth, he moved with enthusiasm, enjoyment and a mind at peace to meet whatever fresh ideas and discoveries this God was placing in his path each day.

Donald MacKay was born and brought up in the far north of Scotland. His father and three uncles were ministers of the Free Church, and aunts were missionaries overseas. In childhood a foundation was laid of knowledge of the Bible, and of theological thinking based on it, which stayed with him all his life. During his time as an undergraduate at St Andrews he came to feel how inadequate was the then popular notion, with which he had grown up, that one defended Christianity by 'clever arguments to show the limits of science'. These essays show how he eventually put in the place of that approach a much more biblical and constructive outlook which made him a pioneer thinker in the science and faith debate.

On leaving the Admiralty he taught physics for fourteen years at

King's College, London. In the immediately post-war years he became a pioneer in the rapidly developing new discipline of information theory as well as in high-speed analogue computing. A year in the States in 1951 as a Rockefeller Fellow stimulated him to apply these new insights and tools to the understanding of the mechanisms of the brain, particularly in perception. Theory triggered experiment, and so began an impressive life-long series of observations and elegant experiments largely on the human visual system. For over thirty years he was in the top flight in the fields of experimental psychology and physiology and has been justly described as 'one of the world's foremost thinkers on the organization of the brain'. He was esteemed and appreciated by his colleagues across the world not only for his experimental work but also – indeed above all – for the *clarity* of his incisive and well-stocked mind.

In addition to his professorship at the University of Keele, he held numerous special lectureships at universities in Britain, Canada and the States. He also lectured in Australia, Japan and most of the countries of Europe. For many years he served as a principal editor of the two international journals *Experimental Brain Research* and *Biological Cybernetics*, and of the classic *Handbook of Sensory Physiology*.

The start of his education in thinking *philosophically* he traced to the time when he travelled daily to London from Windsor with a former professor of philosophy, Sir Walter Moberly. At about that time too he became an early member of a group that met informally under the chairmanship of Professor Karl Popper to discuss topics in the then new field of philosophy of science. MacKay's interests – from the technical end – in information, in meaning, in the theory of measurement , and in the relation between brain and mind kept him for forty years in active involvement with the philosophical world.

He was ever critical of sloppy thinking. Only the best was acceptable in the service of the God of truth. He wanted to be always corrigible and to avoid defending any position, however traditionally or piously held, if it was not valid. The results were sometimes disconcerting to his allies in the religious fold – until they realized that he was after something better and could not bear to see a good cause being spoilt by bad arguments.

In all, he personified a rare combination of abilities to think, debate and contribute constructively in the fields of science, philosophy and theology. He was at home and honoured in the highest circles in all three fields. Someone who greatly respected his scientific work once asked him whether he was any relation of the Donald MacKay who wrote on philosophy!

But the man himself was quite as important as his published work. He was for many years a most sought-after speaker for all kinds of occasions, and this was partly because of his superb handling of questions in discussion after his lucid addresses and his admirable dealing with individuals who came to talk to him. Even when he was seriously unwell and only a few months before his death he evoked admiration for his handling of the assortment of questions which followed each of his Gifford Lectures in Glasgow. [The Gifford Lectures are to be published by Blackwells shortly.] As time goes on we become increasingly aware of how much we miss him and regret our inability to consult him.

He was often asked to speak and write on subjects in the area of Christian apologetics, especially on the relation of science and faith. At one stage he not infrequently spoke at two or three such meetings in a week, mainly to students. Often he combined this with technical lectures to university departments and so tried to demonstrate the harmony of academic scholarship and warm faith for which he was such a successful advocate. He was the major influence in forming the thinking of a whole generation of British Christians in the sciences. Echoes of Donald MacKay are constantly heard in the speaking and writing of others both in Britain and North America. In this, however, he was not content with winning intellectual battles. He had the heart of an evangelist and there are many for whom he provided some of the crucial steps from opposition or agnosticism to a clear Christian faith. One of these steps for many was the simple realization that we not only can afford to be honest, but absolutely must be honest if we are to come to know the God of truth. He often mentioned biblical passages such as John 7:17 which stated the necessity of openness to the truth, however uncomfortable, if we are to get anywhere.

He was far from being a mere academic lecturer or debater. He was sought out by students and many others for personal advice because he was such a wise counsellor. He was also full of fun and knew how to defuse or liven up a situation with wit and humour. He was excellent company for young and old, learned and unlearned. To be the guest in his home was to be welcomed most warmly, made totally at ease, and treated to lively and stimulating conversation which frequently contained fresh ideas on all sorts of topics.

Some of his most memorable emphases or peculiarly apt phrases and analogies are to be found in this set of articles. But one cannot forget his comparison of our daily fellowship with God to that of a dog going for a walk with his master and busy about his own affairs, while always keeping one eye on the master and his direction so that he is never too far away, always responding to the lead given. He could move naturally from the most technical discussion of some question of brain science to this sort of description of the Christian faith. His caution when facts are few was expressed by his dictum that in such a situation we should 'keep mind open and mouth shut'. But this was matched by his confidence that there is objective truth to which we must get as near as possible so that both in science and faith we shall know with sufficient certainty to be able to live by it.

This set of articles can only partially capture the warmth of his impact, and the naturalness of his faith and daily relationship to God. We all learned from him something of the need for that intellectual courage and integrity that must go with the simplicity of a confident personal faith. His faith was in the God who gives us the material world to enjoy and turn to our good – so that he was an enthusiastic scientist, working extremely hard and working always with humility and that openness of mind that he advocated to others. But he knew that God had also revealed himself personally in Christ so that we can as a result enjoy knowing God. As he put it on one occasion, 'The same Master expects me to do justice to the data he gives me in science and to the grace that he gives me in Jesus Christ'. In both areas he helped to teach us to respond humbly, with joy and thanksgiving, to the reality that God puts before us.

Oliver Barclay

Preface

For well over a quarter of a century, Donald MacKay received international recognition as being both a brilliant scientist and an outstanding Christian thinker. The many exciting and highly orginal contributions he made to exploring the relations between science and the Christian faith meant that in so many respects he was without equal.

The present posthumous selection from his writings includes essays dealing with his definitive themes such as complementarity, the logical indeterminacy surrounding our free choices and the notion of Chance. In addition there is fresh material, which has not previously been published.

Donald MacKay was first and foremost a scientist, but since he was a man of wide-ranging interests, this representative selection covers a rich variety of topics which will be of interest well beyond the scientific and philosophical fold. They represent a sustained effort to think clearly and compassionately on issues as diverse as human engineering, artificial intelligence, value-free knowledge, determinism and creation. Several of the pieces were originally addressed to Christian audiences, but there is much here which will be of immense value to any honest seeker after truth. MacKay's professional expertise in the theory of meaning and communication made it natural for him as a Christian layman to make penetrating contributions to thought on biblical interpretation, the nature of theological language and the way God's good news can be related to our contemporaries. Throughout there is that clarity of thought and expression coupled with a no-nonsense eagerness for what is good and true so characteristic of the man himself.

The essays have been so arranged as to ensure that there is a certain progression for the reader, with later papers building upon ideas already met in the earlier ones. The first ten or so, though not solely directed at a scientific readership, have what one might call a 'scientific' locus of concern. The majority of the remainder have a more 'theological' slant. Such a distinction, however, is only one of emphasis since both aspects of Donald MacKay's thinking are interwoven throughout.

In assembling this all-round portrait of a supremely open and joyful mind, I have been deeply appreciative of the suggestions and guidance of Dr Oliver Barclay and Mr Paul Helm. Above all, I would like to express my deepest appreciation to Dr Valerie MacKay for her seemingly tireless effort in collecting and sorting through a mass of literature and for her gentle encouragement and wise advice in the final compilation of this volume.

Melvin Tinker, Keele University, 1988

1

Persons and things[1]

The idea that it is harder for a scientist than for anyone else to be a Christian is quite widespread these days – though of course it is by no means new. 'How *can* you square your Christian faith with this stuff you write about the brain as a machine?' is the sort of question in which I meet it most often.

I should perhaps explain that I am a physicist, who has become interested in the brain viewed as a 'mechanism for handling information' – a puzzle that is now attracting the efforts of scientists from a good many traditionally separate disciplines. I am also a Christian. And it is the sense in which a scientist can honestly say this which seems to present a problem to many people.

Now I certainly don't pretend that I've 'got all the answers' to the questions people have in mind when they ask how I square my faith with my science. But I would like to give you some idea of the way in which the two seem in my own experience to dovetail together. Perhaps most of all I want to help dispel any impression that one's faith and one's science have to be kept safely insulated from one another, each in its private preserve. The really interesting thing to me is the way they each sparkle into more meaningful life as one deliberately seeks to interrelate them.

Let us begin with the most radical question: How can I do my kind of research and be a Christian at all? Doesn't Christianity teach that man is more than a mere mechanism, so that it is really impious to seek to explain his behaviour in mechanical terms?

I think questions like that are sometimes based on a false notion of what a scientist is doing when he sets about the study of the brain; so let me first give you a rough picture of the problem he faces.

The brain comprises an intricate network of thousands of millions of tiny nerve cells and fibres, each quite a complex living individual and all constantly flashing electrical signals to one another in a restless activity that never ceases entirely even in sleep. Sensitive electrical amplifiers can tell us a good deal – more than we know how to interpret – of the scurry of activity going on under the surface. By applying small electric currents we can add to this activity from outside, perhaps making a leg or arm suddenly move – to the great surprise of the patient – or even arousing vivid hallucinations, according to the part of the brain we stimulate. There are quite a variety of ways in which chemical stimuli can influence the brain, too.

From a multitude of observations of this general kind we are gradually gaining a rough idea of what a good many parts of the brain are for – at least we can answer some of the questions we have thought of asking so far. One area receives messages from the eye; another, less sharply defined, controls leg movements; and so on. In fact, on most of the structures of the brain you could find quite a few pages of information of this 'functional' sort in current textbooks. It would be terribly incomplete, even debatable, information, much of it. But the point I want to make is that the scientist now *accepts* the brain as a self-consistent physical system. He has puzzles in plenty, but none of a kind to suggest that a complete account of what the brain does could not in principle be given in physical terms. To put it in another way, the scientist's description of the brain leaves no room for any 'mystery-box' that might conceivably be a 'seat of the mind'.

Not so long ago it was a fashionable guess that the mind might inhabit the little pineal gland in the middle of the head; but nowadays I'm afraid that even this refuge is denied it. Is the scientist then trying to squeeze the mind out of existence, as part of a general programme to replace God by mechanism? Of course not. What he has forced us to realize is that when we speak of mind we don't mean something that has a *seat* at all. Our whole approach is wrong and can only lead to nonsense, if we think of the mind as living like a ghost in some local part of the head. What the scientist is trying to do is to give as complete an account of human behaviour as possible, from the standpoint of an observer, using a language whose terms presuppose that standpoint.

He does not deny for a moment the validity of an account, in quite different terms, presupposing the standpoint of the actor himself. But it would be simply a logical error to mix terms that presuppose one standpoint with terms that presuppose another, and he doesn't do it.

To treat a description in the language of the observer as if it were a rival of a description in the language of the actor is rather as if someone who did not understand algebra were to try to 'debunk' a printed algebra problem by proving that there was 'nothing but ink' on the page. Of course he would be telling the truth. There is nothing but ink there. But the algebra problem is not a ghost inhabiting one of the ink-patches. He will never find it as *something left over* after making an inventory of all the ink on the page. He will find it only by a different approach to the *very same data.*

This is a poor analogy in some ways, though it brings out one or two useful points. Obviously I am not suggesting that the scientist is silly to study the brain in the way he does. He is using a perfectly valid and useful method for his purpose. Nor is it fair, as even some Christians have done, to describe the scientist's method as 'incomplete' or as 'leaving something out', as if it could and ought to be improved so as to make room for Mind in his inventory. 'Mind' is not in the physical inventory because it doesn't belong there, any more than the algebra problem had a place in the inventory of ink-patches.

What our analogy does make clear, I think, is that you cannot debunk one account of a situation merely by producing a different account that fits the facts. If both are supported by the facts and consistent with one another (like the ink-description and the algebra-description) then both are true and that's that! The two, as we say, are complementary. It looks, in fact, as if the old debate, as to whether man was 'nothing but' a mechanism or 'something more', arose not because people were disagreed about facts but rather because both sides were agreed in accepting a wrong formulation of the problem. Our suggestion would be that it needn't be a matter of 'either . . . or' at all, but only one of deciding which description is appropriate in which circumstances. 'All right,' you may say, 'I can see that the Christian view of man needn't be incompatible with a thorough-going scientific attitude to the mechanism of his brain. But if it's just a matter of judging appropriateness – who is to decide?'

This is obviously an important point. Let us consider it in terms of a practical example and ask the question: 'Why if there are natural causes, should we decide that one description is more appropriate than the other?' Now it is here that our distinction between actor-language and observer-language comes in. If I were deliberately to choose to neglect some duty, I don't doubt that an ideal scientific observer could in principle give a complete account, though not necessarily a prediction, of the corresponding physical processes in my brain and body, probably using typical 'observer-words' like 'electric current', 'nerve cell', or 'chemical concentration'. At the same time, I myself as the actor could offer an equally valid account of my behaviour in terms of words like 'purpose', 'choice', and 'responsibility'. These are words that we understand mainly because we ourselves are people who purpose, choose, and feel responsibility. They are typical 'actor-words'.

You can probably see now how the question of appropriateness normally settles itself. If I freely choose to neglect my duty, it would be illogical for me to offer an observer-account of my lapse, for concepts like 'my choosing' do not belong to observer-accounts. On the other hand, if I've been hit on the head and so prevented from doing my duty, it is entirely appropriate to account for my failure in terms of natural causes, since it is a physical situation, describable in observer-language, that I have to explain. In other words, I can account for my physical disabilities in terms of causes, but I can account for my free choices only in terms of reasons. The golden rule is: Don't mix your languages. Words or concepts defined for different logical backgrounds don't mix.

Of course, I am not saying that there is no connection between accounts in the two languages. I know, for example, that if I take certain drugs, I shall probably impair my power of moral judgment. The point is that if I choose to take the drug, I take with it responsibility for the resulting impairment and its outcome.

In fact I do not really see how any description in observer-language can ever release us from our responsibility as actors, as long as we are capable of saying: 'I choose to do this, and take the consequences.'

But let us come back to less theoretical ground. Granted that the Christian view of man is at least tenable, and that there are good logical reasons against assigning natural causes for things like my deliberate lapses from duty, is the Christian view true? Let me say at once that I am not going to try to prove that it is true. Indeed I doubt very much whether any argument can do more than prove the Christian position to be not unreasonable. If an argument claims to do more, then for me at least it is suspect.

'How then do you expect people to adopt the Christian position?' you may ask. This brings us to a much more personal level, on which a scientist can speak with no special authority. But I can say that I was hung up myself at this point for a long time, looking for some kind of logical proof that would compel me to assent to Christian doctrines, and restlessly dismissing each argument I came to as inconclusive. The mistake I made lay in thinking that becoming a Christian *was* just a matter of adopting a position – of taking up a set of beliefs, and maintaining them by argument. I was putting the cart before the horse, of course, as I realized eventually.

The basis of a Christian's conviction of the truth of his faith is not that he has solved an intellectual riddle, but that he has come to know a living Person – the Person of Jesus Christ. It is his new relationship with God that makes the doctrine ring true, and not the other way round. The reason that so many of us lack this conviction is, I think, not that the evidence is not available, but that we look for the wrong kind of evidence in the wrong way. We look for facts and arguments, instead of being prepared to be met by a Person. At least, so it was with me.

This already may sound preposterously mysterious language for a scientist, and I must try to explain what I mean. Let us suppose we are meeting a human friend. 'A mass of pink protoplasm rises to a height of five feet and begins to pucker and wobble up and down noisily' – but, of course, that's the wrong language. I should say, 'He rises to his feet wreathed in smiles and greets us heartily.' Why should I? Because we came to meet a person, not just a thing, and it makes more sense to describe what happened in personal terms.

Now that is just what a Christian means when he says that he knows Jesus Christ as a living Person. He finds that all kinds of experience, still perfectly describable in ordinary terms, can come to demand interpretation as meetings with that Person – sometimes when least expected. So reading the Bible, for example, has often become for me a meeting with Christ. By this I mean that the experience of reading has had for me the full significance of an interview with a friend who is alive and addresses me. I don't mean that I have heard a mysterious voice as I've read; on the other hand I do mean something much more than mere metaphor. There is a metaphorical sense in which I may be said to meet Shakespeare in his sonnets; but the Christ who meets the Christian in the New Testament or in the Church may meet him also in the bustle of daily routine, may meet him in guidance at a difficult moment, may meet him in command or rebuke. He is alive. And it is the constant experience of his living presence that forms the basis of the Christian's faith, and at the same time safeguards it from degenerating into speculative nonsense.

To me, as a scientist, I think nothing is so satisfying as the Christian revelation that this Person whom I know as friend and worship as Lord is also the author of all the activity that we experience and study as the physical universe. You can see, I think, how lightheartedly the Christian who is a scientist can plunge into any worthwhile line of research, and how groundless he would deem any fears that some new discovery might upset the faith.

Let me end with an example of what I mean by all this. I suppose we have all come across passages from Christ's Sermon on the Mount. You will find the fullest account in St Matthew's Gospel from chapter 5 to chapter 7. There we read sentences like this: 'Blessed are the meek, for they will inherit the earth.' 'Blessed are the peacemakers, for they will be called sons of God.' And we say so often, do we not, 'Ah yes, if only everyone would live up to the Sermon on the Mount, the world would be a better place.' In other words – let us face it – our natural inclination is to read this Sermon as directed at the other fellow.

I must confess that I find it easier to read it in this way. But if I want to meet Christ in reading it, the first requirement is that I must read it as addressing me. And when I do that, willing that Christ should address me, my experience is entirely different. I am indeed aware of a lot of facts and duties enjoined. But above all I am aware of the presence with me of the living Master whose words are addressing me, meeting me in divine love that never seems changed by my utter failure to live up to his standard. It is the realization of how far short I come of returning this love of Christ that makes real to me those often-misunderstood Christian concepts, the sense of sin and the need of forgiveness.

Now from the very nature of my research I am convinced that all these experiences are mine through processes of which complementary accounts could, in principle, be given in terms of psychology and physics. It is what a Christian should expect, since his body is part of God's world. This, however, in no way alters the fact that to me the significance of what happens (just as in our earlier example) is most appropriately described in terms of personal encounter. To substitute one of the other descriptions would do less than justice to the facts.

I sincerely hope that in saying all this I have not given you the impression that meeting Christ is an easy matter of just making up one's mind to do so. In a sense these requirements are simple to understand, but they may be far from easy to meet. It is like making an apology – you know all you have to do; it's not so easy to do it.

But if hitherto you have found that with the best will in the world you have not been able to make sense of the New Testament, I do commend this approach, not simply to the Sermon on the Mount, or even to the four Gospels, but to the whole. It is a matter on which no-one can decide as a spectator. The experiment must be made.

2

A scientist in God's world[1]

1. Fog

There is today, it seems, a fog of confusion around the issue of science and faith quite as dense as that which enveloped the unfortunate Darwin a century ago. Even if wholesale fog dispersal is beyond our means, I hope it may not be too ambitious to try to clear the air around some of the main points at issue.

My plan will be the converse of the more traditional pattern of defensive apologetics. What I shall be arguing is not just that Christian belief is compatible with the methods and findings of science, but that the two belong together as naturally as root and fruit. So instead of starting with the scientific world picture as a given thing, solidly established on unchallengeable foundations, and then later asking what room is left for particular religious claims, it will serve our purpose better to ask first what it is that Christians believe our Creator has told us about the nature of our world: about its fundamental dependence (and our dependence) upon his creative power, and about the purpose for which he has brought us into being. Along this biblical-theistic path, if you will have the patience to follow me, I believe we shall then see the habit of mind we call 'scientific' emerging as something not incidental to Christian obedience, but rather naturally expressing it. I hope to show that any sense of 'irreconcilable contradiction' between the suppositions of Christian faith and those of science is in fact an illusion whose causes are understandable, but whose basis can be seen to be false whether or not one accepts the truth of biblical Christianity.

2. Dynamic stability

'I believe in one God, Maker of heaven and earth.' So says the ancient creed of the Christian church. The claim of biblical theism is that the world in which we find ourselves is not eternally self-sufficient; it has a Maker, on whom it depends not just for some initial impulse long ago, but for its daily continuance in existence now. This is strange language to our modern ears. The world we know seems very stable, reasonably law-abiding (in the non-human domain at least), and not at all obviously in need of any divine power to keep it going.

Over the past 200 years and more we have become accustomed to thinking of it in the image of a mechanism, intricate perhaps beyond the grasp of human understanding, but still something self-running and self-contained. Thinking in these terms, we might see some point in bringing in God as the original creator of the universe; but we might find it particularly hard to visualize any sense in which a universe, once created, could continue to depend on its creator for its existence.

Without pretending to fathom the mysterious depths of these biblical claims, I believe we can get some feeling for what they mean from the imagery of modern physics itself. Ask a physicist to describe what he finds as he probes deeper and deeper into the fine structure of our solid world, and he will tell you a story of an increasingly *dynamic* character. Instead of a frozen stillness, he discovers a buzz of activity that seems to intensify as the magnification increases. The molecules he pictures as the stuff of the chair you are sitting on – and of the body sitting in it – are all believed to be in violent motion, vibrating millions of times in a second, or even careering about in apparent disarray, with an energy depending on the temperature. Each of the atoms composing those molecules is thought of as a theatre of even more dramatic activity, at first likened by Niels Bohr to the whirling of tiny planets around a central sun, but nowadays pictured, if pictured at all, as the vibrations of a cloud whose shape and density determine the probability of various kinds of discrete events called light-emission, electron-absorption, and the like. According to modern physics, it is to such elementary *events* – myriads of them, continually recurring – that we owe all our experience of the solid world of objects. Even the fundamental particles postulated by theoretical physicists as the building bricks of our world are thought of as spending their time in snapping from one to another of a variety of different states, or even in continually exchanging identities.

For our present purpose it does not matter for how long physics is likely to go on using these particular images. I mention them now only to illustrate a key concept that I think may help us to grasp what the biblical writers mean when they say that the stable existence of our world depends on the creative activity of God. We can call it *dynamic stability*. In our everyday experience chairs, tables, rocks are typically stable objects. There they are. Nothing may seem to be happening to them, or in them, for most of their existence; yet the modern physicist is quite content to describe such stable objects of our experience as a concurrence of unimaginably complex and dramatic submicroscopic events, without any suggestion that he is contradicting the facts of experience. All he claims is that their stability is not static but *dynamic*. The quiet solidity of physical objects, he would say, reflects the coherence of uncountable myriads of *events* at the atomic or subatomic level, each of which by itself might seem almost unrelated to its neighbours in space or time.

For another and rather different illustration of dynamic stability,[2] ask a television engineer to explain the patterns of light and shade that form the image on the face of a TV tube, say when we are watching the Trooping of the Colour. All that is happening on the screen, he will assure us, is but a succession of isolated sparks of light produced by electron-impact; yet because of the regularities in the *programme* of signals controlling the intensity of the beam of electrons, these sparks fall into a coherent pattern, forming stable images of the objects we are watching. Whether the scene is one of violent change or of perfect calm, or indeed whether it continues in being at all, depends entirely on the modulating programme. Any stability the picture has is a dynamic or contingent stability, conditional on the maintenance in being and the coherence of the succession of event-giving signals.

Perhaps a still better example for our purpose would be the kind of 'television tennis game' that modern electronics has made possible, where the players can control the movement of various objects appearing on a TV screen by means of the knobs and switches on a 'black box' in their own livingroom. Here again, the 'ball' and the 'bat' are dynamically stable patches of light held in being by a coherent succession of control signals, and moved around the screen by changing the timing of these control signals. But in this case what we are watching is not a representation of the real world as seen through some distant television camera. It is an *artifically created* scene, in which every object owes both its existence and its motions directly to the sustaining programme generated by the black box, as modulated by the players. Not only the contents of this synthetic world, but its laws of motion too, have dynamic rather than static stability. They are perfectly stable, for just as long as the generating programme is stable. But at the flick of a switch the contents of the synthetic world can alter completely, different laws of motion can come into operation, or the whole show can disappear without trace.

I need hardly say that none of these examples of dynamic stability is meant as an explanatory *model* of our mysterious dependence on God as portrayed in the Bible. But if we ask the writers of the Bible what makes our world tick – the sort of question that underlies any attempt to build a science of nature – we will find them using remarkably similar language. From the biblical standpoint, all the contents of our world, ourselves included, have to be 'held in being' by the continual exercise of God's sustaining power. In Christ, says Paul, 'all things were created, in heaven and on earth, visible and invisible ... all things were created through him and for him. He is before all things, and in him *all things hold together'* (Colossians 1:16-17 RSV). Or, as the writer to the Hebrews puts it: 'In these last days [God] has spoken to us by a Son, whom he appointed the heir of all things, through whom also he created the world. He reflects the glory of God and bears the very stamp of his nature, *upholding the universe by his word of power'* (Hebrews 1:2-3 RSV). For biblical theism, then, it is clear that the continuing existence of our world is not something to be taken for granted. Rather it hangs moment by moment on the continuance of the upholding word of power of its creator, as dependent on this as the picture on a TV screen is on the maintaining programme of signals.

Not that there is any hint of unreality or illusion about the solid contents of our world – they are as real as we ourselves, as real as their creator has conceived them to be. But their stability is nevertheless declared to be a dynamic, contingent, stability. It is only in and through the continuing say-so of their and our Creator that they cohere or 'hold together'. He is the giver of being, moment by moment, to all the events in and through which we encounter the world of physical objects, *our own bodies included*. This last point is important. Unlike the detached viewers of a television screen, we know the objects of our world by interacting with them – finding ourselves up against them, obliged to reckon with them in the space of our own agency. But however uncompromisingly realist its tone, the Bible has no room for the idea of matter as something eternally self-sufficient or indestructible. The Psalmist may praise God for the stability of the earth and the reliability of the normal links between events on which our rational expectations are based (Psalm 93:1; 104 *passim*); but the same Book of Psalms speaks of a time when the earth and the heavens will perish and will be changed 'as a vesture' at the will of their Creator (Psalm 102: 25-27). In the end, for biblical theism, the only solid reality is God and what God holds in being. I hope to show that this one framework offers all the support needed both for the scientific enterprise and for the life of Christian faith.

3. Science in a created world

In order to make good this claim, I suggest we begin by trying to imagine that we had never heard of modern science, and then asking ourselves what would follow if we took seriously the biblical picture of our world as dynamically stable, and dependent for its coherence on the stability of its Author's creative will. In the first place, we would obviously be urged to recognize and respond appropriately to the 'givenness' of all the twists and turns of our experience. Equally we would recognize the regular succession of day and night, winter and summer, and so forth, as tokens of the coherence and stability of the creative purpose of their Giver, in which the biblical writers see evidence of God's personal faithfulness to his creatures (Genesis 8:22; Psalm 104).

But there are two emphases in the Bible that would I think stand out as particularly relevant to our prospects of founding a viable scientific enterprise. First, from the Book of Genesis onward, man is commanded by his Creator to make use of ('subdue') the created order intelligently for his benefit – not (*pace* Toynbee[3]) in selfish greed, but in a spirit of gratitude and responsible stewardship (Genesis 1:28-30) and reverent admiration for its Giver (Psalm

111:2). Loving the Lord our God with all our mind must include using our minds in a search for the patterns according to which events in his universe are reliably predictable. The more we know of these, the better the foresight we can exercise as responsible stewards. So for someone with the appropriate talents, to gain knowledge and understanding of the created order is more than a permissible human recreation; it can be a duty to its Giver, the God of all truth.

So far, so good. But just how should our minds be used to gain knowledge? Medieval scholasticism, following in the Greek tradition of Aristotle, saw the task as essentially one of teasing out the logical consequences of the definitions of the objects in the world. As Michael Foster[4] has put it, if you start from the assumption that the essence of a natural object is definable, as the essence of a geometrical object is, then you will have no more use for empirical evidence in establishing the conclusions of natural science than in establishing the conclusions of Euclidean geometry. This is not to say that sensory experience played no part in ancient science, but that it played a different part: it supplied the *illustration* but not the *evidence* of the conclusions of science.

And here we come up against the second key emphasis in biblical theism. The God of the Bible is no mere craftsman, shaping pre-existing matter into forms definable *a priori* in abstract terms. He is a free and unconditioned *Creator*: the giver of being to a world of his own devising whose nature could neither be defined nor fully deduced by reference to any first principles.[5]

Of such a world, knowledge by logical deduction from definitions is out. Only sensory experience can offer a valid basis for natural science. To us nowadays this conclusion may seem so obvious as hardly to need stating; but this only shows how complete was the eventual victory of the Hebraic doctrine of God and nature over the scornful opposition of the Graeco-medieval tradition. The point for the moment is that biblical theism, by denying that we can lay down in advance what the world ought to be like, offers positive encouragement to the experimental approach to nature that we now take for granted as 'scientific'. The history of the rise of modern science amply illustrates the crucial effect of this doctrine in liberating and inspiring the pioneers of empirical investigation.[6]

4. 'Customs of the Creator'

So far, we have seen that anyone who takes biblical theism seriously will have a strong incentive to gain systematic knowledge of his world, and to do so by meticulous and unprejudiced observation rather than by working out in advance the way things 'ought' to be. A sovereign Creator is not to be tied by what his human creatures judge to be 'reasonable'. But if we were to stop there, the prospect for our science might seem rather bleak: a matter of endless, patient description, with no hint of explanation other than the inscrutable will of the Creator. With such a God surely *anything* might happen? What hope could there be of our making coherent sense of the pattern of events?

To this question one obvious answer is, 'Well, why not try it, and see?'; but there are also important grounds for optimism in what the Bible itself has to say about the *character* of God. The biblical Creator may be all-powerful, and answerable to none of his creatures; but he is not capricious. He is the God of order, dependability, faithfulness. So our theistic scientist would certainly have an incentive at least to look for, if not to predict, a corresponding orderliness in the pattern of observed events in the created world.

As we all know, this adventure of faith has been rewarded beyond the wildest dreams of those who launched it in the sixteenth and seventeenth centuries. The pattern of natural events has turned out to have a marvellously intelligible structure. The regularities – the 'customs of the Creator' as they were called by the pioneers – are of two kinds. The first and most obvious are those of simple succession or co-occurrence: night follows day, summer follows winter, the sun reaches its zenith simultaneously at points on the same meridian; but we would not speak of one of these pairs of events as a *cause* of the other. The second kind of regularity we call *causal*. Crop failure follows drought, intoxication follows over-indulgence in alcohol, thunder follows the discharge of lightning. The challenge to the scientist is to discover what he calls the 'mechanism' underlying these observed correlations. In the case of thunder, for example, he will talk of electrical discharge producing heat; heat producing sudden expansion of the air; sudden expansion producing a shock wave; and so on. Each link in that chain represents a more general type of correlation which has been observed often enough to be taken for granted. If we are not content to take these correlations for granted, more detailed 'mechanisms' can be sketched which exhibit each as the resultant of a still finer chain-mesh of cause-and-effect. Ultimately, the scientist's aim is to find a set of general principles so comprehensive that all such causal sequences can be recognized as instances or combinations of a few basic kinds of regularity. Such basic principles, established by long enough precedent under sufficiently testing conditions, tend to be called 'laws of nature'; an event is said to be 'explained' scientifically if we can show that it *conforms to the general precedent* expressed in such 'laws'. In effect, to explain something scientifically means to show that it *ought not to have surprised* anyone who knew the initial conditions and the general customs of the Creator.

In these terms a scientific *theory* of a phenomenon is an attempt to link together expectations based on accepted general precedent, in such a way that (if the theory is sufficiently 'deterministic') all future instances of the phenomenon can be recognized (at least in principle) as what *ought to have been expected* by a sufficiently well-informed observer. 'Nothing else *could have* happened', we sometimes say; but what we mean – or what we are strictly justified in meaning – is only that nothing else could have been expected on the basis of precedent. In *our explanatory model* of the situation, only one thing could have happened in those circumstances; but in the end it is for reality to call the tune.

In this sense, although scientific laws do not make things happen, they do more than just describe the way things happen. They also *prescribe* the expectations that would be rational on the basis of precedent. To develop such a theory of the connections between events is, from a biblical standpoint, an act of stewardship that should help men to serve their Creator more effectively. To neglect to do so would be to fail in our religious duty.

5. Two questions

Starting from a basis in the biblical doctrine of God and nature, we have reached a point at which the whole enterprise of experimental science emerges as an expression of Christian responsibility, with no hint of tension between the two. But before we go further there are two questions that you may feel inclined to raise.

First, does not the idea of *looking for a precedent* for a particular created event in terms of earlier created events presuppose that the Creator is *bound* in some way by precedent? How does this square with the idea that he is free and sovereign? The biblical answer is that the Creator has freely undertaken the creation of 'a cosmos, not a chaos'. He is certainly under no *obligation* to maintain precedent; but he encourages us to believe that his sustaining activity actually has both structure and purpose, some of it intelligible enough to be grasped by even our finite minds. The biblical data leave entirely open to investigation the nature and extent of this intelligible structure. There may be fundamental limits to our ability to predict the future on the basis of precedent; and Christianity need have no more stakes in deterministic than in indeterministic theories of the physical world. But in any case a God who was *bound* to conform to observed precedent in all circumstances would not be the sovereign Creator spoken of in the Bible.

A second question would certainly be pressed by those who see science as undermining Christian faith today. Whatever its status in theory, they might say, is not scientific explanation in practice an *alternative* to a religious understanding of events? Obviously in one sense for many of our contemporaries the answer is 'yes'. If the biblical theistic picture is correct, the scientific game of linking events into 'causal chains' can (and indeed should) proceed without bringing in 'God' as one of the links in the chain. For the theist, God comes in as the Giver of all the events, not just as a special kind of link between some of them. It is therefore technically possible to practise science in complete forgetfulness of the One who, according to the Bible, alone gives being to the data, and grounds for the expectations based on them. There is a 'proper secularisation' of science, as R. Hooykaas[7] has put it, even from a biblical standpoint.

What is completely unjustified, however, is the suggestion that successful scientific explanation rationally warrants *disbelief* in the Creator. This would be as illogical as to suggest that finding a causal connection between the impact of the 'bat' and the motion of the 'ball' in the television tennis game eliminates any need for the black box as the sustainer-in-being of the whole show. Explanations in terms of links *within* a created world are logically not in contradiction with, but complementary to, explanations in terms of the power and purpose of the Creator of that world. If, moreover, as the Bible declares, our Creator has a personal purpose in bringing each of *us* into being – a purpose with which our whole eternal destiny is linked – then to ignore this on grounds of our satisfaction with scientific explanations would be irrational and ultimately self-destructive.

6. Miracle

Our argument so far has been running pretty much one way. There are biblical grounds for expecting the normal pattern of God's sustaining activity to conform to precedent, and in that sense to be scientifically explicable. To discover such explanations does nothing to diminish the direct dependence of the events in question upon God. So far, so good. But the Christian faith also recognizes the category of *miracle*. How does this fit into the picture we have been developing?

There is a sense in which, if the picture is true, every natural event is a miracle: an act of God so marvellous that as John Donne[8] put it, 'only the daily doing takes off the admiration'. But in biblical parlance the term stands for an event that departs from the ordinary run in such a way as to communicate God's personal concern with the situation, and his sovereignty in it. This need not always mean a violation of the precedent we call 'natural'. The drying up of the Red Sea to allow the Israelites to cross could be regarded as miraculous in its timing, whether or not the east wind had a 'natural' explanation. On the other hand, the resurrection of Christ is presented as a unique event with no claim whatsoever to fit with natural precedent. The one who had been done to death was none other than the Creator himself; so, as Peter argues, 'it could not be that death should keep him in its grip' (Acts 2:24 NEB). For such an unprecedented event there could be no rational incentive to seek explanations in terms of precedent.

In our day, as it happens, the swing against science has brought with it so much irrationality and credulity that this aspect of biblical Christianity is in danger of being misperceived. Spoon-benders and occultists delight to mock the staid conventionality of orthodox physics, and there are signs that miracle in the biblical sense is liable to be regarded as in much the same quasi-magical category – even becoming more socially acceptable in some circles as a result. Christians who are tempted to grind apologetic axes on alleged evidence for the 'paranormal' must, however, remember two things. First, if a God who holds in being a dynamically stable world has reason to bring about a unique and unprecedented event, he can do so as easily as you or I could change the pattern of an artificially created sequence on a TV screen, quite regardless of the regularity with which precedent has been observed in the past. It would make no sense to speak of him as 'using hitherto undiscovered laws' to bring it about, since he has merely to say the word, and it is done (Psalm 33:9). To try to make such an event respectable as an instance of a standard class of phenomena called 'paranormal' (which if only we knewenough e could bring about ourselves) would be woefully to mistake its character.

Secondly, it is vital to recognize that the biblical concept of miracle is poles apart from the irrational and the incoherent. What is stressed in the Bible is rather the *fittingness* of a miraculous event, as seen by its Creator, given the circumstances and his concern for those involved. So Peter presents the resurrection of Christ not as a mere magician's act designed to awe us by its inexplicability, but as *what was only to be expected*, given the awesome fact of who Christ was. Such a claim would be only side-tracked, and in no way supported, by any suggestion that the event might 'conform to established paranormal precedents'.

This is perhaps the point at which to express some misgivings about the common use of the (non-biblical) term 'supernatural' to refer to the miraculous. If all it means is 'unprecedented', this is harmless enough; but the term has pagan overtones that can cause confusion. The danger is that it lends credence to a thought-model (derived from ancient Greek sources rather than the Bible) in which 'nature' has a self-sustaining power independent of God, and miracles happen when God 'intervenes' by exerting a superior power. For biblical theism, the miraculous is not so much an intervention (since God's sustaining activity is never absent) as a *change of mode* of the divine agency.

7. Objectivity

We have been trying to work out what it should be like to serve as a scientist in God's world; to take one's mandate for the scientific enterprise from the biblical view of our world and its dependence on God. Contrary to widely propagated belief, we have found nothing but encouragement to build up experimentally based knowledge into a theoretically integrated explanatory framework in which the *concept* of God, for excellent theological reasons, ought not to find an explicit use, even though the *agency* of God is the ground of being of the whole subject-matter. Of 'irreconcilable contradiction' we have found no trace.

Before ending this paper I would like to point out one further consequence of recognizing the biblical God as the Creator of our space-time. Philosophers of science understandably argue as to how objective our scientific knowledge can claim to be. Relativity theory has cast doubt on the idea that one single description of the universe can be completely valid for all observers. Quantum theory in turn challenges the distinction between the observer and the observed. Psychology and sociology have each their own reasons for voicing similar doubts. In face of all this it has proved tempting to some thinkers to abandon the concept of objectivity altogether. If universal knowledge valid for all observers is unattainable, they say, should we not admit that there are as many truths as there are knowers?[9]

In the context of biblical theism such reasoning lacks cogency. Let it be admitted, at least for the sake of argument, that what I would be correct to believe about the world must differ in some particulars from what you would be correct to believe. Still, if the flood of experienced events that you and I each encounter day by day owe their being to one and the same Creator, *he* at least is in a position to know what each of us would be correct to believe, and mistaken to disbelieve, about our world. This, for the Creator, is a matter of objective fact. If he has placed you and me in different relationship to a particular situation, the *differences* between what each of us would be correct to believe about it will be equally for him a question of objective fact. True, our scientist in God's world may have no access to the Creator's-eye view of his situation; but because he knows that he is under judgment by that criterion, he is saved from the trap of confusing relativity with a denial of objectivity.

8. Conclusion

In summary, then, a scientist in God's world who knows and loves the Author of it can rejoice equally in the growth of the explanatory structure of science, and in any surprises that may shake it. For both he returns thanks to the same Giver, recognizing his obligation to do justice both to the normal coherence of the flux of created events, and to its moment-by-moment contingency on the divine fiat. His mind will be open but critical, rational but not rationalistic, realizing that the God of truth is even more concerned than he is that he should not swallow falsehood – but also that he should not disbelieve what is true, however unexpected. He will be careful – especially in his public pronouncements – to distinguish as clearly as possible between data and theoretical extrapolations; chary of baseless speculation; and alert to illegitimate attempts to turn science into scient*ism*. In all this – if he can only be true to it – he may find much of value for the defence of the biblical faith; but the Christian's motive for it can never be one of apologetic expediency. His one desire must be to do the fullest justice to all the data given him by God, to whom he will be accountable for keeping the record straight.

3

Looking for connections[1]

I think we all know the man who spins a tall yarn and then fobs off every attack simply by saying: 'I don't care what evidence you bring: that's what I believe, and I'm sticking to it.' And we know that feeling of helpless bafflement that comes over us with the realization that you can't argue with the man; he's just not prepared to bring his belief to the light of evidence.

Now from time to time I meet a good many people who imagine that in order to be a Christian in this scientific age you have to adopt an attitude rather like that, dividing your mind into two compartments and holding your Christian beliefs in one of them, safely insulated from whatever scientific knowledge you have in the other. I am not going to say that Christians have never given any foundation for this idea. But I am quite convinced, as a Christian who is also a scientist, that it is wrong. I do not believe it is necessary to insulate any Christian doctrine from contact with scientific knowledge. In fact I believe that it is only by seeing and holding each in the context of the other that we can hope to gain a proper understanding of either.

This is why I have taken for my subject this question of 'looking for connections' between faith and science. Nothing, I think, can be more intellectually satisfying if we go about it in the right way. On the other hand I believe that looking for the *wrong* kind of connection holds back many people who are honestly seeking to make up their minds about the claims of Christianity. It held me back for a long time.

I think you will see what I mean if we look first at some of these wrong ways of making connections before going on to ask what it should mean for us to be intellectually honest when trying to tie our science and our Christianity together. For example, there is the quite common approach that we might call 'looking for God in the gaps'. You know the idea. You explain things scientifically as far as you can go, and then bring God in to explain what is left. You agree on a kind of division of territory into 'the bits of nature that science can explain and God can't touch', and 'the bits where science has (so far) failed and (perhaps) God must be at work'. And so, of course, God is left with a steadily dwindling territory, liable to devastation by every new discovery in our morning newspaper.

Now I hope you won't misunderstand me here. I think the ground that science hasn't yet covered is vast – perhaps infinite – in comparision with the little area that we feel we are beginning to understand. The point is that, however imperfectly a scientist understands the processes he studies, it would be advancing a *non-Christian* idea of God to suggest that God was to be seen at work *only* in the bits of nature that puzzle the scientist.

Another thing: to integrate honestly our Christian and our scientific thinking does not mean that we should *adopt the same method* in both. An atomic physicist isn't likely to solve his physical problems by thinking theologically about them; and the method of natural science isn't going to help me very much to understand the message of the New Testament. The man who in the name of intellectual integrity tries to win a wife in the way in which he'd tackle a problem in thermodynamics, has the wrong idea of what intellectual integrity means, and is very likely to remain a bachelor!

No, the 'hard-boiled' approach that we have evolved in natural science serves its own purpose very well. But it can prevent us from seeing some points just as effectively as it helps us to see others; and the honest man here is the man who asks what *kind* of approach should enable him best to grasp the kind of points that Christianity claims to be making.

Now there's a trap here which we must be careful to avoid. Our friend who spins yarns might say that he himself only wants us to adopt the right approach – the approach of irrational credulity of course! – to his stories. If we'd only leave the evidence out of the picture, his tales would sound fine. But of course that is not what I mean at all. I do not believe there is anything scientifically *inconsistent* in Christian doctrine any more than I believe there is anything theologically inconsistent in quantum theory. There is no question of trying to protect the one from the other. When an architect, for example, shows you the ground plan and front view of a house, he may insist that it is useless to look on the ground plan for details of the front door. But he's not concerned to protect himself by saying so!

Like all analogies, this one has its dangers. It may be fair to think of Christian doctrine as presenting a view – or a series of views – of reality to which the scientific picture is complementary. But the fullest Christian understanding should be compared, perhaps, to a mental image of the whole house rather than to any one view of it. Our analogy does however suggest what I think is the proper *spirit* in which to set about looking for connections. To keep scientific and Christian doctrines rigidly apart would be silly as well as potentially dishonest. To try to make them into one by chopping bits from each and pasting them together, or by treating them as rival ways of giving identical information, would be equally to miss the point. We can come to relate them properly only by holding both constantly together in our minds, until little by little there comes to us some glimmering of that greater whole of which they present complementary aspects, the activity and character of God himself: not God seen only in the gaps of the scientific picture, nor God deduced only as the conclusion of a scientific argument, but God revealed as the Author of the whole story.

Now it may be that you agree with me that looking for connections in this way could be both intellectually honest and more than intellectually satisfying. But you might reasonably raise one all-important question. How can you distinguish between two pictures that are genuinely complementary, and two which are really incompatible rivals?

A fair question, indeed. When *are* we justified in insisting that two pictures must be complementary? The answer I think must be: Only when we find that both are necessary to do justice to experience. There is a famous example from my own subject of physics that illustrates well what it means in practice to 'have to do justice to experience'. A hundred years ago the orthodox way of picturing light was in terms of waves spreading through space. There was plenty of evidence for it, and everyone was convinced that the ancient idea of picturing it as a stream of particles was wrong. Then, alas, only fifty years later a whole new set of situations was discovered in which light seemed to behave quite definitely like a hail of tiny particles.

What was to be done? Which was the valid picture – the wave, or the particle one? It took many years of hard and honest thinking before physicists could accept the answer that *both* could be valid.

The two pictures were accepted as complementary and not as rivals only when it became clear that you could never deduce *contradictory* conclusions by a valid use of both; because they represented answers to different kinds of questions.

Not that there was any idea of letting them sit unrelated in watertight mental compartments. People gradually came to see quite definite connections between the two ways of describing light, though these turned out to be of a new and unexpected kind. But what I want to bring out is not the analogy between these connections and those we are looking for, but the way in which, even before the physicists could see any connections, they were compelled in loyalty to the facts to find room for both pictures. For however satisfied we may be that two pictures are compatible, it is only *facts of experience* that can convince us that both are *necessary*.

So, in the same way, it is because he finds that both the scientific and the Christian pictures are necessary to do justice to his own experience that the scientist who is a Christian can distinguish each of them from nonsensical speculation, and is compelled in honesty to make room for both in his thinking.

I do not mean that his faith is something purely subjective and emotional. Christian doctrine claims to be based on an objective personal revelation by God of his own nature and purposes, open for all to read; and the intellectual case for Christianity has I believe nothing to fear from the most honest scrutiny. But to get to the heart of the Christian message you need more than intellectual assent to doctrines. Christians express it by saying that you have to come to *know* Christ as a living Person. I used to wonder what on earth they meant by that; and even now as a Christian I don't suppose I've begun to realize all it implies. But for me it means quite simply that in my own day-to-day experience I am coming gradually to see that I'm being *dealt with* by someone who is alive, and whose dealings make sense as tokens of just the kind of faithful and loving personal relationship that Christ claimed to make possible. All sorts of experiences in ordinary life as well as in prayer and worship, now come to demand interpretation as encounters with that Person.

Of course as a physicist I should expect, as I am sure you realize, that a valid complementary account of these could be given in physical or psychological terms. What I am saying is that they make new sense, that I see the *point* of them, in proportion as I am ready to see them also as *addressed* to me.

You can see a crude sort of illustration of what I mean in the kind of electric sign that, when you examine it in detail, seems nothing but a mass of glowing electric light bulbs; but if you are prepared to stand back and look at it in a different way you suddenly find that it is exhorting you to 'drink so-and-so's soda water'.

And this brings me to my last point. Once you have come to recognize the words in the electric sign, it is very hard *not* to be aware of them. And there is something like that too in the Christian's relationship to God. If we once come to take him at his word, and he begins to deal with us as one of his sons, we must reckon with it as a relationship for life. It will be no nodding acquaintance. We shall find that there are deep things to be settled between us, and that being re-made by God can have an antiseptic sting about it as well as joy. It is not my job in this paper to describe all that is entailed by becoming a Christian; but I do want to emphasize that it involves the whole man – intellect, emotions and all. For, to come back to our title, I do not believe we can hope to look successfully for connections between the scientific picture and Christian revelation unless we are prepared, as whole men, to be met in the process by God himself, and prepared in all honesty to take the consequences.

4

What makes a contradiction?[1]

'There's only one thing impossible, Jack, an' that's for a chiel to pull his troosers on ower his heid.' Thus a rustic worthy is reputed to have defined the limits of speculation in a harbour-side argument in my home town of Wick. In more theological matters, it is curiously difficult to find any corresponding 'standard cases' of logical impossibility. Arguments in theology tend to be inconclusive. Opponents freely accuse one another of 'having it both ways', and the suspicion grows in the mind of the onlooker that no sharp criteria of contradiction are recognized in talk about God. Why should this be? If the One whom Christians worship is the God of truth, why is it apparently so difficult to pin down different beliefs about him as clearly and sharply incompatible?

The object of this essay is to throw some light on these questions by taking a closer look at the way in which sharp contradictions come about – in particular, by showing how what we regard as a contradiction, in any field of discourse, depends on certain presuppositions concerning the subject-matter, which may often be held unconsciously by participants on both sides.

Contradictions in mathematics

Most of us would take mathematics to be the most rigorous of argumentative disciplines, so let us begin by looking at the way in which mathematicians use the notion of contradiction. Suppose that in coordinate geometry we define two points P and Q, and give both of them the same coordinates (x, y). (This means simply that each lies at a distance of *x* units from the north-south axis and *y* units from the east-west axis.) Does this definition of P and Q *contradict* (*i.e.* rule out as impossible) the statement 'P and Q are not at the same place'? The answer is of course *Yes*, if P and Q are defined as points *in the same plane*; but otherwise, *No*. Once we admit the possibility of a third dimension, the contradiction vanishes. It is perfectly possible for two points to have the same grid coordinates on a map, for example, without being at the same place. It simply means that one of them is vertically above the other, like aeroplanes 'stacked' before landing. One of the first things an airport radar operator learns is that two aircraft moving to the same position on the radar screen will not necessarily collide!

Simple though it is, we will find this an instructive example for our present purpose. A reader who *presupposed* that we were talking about two-dimensional geometry will probably have felt slightly cheated by our introduction of a third dimension. 'Oh, if *that's* what you mean, of course it's all right; but you didn't *say*,' he may complain. For the sake of illustration, we may even imagine someone accusing us of having 'brought in the third dimension in order to escape from the self-contradiction inherent in our earlier statements'. How then should we answer?

In so far as pure mathematics can be likened to a game, a creation of our own minds, with clearly definable rules made by ourselves, I think we must agree that we gave our critics too little information to play the game properly. We ought perhaps to have prefaced our definition of P and Q with the words 'In a three-dimensional framework'. Equally, they must admit that they had no grounds for accusing us of self-contradiction until they knew *how many dimensions* the space of P and Q might have.

But another kind of answer is also possible. We could tell our critics that the information we gave them (P is at (x,y); Q is at (x,y); P and Q are not in the same place) was logically *equivalent* to informing them that the space in which P and Q exist *must have more than two dimensions*. If they had not been so eager to accuse us of contradicting ourselves, they could have learned something that they needed to know by paying proper attention to the data. In the same way, the radar operator, having observed that the positions of aircraft have frequently coincided on his two-dimensional radar screen without any signs of a collision or a near miss, could in principle infer, without being told anything more, that they must be separated in a third dimension. *An apparent contradiction, both of whose terms are supported by experience, is the logical indicator of an unsuspected dimension.* Conversely, it is impossible conclusively to settle the question whether two statements about the real world are contradictory by appeal to logic alone. Proofs of contradiction are always *relative* to some assumption about the 'dimensionality' of the descriptive framework, in a generalized sense.

Sad to say, this proviso even questions the rustic example with which we began. In three-dimensional space, it is true that trousers can only be put on 'legs first'; but if four-dimensional geometry were applicable, geometers assure us that the body could be inserted into trousers (or removed therefrom) without passing through any of their apertures! If this is a little difficult to visualize, consider an analogous situation in two-dimensional space. An object inside a circular boundary can get outside (if confined to the plane of the circle) only by passing through the boundary; but in three-dimensional space it can be removed by lifting it out of the plane of the circle, and *over* the boundary, without penetrating it. Hence there is no necessary contradiction in saying both (a) 'X has come from inside Y (or has entered Y) which has a closed boundary' and (b) 'X has not passed through the boundary of Y'. It all depends on the number of dimensions in which X is free to move; or we might equally well say that an additional dimension in which X is free to move is betokened by the fact that X has entered or left Y without passing through its boundary. In either formulation the arbiter is not logic, but brute fact.

Complementarity

Shocking though our mathematical examples may seem, the removal of apparent contradiction by admitting an extra dimension makes relatively modest demands on our imagination. It is, after all, only what our visual system does for us automatically with the discrepancies between the appearances of solid objects viewed by our left and right eyes. We see, not discrepancies, but *depth* in the field of view. In a clear sense, the two views are not contradictory but *complementary*.

In the recent history of physics, however, apparent contradictions of a still more shocking kind have had to be endured. When light rays or electric 'cathode rays' are sent through empty space, they are found to ripple round an obstacle, such as the bars of a grating, to form the kind of 'ripple pattern' that a system of *waves* would do, on a receiving screen at the far side of the obstacle. This has given rise to a highly successful 'wave theory' of light-in-motion and matter-in-motion, from which the ripple patterns produced on a receiving screen by passing such radiation through gratings of all different shapes can be successfully predicted.

On the other hand when such rays are emitted or absorbed, they behave equally unmistakably like a stream of *particles*, 'quanta' or 'bullets' of a definite fixed size. Worse still, when the emission is so weak that 'bullets' are given off and received only one at a time, the pattern eventually formed by the 'bullet holes' on the receiving screen or photographic plate is still exactly the same ripple pattern as when the emission was intense.

Now we come to the apparent contradiction. If only one bullet at a time is supposed to encounter the grating (and is not stopped by it), it must surely pass through only one or another of the apertures in the grating. Yet as the bullet holes accumulate on the receiving screen at the far side, the pattern they gradually delineate is found to be still the same ripple-pattern that would be expected if a *wave* had passed through the *whole* grating. Must we then conclude that each individual bullet has somehow gone through *all* the apertures at once?

Initially, this dilemma was felt to be so intolerable that physicists divided into those who accepted the 'wave' model and those who accepted the 'particle' one (or perhaps each on alternate days!); but in due course the weight of experimental evidence has forced us to recognize that *both* thought-models are valid and necessary to do justice to different aspects of the behaviour of radiation (whether optical or electrical). Gradually, it has come to be realized that the situations to which a 'wave' model applies are *not of the same kind* as those in which a 'particle' model is needed. 'Wave' models lead to correct expectations of the behaviour of matter-in-motion (or charge-in-motion, or light-in-motion, *etc.*) whereas 'particle' models correctly predict the behaviour of matter-on-impact (charge-on-impact, light-on-impact, *etc.*). Given this distinction, the two are never in practice contradictory, but *complementary*.

It is not my purpose, of course, to commend this state of physical theory as if it were in any way final. All it does is to illustrate dramatically, in terms of actual scientific history, a point which might otherwise seem artificial and academic: namely, that criteria of contradiction, however 'commonsensical', can be dangerously misleading when applied to descriptions of the real world. Always it is the facts, however bewildering, rather than argument, however plausible, that must have the last word. The man who would venture in the name of 'logic' to pronounce any physical event impossible has no guarantee whatever against the arrival of the event in question with a label attached: 'You didn't expect this, did you?'. Readiness to expand our descriptive frame in obedience to fresh data is in fact what is meant by the essential humility of science.

But we can learn something more from this physical example. Confronted with irrefutable evidence of wave-behaviour and particle-behaviour, the physicist is not content to abandon logic and cheerfully maintain a jumbled model with two incoherent ingredients. Instead, he asks at once *under which circumstances* each description is appropriate. Only when each has been *labelled* for the experimental standpoint from which it is known to be valid can he rest content. Similarly, nobody tries to check the plan and elevation drawings of a building for consistency by laying one on top of the other; but until each is labelled for the angle from which it claims to be valid, no one knows how to check whether the two can in fact be consistent as pictures of the same three-dimensional object. Even when different descriptions are known to be complementary, *identification of standpoint* remains a major task.

A third lesson can be learned from the case of wave-particle physics. If we had asked a nineteenth-century physicist what hard evidence he had for his assertions about the nature of radiation, his answer might well have been in terms of *entities* such as waves, or particles, which he might claim were 'observable' under suitable conditions. A physicist today would (one hopes!) be more cautious. The hard evidence he would point to would not be observable *entities* but observable *events*, to which he might give hyphenated names such as 'electron-impact', 'photon-impact' and the like. It is in fact by tracing our data back to events, and patterns and probabilities of events, that we have discovered how to express the facts of atomic physics without any trace of self-contradiction. This is not (as some positivists would have it) a matter of *denying the reality* of the entities confronting us, but only a principle of 'conceptual hygiene' to allow our limited experimental knowledge enough room to grow without breeding spurious contradictions. The entities whose existence we intuit or read off from our data are thus left the more free to impose their true structure upon our thinking as our data (in observed events) accumulate.

Logic and theology

We may sum up what we have learned from these examples as follows:

(i) In any field of discourse, logic can be used to detect contradiction only when the dimensionality of the descriptive frame has been fixed. Otherwise, every apparent contradiction must be qualified as 'conditional on the non-existence of yet another (logical) dimension in addition to those which we have assumed'.

(ii) In discourse that purports to describe reality, the number of dimensions necessary to do justice to the data of experience must be absolutely open to revision by those data. No event can be held *a priori* to be logically impossible, 'contradictory to fact' or the like. Such claims are strictly nonsensical.

(iii) Where complementary descriptions turn out to be required by the data of experience, it is essential to identify the logical standpoint from which each is defined, as careless mixing of elements valid for different standpoints can lead to confusion.

(iv) It is easiest to see the logical relationship between different data and to avoid spurious conflict if they are expressed in terms of experienced events rather than abstract entities.

What then of theological discourse? Can we justly affirm that 'logic does not apply to the things of the spirit', or even that there is spiritual benefit to be derived from believing both sides of a contradiction in the name of faith? Not at all. Logic applies, and must be scrupulously applied, to any systematic statement worth making, in theology as elsewhere. What goes wrong in religious disputation is not that the anti-religious are too logical, but that they are often not logical enough in discerning what possibilities are left open by the data. They are too eager to adopt and argue within an impoverished descriptive frame, rather than keep open the possibility that their intuitive frame needs additional dimensions. On the other hand, Christians also often fail to sort out and keep clear the logical standpoints from which different theological concepts are defined; and they could frequently avoid accusations of self-contradiction or 'meaningless' talk if they would take pains to frame theological evidence where possible in terms of events and activities (*e.g.* obeying-God, being-forgiven-by-God, being-guided-by-God, being rebuked-by-God) rather than entities (God, obedience, forgiveness, guidance, rebuke).

But if we reject the idea that theologians are privileged to defy logic, we must not undervalue the grain of truth that the assertion contains. What it usually means, in fact, is that in theology we have often to deal with concepts whose logical dimensionality is undefined. It follows, for the reasons we have considered, that logical criteria of contradiction can seldom be *applied* with certainty, and that prior notions of 'what seems reasonable' are liable (in the logical nature of the case) to be treacherous guides. These are logical facts, neglect of which has been one of the great weaknesses of theological 'liberalism' and 'rationalism' down through the ages; and nothing we have said should be allowed to diminish their force. Where the subject-matter adequately defines its own dimensionality, logical conclusions can be drawn with full rigour; but the onus must be on the logician to prove that this is the case. This is precisely the difference between empirical discourse and an artificial language game.

On the other hand just as empirical science rests content, at a given stage of its development, with *working assumptions* as to the logical dimensions of its concepts, so theology in principle might hope to do the same, and in practice it often does. Within the limits of these working assumptions, potential contradictions can be identified and the discipline of logic pursued with full rigour, subject only to an equally rigorous obligation to make clear at each step what is being taken for granted. After all, it is to the living God of truth, and not to some abstract code of logical practice, that we are responsible for avoiding self-contradiction, and above all for avoiding self-contradiction in his name.

5

Man as a mechanism[1]

Man's body and brain can be studied as a mechanism just as other mechanical systems are studied. In this essay I want to consider how man's 'personality-mediating' parts, his brain and nervous system, can be analysed and understood in the same sort of way as his heart, his lungs, or his kidneys.

You might think that this was a field in which, from the religious point of view, one of the 'battles for the mind' was likely to rage. In principle this is a possible danger; it is possible that if we as Christians do not read our Bibles carefully enough and think clearly enough, we could find ourselves trying to fight a battle against scientific results over questions of the mechanical explicability of man's brain, in the kind of way that during the last century many Christian people joined battle with the biochemists over the chemical explicability of biological processes.

There is indeed today a 'battle for the mind', as a book with that title has reminded us; but it is not the same kind of battle. It arises because men are discovering how to manipulate one another, to treat one another as things subject to their dictates. This raises very serious religious, ethical, and moral problems, and I have no doubt that, if things go as we have seen them go in some parts of the world today, there will be a continuing struggle for human values, for the spiritual dignity of man against the forces of those who are not above manipulating people as things. But this is something quite different from any issue raised by a study of man as a mechanism: we have no 'battle' on our hands as Christians to prove that man's brain somehow or other will defy physical explanation, or disobey physical laws; nor have we any 'battle' to prove that some kind of non-physical forces act upon the matter in man's brain.

That summarizes negatively what I want to say. Stress and struggle of this kind would be all wrong in approaching man as a mechanism. Instead we ought to have as peaceably open minds in investigating this particular material part of God's creation as in studying any other.

The threefold emphasis of the Bible

If this attitude which I am recommending is to be defensible, it has to be considered in the light of the Bible and what Christian doctrine has to say about man. This may be summarized in three 'headlines'.

First, at the mechanical level, the Bible describes man as 'dust' – *i.e.* continuous with the rest of God's physical creation.

Secondly, at the psychological level, the Bible speaks of man as 'ensouled': as, if you like, an organism. He is of a piece with the animal kingdom as distinct from the inanimate world. Still more important, he is in some sense able to commune with God, able to be addressed by God as a person. So the first reference to man in this respect in the book of Genesis refers to him as becoming *nephesh*, which might best be translated as 'organism' or 'mind-body'. There is an important point here. The Bible is not suggesting that man has a soul as an invisible extra *thing* plugged into a bodily compartment; rather the Bible leads us to amplify the conception of man from first, the body, the material, to second, the ensouled body. This 'has more to it' than body; it has an additional *aspect* referred to as 'soul', or sometimes 'spirit'.

But then the Bible does not stop there. In a sense its key emphasis, especially in the New Testament, is on yet a third aspect of man's being – the possibility of his receiving 'spiritual life'. It says emphatically that man in his present fallen state is by nature 'spiritually dead', so that when it speaks of the gift of spiritual life it must mean something different from that which by nature we all have, and sometimes refer to loosely as 'spiritual'.

These, then, represent three levels in the biblical idea of man: the mechanical, the psychological and the spiritual – using the latter term in this particular sense in which 'spiritual life' is not automatically a property of the human being, but rather his gift from God in the power of Christ.

The scientific study of man

With the biblical background in our minds, let us look at the way in which scientists can study man as a mechanism, and see what sort of picture has so far emerged.

First, one must say that the scientific study of man is not new; it has been going on now for several centuries. But the reason why it has not been much in the news until recently is that with the coming of electronics (the power to amplify minute electrical signals and to control mechanisms with electric currents) a new acceleration has appeared in the tempo of research. It has become possible to pick up signals from the individual nerve fibres, of which we have about ten thousand million in the body, and to study how, for example, the signals from the eye travel back into the brain and how they are encoded in the form of electrical impulses running along these fibres. In other words, functional investigation on a minute scale utterly different from anything that was feasible before has now become a reality.

Conversely, it has been found possible to stimulate parts of the brain electrically. For example, a patient who is fully conscious under local anaesthetic can be stimulated in certain parts of the brain so that his leg moves; but in this case if asked, 'Why did you move your leg?' he says, 'I didn't; it moved itself.' On the other hand, by stimulating other parts of the brain it is possible to make the patient feel thirsty, or in some other way to *accept into his personality* the events which have been fed into his brain. By stimulating some parts of the brain (admittedly in epileptic people, since these are normally the sort of patients who allow their heads to be opened) whole trains of experience can sometimes be evoked. For example, a woman describes herself as 'suddenly back home', and she 'can hear the kids playing at the foot of the stairs'. She is reliving, in a sense, this part of her ordinary experience. In yet other parts of the brain stimulation can evoke trains of visual images; and so we could go on.

I mention these only as samples of this new power of minute investigation, whereby the study of the organization of the brain has mushroomed in our century to become one of the most elaborate and rapidly developing of the sciences. It has become abundantly clear that there is a continual two-way connection between what we can say about people's subjective experience (of sights, sounds, itches, pains) and what we can say about the electro-chemical activity in their brains. The two are, of course, qualitatively different; but it seems quite likely that they are in 'one-to-one correspondence' of some kind.

Does 'mind' require 'gaps' in the scientific picture?

It is a desperately limited picture that we have as yet; a tiny fraction of one per cent of what we would like to know is beginning to be clear, and every few years theories, some of them rather exotic, find themselves upset and replaced with others which in turn look very queer a few years later. Our picture of the brain is enormously incomplete, so there is plenty of room for people to speculate and say, 'Aha, you will never be able to explain the whole of it scientifically. I believe that the mind exerts non-physical forces on these regions of the brain that we do not yet understand.'

Does what the Bible means by human personality encourage us to talk in this way? Does it make sense from the Bible's point of view to look for the mind in the gaps in what we understand about the brain, or should in fact the relationship be a quite different one?

As a start we have to ask whether, and in what sense, the Bible ever gives us ground for considering the human personality apart from its tangible expression in a human body. Throughout the Bible we find words like 'flesh' used, as it were, interchangeably with 'person' – 'all flesh is as grass'; 'my flesh faints and fails'. This is not meant to be a theological study, nor should undue pressure be put on individual metaphors; but it does seem that the Bible gives very little encouragement to the idea that we should regard ourselves as somehow seated at the controls in a chariot, our body, which is quite separate from us. Paul does use the imagery of living in a tent, or wearing a suit of clothes, to represent our embodiment; but these current idoms of the day are introduced in the course of making quite different points. When the doctrine of the body itself is in question, the image he uses is that of the seed (1 Corinthians 15).

What kind of contemporary image, then, might begin to do justice to the way in which the Bible does talk about us? For, of course, its whole concern is to take seriously our spiritual nature.

No one image could be entirely adequate, because to be an ensouled body or an embodied soul, or, if you like, to be a person, is a thing unique in our experience. There is no perfect analogy for it; but there are one or two illustrations from common experience which may be a little more helpful than the image of a charioteer driving a chariot.[2]

Multiple aspects and the fallacy of 'nothing-buttery'

One familiar illustration is that of the use of lamps to signal from ships at sea. When a man sends a message from ship to shore, in one sense all that is coming from the ship is a series of flashes of light; but the trained sailor who sits on the shore watching this light says, 'I see a message ordering so-and-so to proceed somewhere', or, 'Look, they're in trouble!' Why does he say this? All he has seen is 'nothing but' flashes of light. The whole pattern of activity can be correctly labelled thus by a physicist, and described so completely that he is able to reproduce at any time exactly what the man on shore saw. He does not add 'the message' as a kind of 'extra' at the end of his description, and it would clearly be silly to say he is 'leaving out the message' as if it were very wrong of him to do so. What he has done is to choose one way of approaching a complex unity, namely the sending-of-a-message-from-ship-to-shore, one aspect of which is purely physical, allowing of complete description in such terms as the wavelengths of the light and the time pattern. On the other hand, if he reads it also as a message, it is not as if he had found something mysterious going on *as well as* the flashing. Instead, he has discovered that the whole thing, when he allows it to strike him in a different way, can be *read* and can also make sense in non-physical terms. The message here is related to the flashing of light, not as an effect is to a cause, but rather as one aspect of a complex unity is related to another aspect.

Take another illustration. Two mathematicians start arguing about a problem in geometry. With a piece of chalk, they make a pattern of dots and lines on the board, and the fun waxes fast and furious. Can we imagine some non-mathematician coming in, and saying in amazement, 'I can't see what you're arguing about – there's nothing there but chalk'? Once again this would illustrate what I like to call the fallacy of 'nothing-buttery' – the idea that because in one sense, at one level, or viewed from one angle, there is nothing there but chalk, therefore it is unnecessary, it makes no sense, it is superfluous to talk about what is there in any other terms. Again, if the mathematicians protest, 'But there is a geometrical figure there; we are talking about these angles', they are not suggesting that the other man's eyes are failing to detect something on the board that they are seeing. Both of them are responding to exactly the same light waves. It is not that the mathematicians have a sixth sense or anything queer that enables them to receive from the board some invisible emanations that the other fellow is not receiving. The point is that, as a result of a different 'set', a different attitude to what is there, they have the power to see in it or, if you like, to abstract from it an aspect or significance which the other misses. Of course, in this case he can be trained to discover it. There is no great difficulty in their eventually coming to agreement, and he then realizes that the geometrical pattern is related to the chalk on the board, not indeed as effect is to a cause, but in a still more intimate way.

A relationship more intimate than 'cause and effect'

I want to clarify this alternative to 'cause and effect', because it bears on questions that are often raised about the 'causation' of bodily action by mental activity. If an argument were to come up as to whether the light causes the message or the message causes the light, whether the chalk distribution causes the geometrical figure or the geometrical figure causes the chalk distribution, we would see at once that the word 'cause' in the scientific sense is the wrong one here. Causality in science is a relationship between *two* events or sets of events – the cause and the effect. Here we have not two events or situations, but one. You cannot have the flashing of the light without the message: they are one set of events. You cannot have the chalk distribution without there being at the same time the figure on the board. On the other hand the two do have a certain kind of independence. It would be possible to reproduce the same message or figure in a quite different embodiment – in ink or pencil for example. It is for this reason that I prefer to say that the one 'embodies' the other.

Man as a mental-bodily unity

Now let us pass to the problem of relating mental activity and bodily activity in the human being. The relation between them is certainly not as simple as the relation between the geometrical figure and the chalk, but in the same kind of way it would be a mistake for us to try to regard either of them as the 'cause' of the other in the scientific sense. We should rather recognize that they are a unity in the sense that, given one, you have the other; and yet it would be absurd to dismiss one as 'nothing but' the other because, of course, everything depends on the purpose for which we are trying to describe the situation. If we tell our sailor that what is coming from the ship is 'nothing but light', when in fact it is an instruction that unless he gets back to his ship in half an hour he is 'for it', he will laugh at us. Similarly if a man says, 'I am faced with a fateful decision, and I must accept responsibility for it', then for anyone to reply, 'But once the scientists have explained all that is going on in your brain it will be nothing but a matter of physico-chemical activity' would be to miss the whole point of what the man is doing. He is indeed talking of the same mental-physical unity, but he is referring to it from a different 'angle' or a different logical level, or, if you like, from the inside rather than from the outside. What he says may be as important and valid from his angle as what the scientist would say from his.

I have deliberately said 'as . . . as' rather than 'more . . . than', because for certain purposes what the scientist says about the brain may be crucially important, particularly in cases of mental disease. Health and happiness may depend on realizing that if a man suddenly hallucinates, his experience has at the mechanical level a physico-chemical correlate, so to speak – in other words, something that corresponds to it in the kind of way that the chalk on the blackboard does to the geometry. This might, for example, be the result of a brain tumour, so that if we could get the tumour out without taking out too much that matters along with it, that man's hallucinations might cease and he might then be able to live a normal life.

Similarly, I would say, we must not belittle the importance of understanding the physico-chemical mechanism of what goes on in a man when he is taking a decision. But for all such normal activities, when there is nothing going wrong in our brains, and by the mercy of God we are functioning normally as human beings, then when we face decisions the level at which it makes sense to discuss the thing is that of personal decision and responsibility, and not biochemical activity.

The little girl who said, 'It ain't my fault, it's my glands', illustrates the fallacy which arises from confusing this relationship between 'dual aspects of a unity' with the relationship of cause and effect. Indeed, it is misleading and dangerous to discuss the relation between mental activity and the corresponding brain activity as one of cause and effect, whichever we make the 'cause'. This is trying to tear apart something which does not admit of that sort of disruption, any more than do the geometrical figure and the chalk in which it is embodied. If the chalk distribution is changed we have indeed a new geometrical figure on our hands. But we cannot have the one changed without the other, and the one is necessary for the other. So it is a relation of necessity, but not a relation of (scientific) causality.

Spiritual life

Finally, what of 'spiritual' life? Could we perhaps agree now that in the kind of way that we see psychological life 'embodied' in the physical brain, it is at least not implausible to see, in biblical terms, spiritual life as 'embodied' in the psychological mechanism of a man, if God by his grace is willing to give that man that new life? The suggestion would then be that this acquisition of life, in the New Testament sense, does not necessarily entail something which is inexplicable *psychologically*. In other words, I do not think the Christian has any more reason to do battle with the psychology of religion, even the psychology of religious conversion, than with the physiology of the brain. We may well doubt that such private matter will yield much grist for the scientific mill; but that is not to say that the scientist is wrong to look for 'laws' in what data he can get.

I am suggesting, then, that spiritual life may be thought of in a general way as related to the scientific mechanistic structure of psychological theory (with which Freud among others has dealt) in the kind of way that psychological life can be said to be related to the activity of the nerve cells and other mechanical components (with which physiology is concerned). True, as distinct from superficial, conversion is the only way known to Christian faith of bringing about this transformation in a way which 'follows on' and does not do violence to the personality embodied. I can perhaps illustrate what I mean by coming back for a moment to our problem in geometry set out on the blackboard. It could be viewed on the one hand as nothing but chalk, and on the other as a figure of lines and angles. Now the problem can be altered in any number of ways by rearranging the chalk. If we do violence to it as a problem by laying down new lines or rubbing out old lines and changing them, then we get a new problem, or our problem is removed, but we have achieved this only at the cost of *doing violence* to it. The mathematicians are concerned with the only kind of resolution that interests them, namely by discussing the thing at its own level, respecting its nature, and not forcing or distorting it. Similarly, while in principle one might imagine that by suitable surgical manipulations we might turn an angry man into a peaceful man, and so forth, this would not amount to conversion in the biblical sense, for we would have 'solved' the man's problem at this level by doing violence to the man. In a sense we would have ended up with a different and a mutilated personality. As I understand the claim of Jesus Christ, that only through him could eternal life come to us as personalities, it indicates that only by his power as the Creator and Upholder and Redeemer of our whole being can our personality be reshaped in a way that does not do violence to us. Only his way of repentance, forgiveness and love preserves the *continuity* between us as we are now, faced with the problem of our self-centredness and our rebellion against God, and us as we shall be when he has turned our hearts to God.

In summary, then, I would suggest not only that I see harmony between the study of man as a psychological being and the study of man as a mechanism, but that in some doubtless crude and imperfect way this even throws a little light on the relation between the spiritual life which is offered to man and the psychological structure in which that spiritual life must, by God's grace, be embodied.

6

What determines my choice?[1]

1. Introduction

Choosing is a familiar everyday experience. When I go for a walk along the beach, at what point shall I turn back? When a basket of fruit is passed down the table, shall I take the last pear or leave it for my neighbour? If the deadline for my manuscript is 1 October, shall I give up other pursuits to get it off in time, or let it slide? These are typical of questions that must be answered by what we call 'choosing', or 'making a choice'.

Always, of course, in making a choice we are subject to constraints. Our range of options and capacities is not unlimited. Sometimes the range narrows to a single possibility, as when we arrive at the airport on a delayed flight and 'have no option' but to stay overnight for the next connection. In such a case we tend to say that we were 'not free' or that the outcome was 'inevitable', and to excuse ourselves from responsibility. Otherwise, as in the examples above, we would agree that in an important sense we do have some 'freedom of choice' when facing a range of possible actions. This is a matter of fact that we would be lying to deny.

What, then, is supposed to be the problem about 'freedom of choice'? Why do so many people consider that mechanistic brain science offers a threat to our responsibility for our actions? In this paper I shall first sketch the empirical basis of the argument, and then give reasons for holding that the alleged conflict between mechanistic brain science and human freedom and responsibility is illusory.

2. The I-story and the brain-story

For each one of us, the primary data to which all our thinking must do justice are the facts of our conscious experience. If asked, we could produce a long list of statements of the form 'I see such-and-such', 'I hear this', 'I believe that' . . . , each of which bears witness to a fact we would be lying to deny. Collectively, we might call these the 'I-story'. We may imagine this set out as a very long column of entries on the left-hand side of a table, as follows:

I-story	Observer-story (Brain-story)
I see..............................	Subsystem N_1 is doing....................
....	....
I hear............................	Subsystem N_2 is doing....................
....	....
I remember..................	Subsystem N_3 is doing....................
....	....
I believe........................	Subsystem N_4 is in state..................
....	....

Now the working assumption of brain science (and it is, of course, only an assumption, though supported by much empirical evidence in specific instances) is that every aspect of our conscious experience has a *correlate* in some aspect of our brain activity. This does not necessarily imply one-to-one correspondence, but it does mean that no *change* can take place in our conscious experience without a correlated *change* taking place in some neural subsystem. We can picture the brain scientist, then, as seeking to identify and describe on the right-hand side of our imaginary table the direct neural correlates of each of the data to which the I-story bears witness. This we may call the 'brain-story', which is one form of the 'observer-story' that a non-interfering onlooker could in principle tell about us from the outside.

Thus far, there may seem to be no problem for 'freedom of choice', but of course the brain scientist is not content merely to find such correlates: his aim is to understand and unite all the various brain activities listed in the right-hand column as facets of the activity of a single causally-linked physical system.

Here the key question arises: what if the brain-story were eventually to turn out to have no 'gaps' in its chain-mesh of physical cause-and-effect? The chain-mesh would of course have to extend beyond the confines of the body to all relevant environmental factors, and any idea of actually following it through would be ludicrously impracticable – but in principle the philosophical question remains: would not the outcome of all my choosings in this case be *inevitable*? Would not this prove my freedom of choice to be *illusory*? I shall argue that the answer to both questions, in a sense to be clearly defined, is demonstrably 'No'.

3. How are the 'I-story' and 'brain-story' related?

For our purpose the details of the imaginary future brain-story are irrelevant: the sting appears to come from the suggestion that whatever its details, it might be in a scientific sense deterministic.

This raises the question of how the 'I-story' and 'brain-story' are related?

Let me mention just four of the many answers that have been offered to this question. One, beloved of an earlier generation of 'behaviourists', would claim that the two are simply translations of one another: two different alternative ways of saying the same thing.

A second, which is graced with the name of 'epiphenomenalism', would claim that conscious experience is distinct from brain activity, but only *follows* it as an effect follows its cause. Mental activity would therefore be reduced to an 'epiphenomenon' that plays no effective part in determining behaviour.

A third view would assert that at least some mental activity causally *precedes* the corresponding brain activity, so allowing 'the mind' to determine the movements of the body as a driver does the movements of a car.

The fourth view, which I will advocate, is that my mental activity and the correlated activity of my brain need not be thought of as two trains of parallel events, but rather as 'inner' and 'outer' aspects of the one complex (and mysterious) train of events that constitute my conscious agency. On this view the I-story and the brain-story are logically complementary, each bearing witness to essential facts which the other may systematically ignore. In this sense, I shall argue, there is an irreducible duality about our human nature – but this is a duality of *aspects* rather than of 'substances' in the Cartesian sense.

If there were ever any argument as to which was more 'real', priority would clearly belong to the I-story, since it is only through the data of conscious experience that we gain any knowledge we have about brains and their workings. But as we shall see, the two can be related so harmoniously that no question of priority arises.

4. What room for freedom?

We now have to face our major objection. Suppose for the sake of argument that the causal chain-mesh of the brain-story were (at least in principle) complete. What then determines my choice? If purely physical factors completely determined the physical activity that expressed my decision, what room could be left for *me* to have any effective say in the matter?

Plausible as it may seem, this objection is in fact based on a presupposition which is demonstrably false: namely, that *claims to determination are always mutually exclusive.* A familiar counter-example will demonstrate the fallacy. Suppose that a neurophysiologist sets up a computer to solve the Hodgkin-Huxley (H-H) equation under specific boundary conditions. Provided he does the job properly, he can truthfully claim that the behaviour of the computer is determined by the H-H equation and his boundary conditions. At the same time an electronic engineer analysing the chain-mesh of physical cause-and-effect in the machine can equally truthfully claim that *this* determines completely its behaviour.

Any appearance of conflict here would of course be illusory; for the claims to determination are framed at disparate logical levels, from alternative logical standpoints: they are not competitive but complementary.[2]

If anyone wishes to argue that physical determination of brain activity would prevent me from effectively determining my choices, then he has to prove that the two claims to determination are mutually exclusive. I shall now outline a simple non-technical proof that they are not.[3–6]

5. Logical relativity

In mechanistic brain science we have a working assumption that all a human agent (A) believes or knows is represented, explicitly or implicitly, in the physical configuration of his brain. It is debatable whether we could ever specify completely the physical correlate of a given belief (or indeed of any mental state); but for our purpose it will suffice to consider a more modest implication of the mechanistic assumption, namely that no *change* can take place in what A believes without a correlated *change* taking place in a particular subsystem of his brain. Let us call this subsystem the cognitive mechanism, or CM for short.

Consider now the complete description D='CM(*t*)' that an ideally informed superscientist S could give of A's cognitive mechanism at a given time *t*. If he has done his job properly, D specifies what S (and any non-participant onlooker) would be correct to believe, and in error to disbelieve, about the state of CM at the time in question. If, however, *t* is a time in the present or the immediate future, it is obvious that *A himself would be mistaken* to believe D; for, as we saw, no change could take place in what A believes without a correlated change in CM. Thus, oddly enough, D *has no claim to A's assent*, even though it does have a claim to the assent of a non-intervening observer O. The situation is logically *relativistic.* Notice that there is here no question of S's *actually giving* D to A. What we are asking is *what logical claim* D has to A's assent. This could in principle be settled by a 'logical court' in A's absence, by asking: If D were embodied in A's cognitive mechanism, would it correctly specify every detail of CM at *t*? The answer is: No, because the change in CM necessary to embody D would necessarily make D out of date.

It might be imagined that we could relieve the logical tension here by allowing S to generate a new description D_1='$CM_1(t)$' which corrects for the change that must take place in CM when A believes the description. It is not obvious that this could be done;[7] but in order to clear the air let us suppose that it could, and imagine our superscientist bringing his pre-corrected description D_1 before us as the logical court. We could then insist that A would be correct to believe D_1; but we must equally insist that A would not be in error to *disbelieve* it, since D_1 is designed to be accurate if and only if A believes it! In short, the most that our imaginary superscientist could do, even if ideally informed and equipped, is to produce a specification D_1 whose correctness or otherwise would be *up to A*, rather than having any *unconditional* claim to A's assent.

Notice that none of this denies the possibility (in principle) that S can (secretly) predict whether or not A *would* believe D_1 if he heard it. For the sake of argument, we may as well assume that he can. The logical point is still that since an A-who-did-not-believe-D_1 would not be in error, there is nothing *inevitable-for-A*, nothing 'take-it-or-leave-it', about the claim of D_1 to his assent. In fact, the correctness of D_1 depends precisely upon whether A takes it or leaves it!

Suppose, for example, that from his data S secretly predicts that A would believe D_1 if offered it, but that in fact A will not be offered it. Does this give D_1 any stronger logical claim to A's assent? Of course not. It merely guarantees that D_1 has no claim to the assent of anyone else, and that D (rather than D_1) will correctly describe the state of CM at time *t*. As we have already seen, an A-who-believed-D would necessarily be in error, so D has still no claim to A's assent. Even if we imagine a special case in which S can predict that A will be offered D_1 and will believe it, D_1 could still prove no *unconditional* logical claim to A's assent, since an A-who-disbelieved-D_1 would not be in error. In short, CM has no completely determinate or fixed state-description with an unconditional claim to the assent of all (including A), until after the event.

6. Logical indeterminacy

What we have proved regarding the future of A's cognitive mechanism must of course hold for any other cerebral mechanism whose future state depends physically on the relevant details of CM. In particular, the outcome of a decision which depends on conscious cognitive reflection will in general be *'logically indeterminate'* for A until he makes up his mind. Note again that this does *not* deny that the outcome could be *physically* determinate or even predictable in principle for a non-intervening observer. It leaves this an open question. On the other hand, it says much more than that A *cannot know* what he will decide to do. By calling the outcome 'logically indeterminate' we mean that it has no unique and completely determinate specification with an unconditional claim to the assent of all – until A has made up his mind. Of course, for those observers who are defined as unable to intervene, the outcome may well be 'inevitable'; and there could exist a specification of it which, if only they knew it, they would be correct to believe and in error to disbelieve. But *no such specification exists* with an unconditional claim to the assent of A – nor, as we shall see, to the assent of those in dialogue with A.

Needless to say, even in a normally-functioning brain there may be many subsystems whose future state is negligibly dependent on that of CM. Moreover in an epileptic or drug-sodden brain, or one under stimulation with implanted electrodes, even subsystems normally coupled to CM may be so dominated by other inputs as to lose much of their logical indeterminateness for A as well as for others. In all such cases, A's responsibility for the future state in question can be regarded as diminished to the extent that it is inevitable for A as well as for others, *i.e.* to the extent that its specification has an unconditional claim to the assent of *all*, including A. In the case of implanted electrodes, interestingly enough, responsibility could be attached by this criterion to the person who controls the stimulating current, even when none attached to the subject of manipulation.

In summary, then, our criterion distinguishes between two possible classes of action predictable-for-observers: (a) those which are physically dependent on CM in such a way as to be logically indeterminate for A. Such actions, even if physically determined, are not *inevitable* for A in the sense defined; (b) those (such as reflexes) which are *not* physically dependent on CM in such a way as to be logically indeterminate for A. Such actions, if physically determined, *are* inevitable for A.

I have suggested elsewhere[4] that this distinction may offer in principle a more rational basis for forensic psychiatry than some other criteria currently urged for deciding when to deny a man responsibility for his actions. In particular, it shows the irrationality of treating the *predictability* of an action (by non-participants) as a sufficient ground for refusing to hold the agent responsible.

It may be worth noting a common misunderstanding. 'All you have proved,' an objector might say, 'is that the agent A cannot *know* the outcome of his decision beforehand; but if his brain-and-environment were physically determinate, the outcome would really be immutable.' This objection misses the point. It is not that A cannot *obtain* a universally beliefworthy specification of what he will do, but rather that no such specification *exists*. It is not merely that he cannot have access to completely definitive information, but that no completely definitive information-for-him exists. What O is correct to believe about A is something that would not be true information-for-A if he (A) had it. What we have proved is thus an *ontological* rather than a merely epistemological point:[6] it is the non-existence of a unique solution to the state-equation valid for A, and not merely its undiscoverability by A.

Thus even in a physically determinate world the outcome of A's decision has an immutable – *i.e.* unchangeable – specification only for those who are causally uncoupled from it until after the event. So far from being unchangeable by A, the outcome is objectively up to A; so A is under no illusion in believing this. Indeed any claim by A in retrospect that he had had no option would be demonstrably false. However predictable his actual choice may have been for the non-intervening O, it had no immutable specification beforehand which, if only A had known it, he would have been correct to believe and mistaken to reject, whether he liked it or not.

7. What of Heisenberg's Uncertainty Principle?

Although our argument has had no need to invoke Heisenberg's Uncertainty Principle (or any other loosening of the physical chain-mesh) in order to make 'room' for our freedom of choice, it may be as well to ask what might follow if physically-indeterminate events, opaque to brain science, did play a significant role in brain processes. Sir John Eccles[8,9] among others has calculated that synaptic terminals or vesicles are delicate enough structures to be appreciably affected by the small residual uncertainty specified by Heisenberg's Principle, and that the synaptic network of the cerebral cortex could effectively amplify this physical uncertainty to a macroscopic level of significance. Eccles avoids the trap of equating freedom with Heisenberg-unpredictability, but lays emphasis on the possibility that some significant brain-events might be undetermined by prior physical conditions.

Insofar as they disrupted the normal cause-and-effect relationships between the physical correlates of my rational deliberation, such events might be held to diminish rather than enhance my responsibility for the outcome; for, granted the correlation between I-story and brain-story, physical continuity between the present state of my brain and its previous states would be expected as the correlate of the continuity of my mental processes. On the other hand, it can be argued that intelligent decision-making normally involves much more than logical calculation or rule-determined extrapolation from data. It requires us for example to evaluate evidence, to weigh priorities, and to think of relevant considerations. The last in particular can be more like something that *happens to* us than something we *do*: we say, 'It occurred to me . . .';

or in retrospect we ask, 'Why didn't I think of that at the time?'. If the influence of physically 'random' factors were confined to these processes we would not have the same reason for holding our responsibility for the decision to be diminished, since we do not in any case claim to determine what 'occurs to us' while we are making up our minds.

Thus while rejecting any suggestion that physical indeterminacy is necessary for responsibility, I do not see any reason to insist conversely that all the cerebral correlates of responsible decision-making must be physically determinate. Like so much else in brain research, this must be peaceably left an open question. Certainly I do not believe that our power to determine our courses of action hangs upon the answer to it.

8. Dialogue and self-awareness

We have so far spoken only of an isolated conscious agent (A). It is time now to consider briefly how the social aspect of our conscious experience fits into the picture.

If an agent A faces a second agent B, an intriguing new possibility opens up. Although at one level B may be represented within A's cognitive mechanism, just like any other physical object, in terms of the constraints imposed by its physical presence, size, shape, mass, structure and so forth, there is now another level at which B has to be reckoned with – as himself a conscious centre of evaluation and the planning of action. At this level B demands to be represented in terms of his goals, priorities, intentions, beliefs, hopes and fears – all of which impose conditional constraints upon A's agency quite as vital as those imposed by B's physical structure, but at a higher level of the supervisory system.

The ability to develop such an internal representation of another conscious agent is a complex skill that has to be acquired early in life with the help of those who already have it. It must involve the elaboration of an extensive, special-purpose internal repertoire within the supervisory system, ready to be applied in the business of perceiving and reckoning with any conscious agent encountered. If now a system so equipped were to turn the same repertoire to the task of internally representing *itself*, we would have a process which seems to have the features required for a mechanistic correlate of reflective *self-consciousness*.[10] Such a system would be able to engage in internalized dialogue as a way of evaluating alternatives and re-ordering its priorities in a manner that would correspond closely with our experience of 'thinking things out' and 'making up one's mind'. The argument sketched in sections 5 and 6 shows that any such self-representation must be incomplete – not only for want of data, but more fundamentally because no completely up-to-date self-representation of a cognitive mechanism can exist. The word 'I' is thus misconceived if taken as the name of a fully-determinate *object* of the speaker's cognition.[5]

(To pursue this theme here would take us off our main subject; but it is worth noting that the richness of self-awareness in this mode will be strictly limited by the capacity for forming internal representations of *others as planners of action*. Species not well equipped in this respect may be expected to be doubly lacking in such reflective self-awareness, no matter how complex may be their reaction patterns.)

Consider now what happens when two such agents A and B are *reciprocally* open to one another's perception at the personal level. The two supervisory systems, in seeking to build up a representation of one another, must run into the same logical limitation as with self-representation. Current or future details of A's cognitive mechanism become logically indeterminate not only for A, but also for B, to the extent that A's and B's cognitive mechanisms are reciprocally coupled, so that each finds in the other a representation of itself. In this strict sense cognitive agents in dialogue would have an element of irreducible *mystery* for one another, even if their brains were as physically determinate as computers. This holds a *fortiori* for a dialogue involving more than two persons. It means not merely that none could *ascertain* in full detail a determinate specification of another as an object of awareness: it means that no such specification *exists* with an unconditional claim to the assent of any member of the community so constituted. Here also, the indeterminacy is not merely epistemological but ontological.[6]

9. Conclusions

Our answer to the question in our title is thus pedestrian and conventional. What determines my choice is *my thinking and deciding*. The idea that this 'claim to determination' conflicts with physical claims to the determination of my correlated bodily movements we have seen to be a logical illusion.

Like some optical illusions it is hard to shake off at the perceptual level. Its falsehood can be shown only by means of crucial tests. The test I have suggested takes the form of a question: can the brain-story, even if physically deterministic, generate a complete and unique determination of my future which could prove an unconditional claim to the assent of everyone, including me? Does such a predetermination exist (though unknown to me) which I would be correct to believe and in error to disbelieve if only I knew it?

The answer, as we have seen, is *No*. Even the most deterministic future brain science imaginable cannot – logically cannot – pass this test. So the alleged conflict is bogus. The denial of freedom of choice (in this sense) on grounds of deterministic brain science is not just empirically but logically bankrupt.

We have taken the I-story and the brain-story as bearing witness to correlated aspects of a single unitary train of complex events and processes, its 'inside' aspect known to me in conscious experience, and its 'outside' aspect knowable to others (and in part to me also) from the standpoint of an observer. That the two stories are not just 'different ways of saying the same thing' is now obvious, since (a) they employ catergories at disparate logical levels, and (b) the brain-story even includes statements that the agent would be mistaken to believe. From this standpoint it would make no sense to claim that 'my brain tells me what to do'; and it would be equally inept to claim that 'I tell my brain what to do'. To speak of 'telling' or 'communication' between mind and brain, I suggest, misconstrues their relationship. Nothing in our experience justifies thinking of it as that between a sender and a receiver. It seems both more parsimonious, and more consonant with the two-way interdependence observed between brain events and conscious experience, to recognize the latter as *embodied* in the former, as we might speak of the solving of an equation as embodied in the workings of a computer.

At the core of our argument has been the fact that even a brain-event which is physically determinate may be logically indeterminate, in the sense of having no unique specification beforehand with an unconditional claim to the assent of all. Much of the illusion of conflict between physical determinism and freedom of choice can be traced to a confusion between physical and logical determinateness. It is the *logical* rather than the physical determinateness of my future action that would have to be demonstrated in order logically to refute the belief that I am responsible for the action.

Whether the human brain is in fact a physically determinate system I leave a peacefully open question. It is quite certainly not physically predictable in practice.[11] I have no dogmatic objection to the time-honoured Cartesian suggestions favoured by my friend Sir John Eccles, that non-physical factors may influence our brain-working.[8,9] Time will tell, perhaps. I only doubt whether such speculations are necessary to do justice either to our experience of conscious agency, or to the inherited convictions of Western Christendom regarding the spiritual nature of man.[12]

Summary

It has been shown that there is no logical contradiction between the theory that all human actions, quâ physical events, are physically determined, and the claim that I as a conscious agent determine my behaviour. The theory may be mistaken, and the claim must be qualified; but the idea that one must be false if the other is true is a logical illusion. Even if my brain were as mechanistic as a computer, there is a crucial sense in which the outcome of my choices is up to me, and logically *indeterminate* until I make up my mind. There are no scientific grounds for reducing our mental activity to an irrelevant epiphenomenon, nor to a mere re-naming of physical activity. It is more adequately regarded as an undeniable 'inner' aspect of our unitary personal activity, complementary to the 'outer' aspect that can be studied physiologically. The relation between the agent's view and the observer's view of a choice is *relativistic*, in the sense that the two must differ systematically if both are to be correct in what they believe. This essential (logical) relativity implies that some choices predictable by an observer can also be objectively free choices for the agent. The same analysis leads to a rational mechanistic criterion of diminished responsibility in cases of brain damage and the like.

7

Brain research and human responsiblity[1]

1. The authority for brain research

The scientist is like an exploratory map-maker. His map-making, like that of a geographer, may require him to feel his way where few others have gone before, to pry into territory in which many others claim an interest, and to exercise discretion as to whether, when and to whom to disclose what he discovers. His aim, of course, like that of the modern geographer, goes far beyond mere description. The purpose of his exploration is to understand what must be reckoned with in the world around him, to discover the 'go' of what he studies, to identify resources that may be tapped and relied upon by future users of his map. His maps, in a word, are *functional*. His duty is to guide intelligent agents and not mere sightseers. The brain scientist is not exempt from any of these obligations. His chosen domain has an organized structure more complex than any other known to man. New tools of investigation create constantly expanding frontiers of pioneering effort. Every one of his fellow men claims a natural interest in the territory he explores. The proper use of his knowledge is thus for the brain scientist a matter of constant and inescapable concern.

Fundamental for anyone in this position is the question of *authority*. By what authority are the maps being made? To whom is the map-maker accountable? Whose is the territory he explores? For the Christian the answer is clear. The world is God's. It is to him that we are ultimately accountable. It is by his authority that we are commissioned to explore and have dominion over the works of his hands, in a spirit not of arrogant exploitation but of humble and compassionate stewardship. In contrast to the pagan image of the gods as jealous of their secrets and inquisitive man as a resented interloper, the biblical emphasis is on man's duty to apply his mind to the understanding of the natural world, as an expression of reverence for its Creator and in gratitude for the benefits that deeper understanding can bring.

Inasmuch as the human brain is one of the works of God's hands and a part of the natural world, the *Genesis* mandate to 'subdue' presumably makes brain research not just a legitimate but an obligatory sector of our responsibility to our Creator. But there are two singular features that set the human brain apart from other objects of investigation. First, the map-maker of the brain is in a certain sense mapping (or trying to map) part of himself; and the logic of such an enterprise must present certain difficulties and pitfalls that map-makers of other domains can escape. Secondly, our common experience in choosing and acting, let alone the Christian doctrine of the human soul, might seem to raise doubts as to whether the human brain is in fact a purely 'natural' object, conforming to the same physical laws as the rest of the natural world.

It must be said straight away that this last is still an open question. Despite all recent advances in brain science, our ignorance of the causes of brain events still vastly exceeds our knowledge. Nobody can rule out on scientific grounds the idea that some events in the human brain may violate the physical principles that apply in other parts of the natural world. What I hope to show in this paper, however, is that it would be both unnecessary and dangerously misleading for Christians to try to defend any such theory in the interests of the biblical doctrine of man: unnecessary, because I believe that nothing in biblical teaching requires the brain to have any exemptions from normal physical principles; and dangerously misleading, because such an emphasis would deflect attention away from the distinctive points that the Bible does make about our human nature and destiny.

In this context, then, my title has an obvious double meaning. First – and vital for a healthy relationship between brain research and Christianity in particular – there is the question of our human responsibility to explore, make maps and gain understanding of the vastly mysterious territory in which we are embodied as conscious agents. Have men any right, it may be asked, to probe the mystery that surrounds the springs of human action? The biblical answer to this, I have suggested, is in principle straightforward. If there is need to be met, and good to be done, by gaining knowledge of God's world that God has not forbidden us, then we would need good reason to excuse our neglecting it. We have not merely a right, but an obligation to our Creator and our fellow men, to learn all we legitimately can about the way the brain works, the ways it can go wrong, and the ways it may be mended. Increasing knowledge will of course bring enlarged responsibility for the proper use of it; but to gain that knowledge, in that spirit, is a matter of obedience.

This, however, raises in turn a much more complex question – namely, the implications of what we learn about the brain for our concept of human responsiblity itself. Science has a long-standing reputation for showing us that 'things are not always what they seem' to common sense. Brain science is likely to be no exception. Is there not a risk, then, that it may end by showing up as 'illusions' those very aspects of our commonsense view of man that make meaningful our idea of responsibility? Might not brain science, for all its biblical warrant, end by debunking the biblical view of our human nature?

It is this second question that will occupy us for most of the present paper.

2. Major developments

The great surge forward in brain science in the present century has resulted from a coincidence of advances on many widely different fronts. Developments in microscopy, including the art of selective staining of nerve cells, have told us more about the way cells interconnect than we know how to use. The rise of electronics has produced a whole battery of sensitive tools that allow us to stimulate, record and analyse the chatter of electrical activity that goes on in the ten-thousand-million neural population and even in the minute individual members of it. Biochemistry and its relatives have begun to trace intricate patterns of chemical interaction that add a new dimension to the complexity of our map of the brain, and formidably enlarge the armament of drugs whereby its behaviour can be modified for good or ill.

But perhaps the most far-reaching influence has come from

quite another direction. The need for automatic machinery to take the place of human operators in dangerous or boring or otherwise undesirable occupations has forced engineers and psychologists to co-operate in an unprecedented effort to understand and specify the mechanisms of intelligent action. Although this hybrid 'cognitive science' (whose components go by such names as 'automata theory', 'autonomics', 'communication and control theory', 'cybernetics' and 'artificial intelligence') is only a few decades old, it has already revolutionized the way in which the brain scientist thinks of his problems. Let me emphasize that this does *not* mean drawing detailed analogies between brains and present-day computing machines. Our present electronic computers work on quite different physical principles from the nervous system, and the differences between them and the brain are probably more significant than the resemblances. What it does mean is that the *habits of thought* of the automation engineer have powerfully shaped the kinds of question the brain scientist asks, and the kinds of answer he may accept as satisfactory. It now comes as second nature to him to think of the brain as a means of engineering in protoplasm the kinds of information-processing functions that we have found necessary to produce intelligently goal-directed behaviour in our automata. The brain may well be *more* than that; but it is at least amenable to a great deal of detailed explanation in these mechanistic terms. Hypotheses framed in such terms have led to an astonishingly fruitful crop of experimental results, and show every sign of continuing to do so. Conversely, the merchants of 'artificial intelligence' are becoming ever more sophisticated in the kinds of task for which they can produce formal written instructions. In working out their ideas a computer serves as an invaluable 'test bed', since it can show up relentlessly any flaws in a hypothetical model, and allows the theorist to discover (or obliges him to face) unexpected as well as expected consequences of his speculations.

3. Room for the soul?

Man in biblical thought is distinguished from all other animals as 'made in the image of God'. What this means in theological depth has been the subject of unending debate.[2] For our present purposes we can extract three essential ingredients: (1) Man has rational faculties capable of apprehending not only concrete facts of his immediate environment, but also abstract ideas including truths revealed to him by God; (2) Man's death on earth does not annul his relationship (whether of love or rebellion) with his Creator; and (3) Man is *answerable* to God for his actions: he can be *called to account* by his Creator.

Our question in this and the following two sections is whether, and if so how, these ingredients can find a coherent relationship with the kind of understanding of man being developed in brain science, particularly in its mechanistic aspects.

In tackling this question we must beware of a common presupposition that has no basis in biblical doctrine, but is widely accepted, even by some Christians, as 'common sense'. According to this model, which was popularized by Descartes, the brain-and-body is to be thought of as a steerable machine, like a car or an aircraft, which needs a pilot to control it. The 'soul' is then thought of as the invisible pilot, exerting quasi-physical influences on suitably sensitive parts of the machine. I am not concerned here to argue that this model is wrong. Our ignorance of brain mechanics is so great that nobody can dogmatize about the details of its control system; and no less an authority than Sir John Eccles, Nobel Prize winner in Neurophysiology, has opted for something very like the Cartesian picture.[3]

What I do want to emphasize, however, is that this is not a model required by the biblical data. The teaching of Genesis 1 is that man 'became' a living soul, not that a 'soul' was coupled up to his body as an extra *part*. The mechanistic notion of the soul as an invisible and independent entity, capable of exerting *forces* on parts of the brain, goes far beyond anything taught in Scripture. It implies, moreover, that unless there are suitable 'gaps' or indeterminacies in the chain-mesh of physical cause-and-effect in the brain, there can be no effective connection between the workings of the soul (so conceived) and the activity of the body. It suggests that if brain science were ever to swing in a completely deterministic direction, the soul would find itself squeezed out, having no effective part in determining human behaviour.

Christians brought up to accept a 'bipartite' (if not a 'tripartite') idea of man may at this point feel restive. Surely 'body', 'mind' and 'spirit' are biblically distinct concepts? How can we do justice to them if we do not postulate force-like connections between the body and the soul?

Oddly enough, I think that the example of computer technology itself illustrates the answer. When a mathematician describes his computer as 'solving an equation', he means that the behaviour of the machine is *determined* (note the term) by that particular equation. This does not imply that there are 'gaps' in the physical chain-mesh of cause-and-effect linking its components, through which some invisible entity called an 'equation' exerts quasi-physical influences on the transistors. Indeed the electronic engineer in charge of the machine will insist that every physical event in it is *determined* (note: the same word) by other physical events in its depths. Far from contradicting this, the mathematician will insist that he *relies* on its being true as the basis for his own claim, that the behaviour of the machine as a whole was determined by his equation! He will insist equally strongly that computer hardware and mathematical equations are distinct concepts, in quite different categories.

Any appearance of conflict here is of course illusory. A computing machine is simply one example of a situation that *needs explanations at more than one level* in order to do it justice. Each level may specify in its own concepts what determines the behaviour at that level *without necessarily conflicting* with the claims of the other. No matter how complete the electronic engineer's explanation, the mathematician's is *necessary*, and not merely an optional extra, if we are not to miss the whole point of what a computer is and does. The equation determines what the network of transistors does, not by prodding it with quasi-physical 'forces', but by *being embodied in it*.

The point of this illustration is not of course to argue that computers have minds, still less that men are 'nothing but' computers.[4,5] Its purpose is only to suggest an alternative way of doing justice both to biblical data and to common experience, by regarding 'body', 'mind' and 'spirit' as entities recognizable at three different *levels of significance* of our mysterious and complex human nature, rather than three different kinds of 'stuff' that have somehow to exert forces on one another. According to this view, which I like to call 'comprehensive realism', mental activity determines brain activity by being *embodied in it*. Spiritual life similarly shapes mental life by being *embodied in it*. This does not mean that these are only three names for the same thing, nor that mental activity is 'nothing but' brain activity. That is the fallacy of metaphysical reductionism or 'nothing-buttery'. It would be as absurd as to suggest that the equation embodied in the computer is 'only another name' for the transistor network, or that mathematical relations are 'nothing but' relations between computer parts. If there *were* any conflict here, it is our immediate experience as conscious agents that would have to take priority over any story about our brains and bodies, however persuasive. But the point is that there need be no conflict. Each story bears witness to facts to be reckoned with, at different levels of significance. As we shall see, this way of thinking about man, as a unity with at least three levels of significance, is if anything more harmonious with biblical emphasis than the Cartesian (tripartite or bipartite) model.

The moral I wish to draw is not that we should all espouse comprehensive realism (although I personally do so), but only that there exists at least one viable alternative to Cartesian interactionism (the doctrine that the mind or soul *interacts* with the brain or body by exerting *influences* on certain physical parts.) The alternative we have considered, moreover, has nothing to fear from advances in mechanistic brain science, and can indeed positively welcome them. If that is so, Christians have a responsibility to avoid giving the contrary impression, as if the biblical doctrine of the soul logically required some breakdown of physical cause-and-effect in the brain. Here, as on so many other scientific questions, our Christian duty is to keep both our minds and our eyes equally open, and equally obedient to whatever further data God may give us.

4. Lower animals and automata

If our capacity for conscious experience depends so directly on the structure of our brains, what are we to say of the capacities of lower animals? What, for that matter, of automata? The nerve cells making up the brain of a monkey, a dog or a cat are very similar to our own. The principles on which our behaviour is organized can to some extent be imitated by automata. Is there not then a 'thin end of the wedge' argument for attributing some kind of mind or soul both to such animals and to automata?

Once again our concern here is not to decide the issue one way or the other, but rather to evaluate the *logic* of such arguments, from continuity, or 'thin-end-of-the-wedgery'. I see no biblical reason to deny that animals have conscious experience and (limited) mental ability; indeed the term *nefesh* translated in Genesis 1 as 'living soul' is elsewhere applied to lower animals. Recent work[6] has shown that even the rudiments of symbol-using are within the capacities of chimpanzees trained to use deaf-and-dumb sign language. Similarly, as I have argued elsewhere,[7] the Bible offers no objection in principle to the possibility that artificially constructed 'brains' might embody some kind of conscious mentality – however speculative and impracticable such science fiction notions may be. But the 'argument from continuity' by itself is quite invalid. To take an obvious counter-example, a weak mixture of gas and air may contain the same kinds of molecule and lie on the same continuum as a richer mixture that burns; but this does nothing to prove that 'some kind of flame' must be possible for the weaker mixture. Below a certain minimum concentration the mixture is simply non-flammable. By the same token, the fact that a human brain organized in a specific way can embody conscious mental and spiritual life does nothing to prove that similar mental and spiritual capacities must be present in the brains of animals, still less in the artificial brains of automata built of different elements.

Having made this negative point, however, it is important to put it in perspective. Why do so many atheistic propagandists try to make anti-Christian capital out of advances in the scope of 'artificial intelligence'? Why have some Christian apologists felt it to be in their interests to minimize the powers of lower animals or of automata? I suspect the reason may be, on both sides, a hangover of the same 'nothing-buttery' thinking. If the biblical claim were that man was distinguished from lower animals and automata by having a brain sensitive to non-physical influences, and that these non-physical influences were what made his behaviour essentially human, then of course the question of the capacities of animals or automata built of ordinary physical matter would become crucial. Once this claim is recognized as without biblical foundation, however, the polemical pressure disappears, and the whole issue becomes one of marginal interest to the biblical apologist, on which his primary duty is to keep a critically open mind.

5. Immortality

So far our discussion has been tied strictly to experience here and now. But the illustration of the computer with its two levels of significance may seem to raise a difficulty when we face the biblical teaching regarding the hereafter. After all, it may be argued, if a computer were destroyed physically, that would be the end also of its mathematical significance. Does not this suggest that when our brains are destroyed at death, this must also be the end of our mental and spiritual life?

Although such arguments from analogy must be handled with care, I believe that this has an element of truth in it. There is a real biblical sense in which death is the end of our agency in this space-time framework. But the very same illustration points to a possibility which in fact seems more in harmony with the biblical emphasis on 'resurrection of the body' than the Cartesian solution. If a computer solving an equation is destroyed, the mathematician can, if he wishes, set up the very same equation again in some new embodiment. This need not be a computer identical to the old, and certainly need not re-use the original components, in order to be recognizably an embodiment of the same equation.

When we turn to 1 Corinthians 15, which gives our most explicit teaching on the Christian hope of eternal life, we find a remarkably similar emphasis. We are given no promise of *physical* continuity, let alone identity, between our present body and the resurrection body. As when a grain of wheat is sown, the blade that rises from the ground is a quite different structure, so at death we are 'sown as an animal body ... raised as a spiritual body' (1 Corinthians 15:44 NEB). The continuity implied is rather at the level of our personal relationship with God; the personality that is ours will find expression in a new embodiment, perhaps unimaginably different from our present one, but still having the same essential relation structure that identifies and distinguishes us as individuals here and now.

Attempts have been made to discredit this biblical doctrine by suggesting that such a resurrected individual ought to be regarded as a mere *copy* of the original, rather than identical with him. This argument seems strangely perverse. Nothing is more universally accepted than our daily experience of waking up to find ourselves *the same individuals* who went to sleep the night before, despite all kinds of metabolic changes in our bodily tissues. Mysterious though the idea of resurrection may be, there would seem to be no basic *logical* difference between the problem of personal identity on waking up in another world, and that on waking up in this world. Ontologically, the objective reference in either case must of course be to the *fiat* of our Creator, to whom we owe our continual identity moment by moment, day by day. If he knows and recognizes us in the resurrection as those whom he knew in the days of our flesh, then by the same token that *is* who we are in fact, for it is the Creator who alone determines and gives being to what is the case.

Even the most mechanistic brain science, then, offers no objection in principle to the possibility that our Creator might bring into being a sequel to our earthly career, and in it bring to eternal fruition (for good or ill) the solemn consequences of our dealings with him here and now.

6. Responsibility

Here (if not before) someone may be inclined to protest. Even if mechanistic brain science has no objections to the doctrine of the soul or of the resurrection, surely it must question whether we as individuals can be held *responsible* for 'the deeds done in the body'? If my brain were as mechanical as a computing machine, would it not be physical forces, rather than my decisions, that determined my actions?

I have discussed this question at length elsewhere[8–13] and must here be brief. I believe that it rests on a fallacy – the same fallacy of 'nothing-buttery' that we noted earlier. The question presupposes an *either . . . or* : *either* my actions are determined by my decisions *or* they are determined by physical forces. But where we are dealing with explanations at different levels, this assumption is baseless. At one level it is true that a computer's behaviour is determined by the equation it is solving; at another level, that it is determined by physical forces. To suggest that if one of these explanations is true, the other must be false or redundant, would be to talk sheer nonsense.

It is equally nonsensical, and for the same logical reason, to argue that my brain processes *must* be inexplicable in mechanistic terms if my actions are determined by my decisions. This ignores the possibility that the brain processes are precisely the *necessary correlate*, at the mechanistic level, of the mysterious process I know in conscious experience as 'making up my mind'. In view of our present ignorance, nobody can say whether in fact my brain workings always proceed entirely according to physical laws; but even if they did, I could not rationally on those grounds deny, or be denied responsibility for my actions.

But, you may say, if physical laws ruled all my brain workings, would not the outcome of making up my mind be inevitable? Here we must make a crucial distinction. *For an observer* who was physically incapable of interfering with me, the outcome of my decision process could well be inevitable, in the sense that (by definition) he could do nothing to affect it and might even be able (*ex hypothesi*) to predict it with certainty. But – and this is the crucial point – even though inevitable-for-him, the outcome would not in general be inevitable-for-me. 'Inevitability' is essentially a *relative* term. An event inevitable-for-A need not be inevitable-for-B. In particular we shall see that there will be some future events in B's brain which would not be inevitable-for-B, even if his brain were as mechanical as a computer.

The proof of this is quite short, though the result digs deep. According to brain science there must be some mechanism in B's brain which represents by its physical state *what B believes*. Let us call this mechanism M. By definition, no change can take place in what B believes without a correlated change in M. It follows that no completely detailed specification of the present or immediately future state of M could be equally correct whether or not B believed it. (If it were correct *before* B believed it, then it must be incorrect in some detail *after* B comes to believe it; conversely, if the specification were adjusted so that it would *become* correct if and when M were changed by B's believing it, then it would not be correct *unless* B believed it.) In this strict sense, then, the immediate future of M is not *inevitable-for-B*. By this I mean that no complete specification of it exists, unknown to B, with an *unconditional claim to B's assent*. The truth is rather that in some details at least the immediate future of M is *up to B*, in the sense that what B thinks and believes will determine the correctness or otherwise of any purported specification of it, and there is no unique specification of it that B would be logically bound to accept as inevitable, to the exclusion of all others, if only he knew it. The details in question are *logically indeterminate* for B.

It follows that B cannot logically argue that any decision causally dependent on those details of M was inevitable-for-him. The truth rather is that such decisions were strictly *up to him* in the foregoing sense, no matter how physically determinate the workings of his brain.

Note that so far we have been discussing a normally functioning individual in whom the process of deciding and acting depends directly or indirectly on what he knows and believes. If through brain damage, drugs, *force majeure* or the like, the normal link between M and the action centres of the brain is cut or overridden, then the outcome may cease to be logically indeterminate for the agent, and may become inevitable for him. To the extent to which this happens, there would then be logical grounds for denying or diminishing the responsibility we attribute to him for that outcome. One of the challenges offered by brain science to Christians especially is to clarify the rationale of arguments for reducing the accountability of criminals for their actions, which are often quite inadequately based on claims that 'physical causes' or 'psychological causes' made them 'inevitable'. In the light of the foregoing there is a clear need to distinguish two questions. The first concerns the strength of the alleged evidence for causal connections between particular factors and behaviour. The notorious 'XYY-chromosome' abnormality, for example, seems to have been much overrated as an indicator of criminal tendencies.[14] Explanations of behaviour in social terms are often even more shakily supported. It would be a great mistake, however, to imagine that such explanations ought to be minimized *in order to* maintain a belief in human responsibility. The force of the argument above is that even if causal explanations of behaviour in such terms were complete, this would not necessarily diminish the responsibility of the human agent.

The relevant question highlighted by the argument is not whether (or how far) an action was *predictable* (by a detached observer) in practice or in principle, but whether and to what extent it was *inevitable for the agent*. All too often an answer to the first question is taken (by both sides) as if it were an answer to the second. The foregoing argument makes clear that it is not. Christians accustomed to living responsibly under divine sovereignty should not find this too surprising.

7. The damaged brain

Despite the delicate intricacy of the nervous system, a remarkable amount of damage can be done to certain large areas of the brain without causing death. A bullet wound in the occipital lobes at the back of the head, for example, may merely leave the patient with a permanent localized 'blind spot'. Excision of tissue to remove a tumour from so-called 'association areas' may have still less easily detected effects. Even after such a drastic operation as the separation of the two hemispheres of the brain by cutting the millions of connecting fibres in the *corpus callosum*,[15] a patient may seem surprisingly normal to superficial observation.

If the brain embodies the human personality in the sense we have been exploring, a Christian is bound to ask how such brain damage may affect the spiritual status of the individual and the spiritual significance of any resulting changes in his personality. Whereas damage to the occipital lobes of the brain may make no more difference to the personality than does the loss of an eye, a corresponding loss of brain tissue or connecting fibres from the frontal lobes (above the eyes) can turn a formerly civilized and restrained individual into an uninhibited and inconsiderate boor.[16] Damage to one of the parietal lobes (roughly above the ear) can lead to a patient's completely neglecting the opposite side of his body, and even denying that it is his. Most dramatically of all, after the split brain operation mentioned above it is possible for opposite halves of the brain to develop *incompatible* goals.[17] One unfortunate patient found that when he was buttoning up his trousers with his right hand, his left hand would push past the right and unbutton them again!

Startling though such observations are, it would be a mistake to overemphasize the novelty of the issues they raise. Mankind has known since the discovery of alcohol that damage to the functioning of the brain (in this case via its blood supply) can radically transform personality. Because drunkenness is normally a reversible condition, we tend to solve the problem by associating the identity of the individual with his sober state, and saying that he is 'not himself' when drunk. Deterioration of the brain in senility presents a different though equally long-standing problem. Here we find ourselves having to say that the patient is 'not the man he was'.

Doubtless as we grow more accustomed to the newer forms of personality disturbance caused by brain surgery we shall develop similar verbal ways of coping with the mystery of the resulting transformation. A mystery, however, it remains: a mystery of which death itself is the ultimate exemplar. In a case of sudden death we are spared the need to speculate about the status of half-mangled personalities. What these other cases force us to consider is the possibility of the death of a personality without the death of the body that once expressed it, leaving a half-personality that may be so different as to lack essential spiritual continuity with the one who is no more.

In this context what the Christian must recognize is that the entry into eternal life offered by Christ is something far more and other than a mere extrapolation of the personality as it exists at the point of death. The stuff of eternal life, as John in particular makes clear (*e.g.* John 17), is the relationship formed in our present life with the eternal Son. It is by virtue of this relationship that we can be known by the Father and can be welcomed to eternal bliss in the resurrection. The events in our lives that sealed our relationship with Christ are in no way annuled by death. Thus if, through brain damage, the death of our personality takes place by stages, there is no more reason to fear the eternal consequences than if those stages were telescoped into one. What matters is always and only the covenant of grace entered into while the personality was entire and undamaged.

I am painfully aware that this does not answer all the theological questions raised by the after-effects of surgery or accident to the brain; but I believe that the general principle of focusing for spiritual purposes on the relationships formed with God while the individual was capable of them, and thinking of brain damage as a first instalment of death, is fully consonant with biblical teaching. If no man can snatch from Christ's hand those to whom he has given eternal life (John 10:28), we may be sure that no brain damage can do so either, however horrendous the behavioural consequences of the damage for the remaining span of bodily existence.

8. The challenge to the Christian

Let me end with a few summary implications.

(1) It is vital that Christian apologists for the dignity of man should not rest their case upon arbitrary 'postulates of impotence': 'You'll never find a scientific explanation for such-and-such.' We may or may not in the end succeed in explaining or predicting the bulk of human behaviour on a scientific basis; but to pretend that there are any *biblical* grounds for predicting failure would be totally unwarranted. Christianity has no stakes in our ignorance of the physical causes of brain events. Its concern is that we should see and reckon adequately with what they *mean*.

(2) We must beware of confusing claims about *brains* with claims about *people*. For example, it is not brains but people – conscious cognitive agents – who think. Their brains doubtless go through corresponding motions, embodying people's thoughts much as a computer embodies an equation; but it makes no sense to describe the brain (or the computer, for that matter), quâ physical

mechanism, as 'thinking'. Similarly it is people, not their brains, who make choices, freely or otherwise. There need to be no contradiction in saying that a man's brain is physically determinate, yet the man (as a cognitive agent) is free – any more than in saying that a computer is physically determinate, yet the equation it is solving has more than one solution.

(3) One of the greatest temptations of the Christian apologist is to *go beyond his biblical brief* in his eagerness to erect would-be lines of defence. With regard to those aspects of human nature that concern the scientist, the biblical data are much more reticent than is commonly supposed. As Professor R. Hooykaas has remarked in another connection,[18] we are all too ready, like Uzzah, to put out our hands unbidden to steady the ark (2 Samuel 6:6). We cannot remind ourselves too often that our brains, like the rest of our world, are God's workmanship in all their intricate detail. It is he who is affronted if we presume to tell him in advance how they must – or must not – function in order to leave room for our spiritual nature and eternal destiny.

(4) In contending with destructive reductionism or 'nothing-buttery', one of the best services that the Christian apologist can render is to remind people of simple ontological priorities. For the biblical theist, the only ultimate reality is God; what is real is what God holds in being. It is God who brings into being and holds in being the world in which we find ourselves, including our own brains. It is he who gives us moment by moment the flux of our experience as conscious agents. Since it is only in and through that experience that we gain scientific or any other knowledge of the world of physical objects, including our own brains, there can be no question of our scientific knowledge throwing doubts on the reality of ourselves as conscious agents. If there were any conflict, the doubt would have to be the other way around! Even in science it is to the conscious experience of other observers that we appeal in order to resolve questions of objectivity and reality. Thus the practice of science itself is built on a recognition that people have ontological priority over things: our fellow scientists, as conscious beings, are more indubitably 'real' than anything we may collectively believe about the world around us. Nothing could be more fraudulent than the pretence that science requires or justifies a materialist ontology in which ultimate reality goes to what can be weighed and measured, and human consciousness reduced to a 'mere epiphenomenon'. Even apart from biblical considerations, this is to stand reality on its head.

(5) But the greatest challenge offered by brain research, I suggest, is not to our theoretical understanding of ourselves so much as to our practical compassion for our fellow men. Once the nonsense of 'nothing-buttery' has been seen through, each advance in our knowledge of brain processes is to be welcomed in principle as enhancing our sensitivity to one another's vulnerabilities as well as our respect for one another's strengths, and as extending our capacities to do one another good if we will. The fateful effects of malnutrition on infant brain development[19]; the vital importance of social and environmental factors in the maturation of personality[20]; the risks of unethical manipulation, whether by psychological or physico-chemical means[21]; the possibilities (as yet, alas, primitive and limited) of scientifically based psychotherapy[22] – our explosively growing knowledge under these and similar heads daily adds fresh dimensions to our responsibility both to discern its right use and to guard against its abuse. Here science as such is not enough. Although knowledge of the scientific 'map' is essential and would-be guides who are ignorant of its details can be a menace, the choice of a route is not exclusively the business of the map-maker. Christians can claim no monopoly of wisdom in such a task; but they have surely a special duty to contribute positively and constructively to the effort to do it justice as in the sight of God its giver.

8

Biblical perspectives on human engineering[1]

Introductory

We are met to consider a question that is perplexing for men of any religious persuasion or of none: What new obligations are laid upon us by the prospect that human behaviour, and the very constitution of human beings, may be shaped by scientific means? In principle, of course, both behaviour control and human stock-breeding are as old as civilization itself; but in our generation, for the first time, we are having to face possibilities beyond anything considered in traditional ethics. We want to do good, if any good can be done with our new knowledge; yet we are unhappily aware of the ethical risks inherent in the manipulation of human beings, even with the best of intentions. Torn by the claims of compassion and of respect for the individual, men of goodwill look to one another for guidance, and find it hard to see a clear way forward. Christians feel the tensions no less painfully than others . . .

In this setting my brief is to ask what difference it should make to be committed to the biblical Christian faith. There is no suggestion that the Bible contains ready-made answers, still less that Christians know already what the answers should be. The danger in all such enquiries, I think, is that we do not start far enough back; we do not set our problems in a wide enough context to avoid inconsistencies in our thinking. My plan in this paper is therefore to begin at ground level, by considering first how the whole approach of science and technology fits into a biblical view of the world.[2] Once our theological lines are clear, we can then move to consider more specific issues raised by the notion of 'human engineering'; but it should be obvious that my aim will not be to offer definitive conclusions, so much as to clarify the biblical principles upon which Christians will have to base their assessment of this novel and challenging situation.

Biblical or pagan?

For anyone, Christian or otherwise, who wants to understand how biblical Christianity relates to science and technology, the first priority is to distinguish between genuinely biblical concepts of nature and man and a whole variety of pagan ideas that are commonly confused with them. To many people in our day, as in previous ages, the typically 'religious' attitude to natural science is that embodied in the ancient Greek legend of Prometheus. Nature, herself thought of as semi-divine, has her secrets. The gods would like to keep some of these to themselves, and jealously resent any advances in man's knowledge of them. Science is thus an irreverent and dangerous pursuit in which 'sinful man aspires unto the place of God'. If disaster results from attempts to apply man's scientific knowledge, this is only what he deserves for prying into the sacred mysteries of the Creator.

As we shall see later, our overriding policy from the biblical standpoint is to love God and our neighbour; all our exploitation of natural laws and resources must be an expression of this love, and nothing else, if it is to be acceptable. But the whole ethos is clearly in complete contrast to the pagan caricature with which it is so often confused. In place of the craven fear that haunts the unwelcome interloper, we are meant to enjoy the peaceful confidence of the servant-son at home in his Father's creation, knowing that we are on our Father's business no less when investigating his handiwork than when engaged in ritual acts of worship. In place of the jealously secretive gods of the pagans we have One whose very nature is truth and light, who is himself the giver of all that is true, and who rejoices when any of his truth is brought to the light and obeyed in humility (*e.g.* 1 John, *passim*).

We shall be looking at further points of contrast between the pagan and the biblical views under specific headings below. Suffice it for the moment to stress the Bible's positive encouragement to man to roam the domain of the natural world in responsible freedom, showing all of it the respect due to his Father's creation, but none of it the superstitious reverence that would deny its status as a created thing like himself. The characteristically biblical concept of man is that he is God's fellow-worker.

The Bible and the scientific enterprise

The Bible of course contains no worked-out 'theory of nature'; its concern is with still more urgent matters, and the biblical view of the natural world finds expression in it more or less incidentally and often implicity. Nevertheless enough is said to make a strong contrast with pagan attitudes inimical to the spirit of science as we understand it. Hooykaas[3] cites a wealth of illustrations from mediaeval and later writers to show how the fertilizing influence of biblical thought counteracted the Greek tendencies to deify nature, to overvalue speculative arguments *a priori* and to undervalue manual labour, which had hindered the rise of experimental science. From the Bible the sixteenth and seventeenth century founders of the experimental approach drew encouragement both for pure science, as a reverent unfolding and reading of 'God's Book of Nature', and for technology as a compassionate endeavour to ameliorate the lot of mankind through active obedience to what that Book revealed.

Science thus emerges in biblical perspective as an activity *pleasing* to God. The Preacher (Ecclesiastes 1:13) may sound rather doleful as he spells out the scholar's mandate: 'I gave my heart to seek and search out by wisdom concerning all things that are done under heaven; this sore travail hath God given to the sons of man to be exercised therewith'; but it is clear from less pessimistic passages that 'seeking out the marvellous works of the Lord' is a natural response of 'those who take pleasure in them' (Psalm 111:2). There is no suggestion in the Bible that any domain is closed to human enquiry. Although the Creator's thoughts are as far above our thoughts as the heavens are above the earth (Isaiah 55:9), nevertheless the regularities of the natural order are tokens of his faithfulness to us, to be observed and relied upon by us for our good (Genesis 8:22; 9:16). As such they are *worthy* of our investigation: science will not only be fun, but will also be useful, and will moreover stretch our intellectual powers to the limit.

In all this the emphasis on *obedience to truth* is central. In science, facts (data) reign supreme. Opinion is (officially) tenable only as far as the evidence allows, and should (ideally) hesitate to go much further than the evidence demands. In practice both anomalous exceptions to laws and baseless flights of fancy may have to be tolerated; but everyone knows where the last word lies. Since from the biblical standpoint the data that claim the scientist's obedience are God's data, Christians have particular reason to be enthusiastic in support of this emphasis.

In summary, the biblical attitude to science is thus a healthily balanced one. The Christian who wants to think biblically will neither deify science nor vilify it. He can never give absolute or overriding priority to the claims of scientific investigation over ethical or moral considerations; but he will resist all efforts, however well-meaning, to denigrate the scientific enterprise as such, or to bring back negative pagan attitudes towards it.

Technology in biblical perspective

At no point is the contrast between biblical and pagan theologies of nature more decisive than where science comes to inspire technology. 'What right has man to improve upon nature?' 'Aren't we beginning to usurp the prerogatives of the Creator?' Such questions are often asked rhetorically.

There is of course a sober warning for all ages in the story of the Tower of Babel (Genesis 11), where men sought to build 'a tower whose top may reach unto heaven'. What the context makes clear, however, is that their sin in this case consisted not in the building but in the motivation for it – an arrogant desire to be independent of God. Nowhere in the Bible is technological achievement disapproved of, except where it expressed human pride and vainglory. More relevant, perhaps, would be the reiterated biblical teaching that 'He that knoweth to do good and doeth it not, to him it is sin' (James 4:17). From the biblical standpoint whatever lies to our hand to do, by way of alleviation of the lot of our fellow men, is a duty from which we can excuse ourselves only for good cause.

The contrary notion, that it is both impossible and illicit for man to compete with or improve upon nature, has had a long and fascinating history from ancient times (see Hooykaas, *loc. cit.*, Chapter III). The Greek concept of the Golden Age, when men were supposed to have lived healthy and contented lives without technological aids, coloured much classical and mediaeval thinking; and the supposed divinity of Nature was taken to imply that man would be claiming divine prerogatives if he were to attempt to copy her work (let alone to improve upon it). The general belief of the Middle Ages was that the feats of Nature could be surpassed only by magic.

The most powerful biblical arguments against this pessimistic view were advanced by Francis Bacon in memorable rhetoric: 'If there be any humility towards the Creator, if there be any reverence for or disposition to magnify His works, if there be any charity for man,' he dismisses those preposterous philosophies which have led experience captive, and thunders, we should 'approach with humility and veneration to unroll the volume of Creation'.[4] His ideal was a science in the service of man, as the result of the restoration of the rule of man over nature. This to him was not a purely human but a divinely inspired work: 'The beginning is from God . . . the Father of lights'.

For Bacon, 'the entry into the Kingdom of man, founded on the sciences, is not very different from the entry into the Kingdom of Heaven, whereinto none may enter save as a little child.' What must be said, however, is that Bacon's own repeated warnings against the dangers of power divorced from humility and charity have all too often been ignored by later inheritors of the scientific tradition. Under the banner of 'scientific humanism', the most extravagant boasts are to be heard even today concerning the 'limitless power of man to control his own destiny' – free, of course, from 'pre-scientific' belief in God. On this sort of thing the Bible has terse comments (Psalm 14:1). Our question must only be whether there is not a properly biblical way of exercising humbly and charitably the powers that scientific technology puts at our disposal, so that we escape the Bible's condemnation of the proud without falling under that of the neglectful.

The 'perfectibility' of man

How then do these general principles apply in relation to the science of man himself? Few topics so rapidly bring out the irrational in educated people as that of human 'perfectibility'. On the one hand are those who take it as an affront, personally or on behalf of the race, if one ventures to question whether man is perfectible by his own efforts. On the other are religious people who see an affront to biblical doctrine in the suggestion that any human failings could be remedied by psychological or physiological means. To cool the temperature for present purposes, I suggest we discuss the more modest question of the *improvability* of man. What comments does the Bible offer, directly or by implication, on the prospects of human efforts to improve the human race?

Fundamental to this issue is the question: What are people for? Until we settle this one, all talk of improvement is indeterminate. Conversely, to the extent that we spell out what we would see as improvements in man, we are by implication answering this question. The Bible sets out the primary answer in uncompromising terms: men – you and I – exist 'to glorify God, and to enjoy him for ever'. The words are those of the Shorter Catechism; but the thought is solidly biblical. Human life is fulfilled in glorifying and enjoying God at three levels of relationship: (1) In our western tradition Christians tend to think first of the *individual* relationship in which each person would ideally express his love for his Creator by constant, perfect and glad obedience and thankful personal communion; (2) Chronologically prior to this, and given much prominence in the Bible, is the *family* relationship. God has made people for the enjoyment of one another in family bonds of mutual expectations and love, in and through which they are also meant to enjoy fellowship with him; (3) Finally, the Bible lays great stress on the various *corporate* relationships whereby people outside the family circle can become bound to one another by a complex of happily shared expectations and reciprocal giving, and can ideally express a corporate commitment to love and serve their God as a group or a nation.

In biblical terms, then, 'improvement' must mean *enhancing men's capacities for one or all of these levels of relationship to God and other people.* This in no way excludes, but rather subsumes, the development of natural human talents, whether intellectual, aesthetic or any other; but it focuses on essential criteria of 'improvement' which go deeper, from the biblical standpoint, than any merely psychometric assessment. There may be any number of techniques for improving human capacities, even for religious performances, which would miss the main point of what life is for: witness the Pharisee of Jesus' famous parable (Luke 18:11, 12). Any programme to improve the human lot which fails to measure up to the appropriate criteria at these three levels must from a biblical standpoint be seen as short-sighted or worse.

What the Bible emphasizes, and our hearts know all too well, is the extent to which factors each desirable in themselves may interact negatively. 'Geshurum waxed fat – and kicked' (Deuteronomy 32:15). 'It is better . . . to enter into life with one eye (or hand, or foot) than having two . . . to be cast into hell fire (Mark 9:42–50). 'Not many wise men after the flesh, not many mighty . . . are called' (1 Corinthians 1:26). If it was so easy for well-meaning people to make dust bowls of their physical environment in pursuit of desirable and legitimate ends, what dust bowls of the human spirit might not be created by analogous psycho-biological developments? May not some of these indeed be with us already?

When such questions as these are raised, examples come readily to mind. Health is good; but artificially stock-breeding or cloning the finest specimens of manhood at the cost of destroying the biblical ideal of family relationships would buy health at too high a cost. Self-respect is good; but a policy that gave top priority to the development of self-esteem and independence of mind, to the detriment of unselfishness and compassion, would be disastrous. Contentment is good; but the greatest unkindness we could do to a man would be to blind him to the tragedy of living with his back towards God. Contentment at that price would be an opiate indeed.

It would perhaps be a relief to be able to conclude that the weight of biblical evidence is against our entering such a hazardous field at all; but I can find no such evidence. As we shall see, there are a number of principles that restrict closely the kind and manner of interference with human beings that might be legitimate; but it cannot honestly be said that the Bible proscribes all thought of improving either the individual or the race by artificial means. This being so, we cannot on biblical grounds dodge the responsibility of asking whether there is good to be done in God's service by these means, and if so, upon what conditions.

This point is most clearly felt if we apply it to ourselves. We might be tempted to imagine that where we personally are concerned it would show proper humility to accept passively and learn to live with all our defects and limitations. Are we not instructed, after all, that 'godliness with contentment is great gain' (1 Timothy 6:6)?

The distinction we need to make here is between *contentment with the unalterable*, and *complacency with the alterable*, in our human condition. No doubt if our priorities were purely self-centred it could be argued that our lingering in a defective but remediable condition is our own affair; but if our primary obligation is to serve and glorify God, and if an innocuous remedy were at hand that would increase our effectiveness to that end, complacency on our part would be clearly culpable. The question then would be not: why? but: why not? If we daily 'present our bodies a living sacrifice' (Romans 12:1) it should pain us to offer our Master any needless imperfection; and whether it does or not, we rob him by doing nothing about it. In principle there is no more penetrating criterion than this one: what (with all its costs and implications) will make the most acceptable possible offering to God? To apply this in the case of other people, and especially of non-Christians, may be more difficult in detail; but in essence the criterion must be the same. 'Will a man rob God?' (Malachi 3:8).

The fallenness of the natural order

At this point we must come to grips with one of the most crucial, albeit mysterious, of biblical doctrines: that of the 'fallenness' of the natural order, including man himself. 'Cursed is the ground for man's sake' says the Creator (Genesis 3:17). The whole creation has been made 'subject to frustration', and 'groaneth and travaileth', says Paul in Romans 8:20,22. The divine drama in which we find ourselves is emphatically not defined as 'the best of all possible worlds'. Our divinely appointed task is to 'subdue' (for legitimate purposes) a natural order infested with metaphorical thorns and thistles. Moreover we ourselves, even at our best, are not free of the entail of the curse. Our highest motives are likely to be tainted, our moral perceptions blunted or distorted.

In this doctrine, then, we find both a mandate and a warning. Because ours is a world full of imperfection, our brief to improve on things as we find them (through obedience to the facts of nature as we find them) involves no suggestion of impiety. Christ's own example makes abundantly clear that to mitigate the effects of the fall is no sin, but rather a duty. On the other hand, as we ourselves are radically flawed in our own nature, the enterprise of inventing and selecting among possible 'improvements' is bound to be a still more hazardous one than if we were not. History regrettably shows that even official membership of the Christian church is no guarantee against being taken captive by a spirit alien to that of Christ, and thinking we do God service in exercising it.

We now come to a crucial distinction obscured in much of the fashionable theology of our day. The tragedy of fallen man, as seen by the Bible, is his loss of good standing with his Creator. He is not only unfit for the relationship of a son with his Father, by nature he is not even keen on it. This is his 'sin'. As a result, he finds himself in a world that offers frustration in a thousand forms, including his own physical and mental infirmity and a general propensity for anti-social acts and attitudes. Man needs rescuing; and the chief theme of the Bible is the great and mysterious rescue operation whereby God in Christ has reconciled us to himself, and can offer us each the restoration of our standing – the new relationship, unbroken even by death, that is called 'eternal life'. This is our 'salvation'.

Unfortunately in some 'demythologizing' circles today the term 'salvation' has found itself downgraded to mean little more than 'health' – though still invested with emotive religious overtones. The result is particularly confusing in the present context, since it seems to suggest that the Gospel and human engineering could be two alternative or even competitive ways of achieving the same end. The truth is quite otherwise. The root of the biblical concept of salvation is the restoration of our broken relationship with God (*cf.* Romans, *passim*). One of its by-products should indeed be spiritual health and wholeness; but to be interested only in the by-product and to ignore or spurn the new relationship of which it is the fruit would be unequivocally to reject what the gospel means by salvation.

To put it otherwise, in Christ's estimation healthy people need God's salvation just as much as sick people. 'Improved' human stock will miss the way of eternal life without it just as completely as 'unimproved' – and may indeed be at greater risk of doing so (John 9:41). True, there was a notable occasion, reported by all three synoptists (Matthew 9:12; Mark 2:17; Luke 5:31), when Jesus told the Pharisees that 'they that be whole need not a physician, but they that are sick'; but anyone who has missed the irony in that remark should read the context again.

No, the biblical maxim, here as elsewhere, is 'These ought ye to have done, and not to leave the other undone' (Matthew 23:23). Human engineering at its utopian best could be no substitute for divine salvation; conversely, to give top priority to salvation is no excuse in Christ's eyes for neglecting human health and the possibility of improving it. For Christians to stigmatize (or atheists to advocate) human engineering as 'an attempt by man to do what the Bible says only God can do' would be a theological blunder.

Compassion *versus* ambition

There is a further distinction that may prove important for our discussions. To alleviate suffering is a clear Christian duty. If, for example, brain operations for the relief of anxiety raise ethical questions, many of us would feel that the onus of proof should be on those who would abolish them. It is by no means so clearly a duty, however, to seek to change the genetic balance of a human population, or the personality of a healthy individual, in directions we think to be good. *Compassion* for our fellow men and their descendants is not the same as *ambition* for them. This is not to say that one is good and the other bad, but only that the second may need more careful justification, and more ruthless scrutiny of our motives.

Suppose, to take a science fiction example, that we found a human population richly contented with a simple life, but genetically lacking in any capacity to appreciate great music, drama or the like. No one is consciously suffering, for none of them realizes what they are missing; they may even scoff contentedly at the enthusiasm of cultural missionaries for 'unintelligible gobbledygook'. What right, we may ask, has anyone to interfere? But to deal rhetorically with the matter in this way is not good enough. If it were not a matter of genetic defect, but simply one of lack of education, many of us would side with the pioneers of mass education in asking the converse question: what right have we to deny them the ennobling experiences we enjoy, if they could be simply and humanely equipped to share them? From this point of view, to be in possession of means of enlarging people's capacities for what we regard as good, yet to make no effort to make them available, makes us partly at least responsible for their deprivation.

This of course does not settle the matter. It can be cogently questioned whether some of the pioneers of mass education reckoned adequately with the potential for corruption, in various dimensions, which they were bound to enlarge along with that for good. If they could see the results today, what would they think? It is equally far from obvious whether the contented uncultured of our parable would be better people, by either biblical or secular standards, if their aesthetic blindspot could be removed. What the parable should alert us to is firstly the ease with which crass thoughtlessness for others can masquerade as the liberal spirit of 'live and let live'; and on the other hand, the dangers of having ambitions for other people.

Our science fiction case can bring out one further point. Suppose that we had no remedy for the defect in the present generation, but could readily persuade them to let us give their offspring a better aesthetic endowment. We envisage that community fifty years hence, rejoicing in capacities that they would hate to lose, and glad that someone persuaded their parents to have the necessary operation. This may give us a feeling of *obligation* 'not to let the next generation down'; but there is a logical fallacy in this which it is important to spot. For just suppose that we had (in our science fiction world) ten radically different possible genetic recipes for the next generation. In that case we must by our earlier logic envisage not just one (hopefully) thankful community fifty years hence, but ten different alternative onces, each perhaps thankful for different things. To which, then, do we owe our obligation? The answer surely is: to none of them; for they are non-existent and not even *identified* until we have acted. The notion of 'obligation to posterity' becomes logically incoherent if the action in question has to determine *who posterity shall be.*

This does not mean, from the biblical standpoint, that we have no obligations in such a case. It means rather that we must recognize our obligation as directly to our Creator, rather than to multiplicity of non-existent potential human beings. This is logically and theologically parallel to the everyday situation in which Christian parents decide whether or not to have another child. It would be nonsensical to construe their decision in terms of 'obligations to the future child', since it is the existence of that child that is at issue, and in perhaps the majority of such cases the child never will exist. On the other hand, it is both meaningful and relevant to construe it in terms of their obligation to God as 'fellow-workers' or *pro*-creators.

The suggestion that emerges, then, is that if we were ever called to exercise the function of genetic engineers, the logic and theology applicable would be those relevant to *procreation*. The Bible has plenty of worked examples of what it means to exercise this function both responsibly and irresponsibly, and of the special kind of mutual responsibility that is meant to develop in due course between procreator and procreated when both survive together (*e.g.* Ephesians 6). If it ever becomes a live issue, this might provide a useful biblical model for the corresponding relationship between the genetic engineer and the offspring of his selective actions.

Dehumanization

Behind much of our instinctive uneasiness with the notion of human engineering lies the feeling that it *dehumanizes* its subjects. It will be important for us to try to pin down this feeling and to articulate biblical guidelines for deciding which forms of manipulation, in what circumstances, are indeed dehumanizing.

To dehumanize a fellow man, in biblical terms, is to refuse to love him as oneself. It is to 'shut up one's bowels of compassion from him', to harden one's heart against him, to refuse to be answerable to his questions or to be sensitive to what it is like to be he. It is, in short, to 'treat him as an object'.

In order to spell out what this means, and what precisely is wrong with it, we have to go into some technicalities. Manipulation requires calculation. A precondition of successful manipulation is that the process of calculation can be kept isolated from the manipulated situation, sufficiently to prevent 'feedback' which would render the calculation out of date. In the relationship of *dialogue*, to the extent that the goals of each partner are reciprocally open to adjustment by the other, feedback of this kind is inevitable, and manipulation correspondingly limited.[5] The mutual interaction that takes place in dialogue (as distinct from alternate monologue) makes the partners effectively one system for purposes of mechanistic analysis and prediction, so that in respect of certain actions each becomes incalculable and 'logically indeterminate' for all the others in dialogue as well as for himself. It would be irrational for any of them to regard such actions as unconditionally *inevitable*. This, I have suggested elsewhere, is the ethically essential sense in which normal human beings must be recognized by one another as objectively free.[6] Conversely, a calculator who withdraws from the vulnerability of dialogue may thereby enhance his powers of manipulation by increasing his calculating capacity. He may continue to communicate but to the extent that his own goals are invulnerable he does so purely manipulatively.[7]

We have so far tended to speak of manipulation as something ethically unsatisfactory; and indeed it usually is. There are, however, certain common situations where this is not the case. In clinical psychiatry, for example, we encourage the patient to give himself up to be manipulated for his own good; and all of us at an early enough age endured purely manipulative relationships for which we are now grateful.

Perhaps the most difficult borderline case, and one which creates much confusion today, is that of the education and upbringing of children. Until recently it was taken for granted that parents had not only a right but a duty to mould the value-system and character of their children in accordance with the best they knew. In these enlightened days, however, there are many who condemn all this kind of teaching as 'manipulation' or 'indoctrination'. The ethics of the alternatives they themselves offer are not always beyond question, but that is not here our concern. What needs to be asked first is whether, and when, manipulation *is* unethical in this context.

This is of course a big question which could take us far beyond our present topic, but one possible suggestion emerges from what has just been said. The basic objection to the manipulator is that he dehumanizes, by treating people as objects. We have seen however that where a certain kind of reciprocal coupling exists between two individuals, they necessarily cease to be fully specifiable to one another. In that sense it becomes self-contradictory for either to treat or even conceive of the other as a mere object, fully specifiable to him in principle.

Now it is clear that not all manipulation requires the withdrawal from this interpersonal relationship to be complete; what is needed is only sufficient 'uncoupling' to provide predictive information in the area of the manipulation. Only that area, and not necessarily the whole individual, is and must be 'dehumanized' for this purpose. It would therefore seem that to define manipulation (in the technical sense) as *ipso facto* unethical would be to fasten dangerously upon the wrong thing. What is ethically significant, and may be either good or bad, is rather the kind of one-way relationship necessitated by the manipulation. It is in part the lack of reciprocal openness, the rejection of all answerability in the manipulator we were discussing earlier, that makes his attitude and practice unethical.

But, it may be said, is not the trouble with the old-fashioned parent or teacher just that his teaching is *not* open to question, and that he declines to be held to account by the child he instructs? This may be true enough – at the time. It is equally true of the clinician that he declines to give all the judgments of his patient equal weight with his own. Each rejects questioning for what he regards as good reasons, of immaturity or mental disorder in his charges. To this extent fully symmetrical dialogue is in fact impossible *for the time being*. It would be a naïve mistake, however, to conclude from this that these admitted manipulators have rejected all answerability in principle. As far as the best of them are concerned, nothing would give more pleasure than to be confronted in due course by their charges, mature and of sound mind, and to answer for their manipulative actions in full dialogue. Only, in the nature of the case, this pleasure has to be deferred for a time. They believe that they best betoken their future answerability by exercising the highest skill now, in the most single-minded way, to the purpose that they will in due course be glad to defend if asked.

Potential answerability

It is the nature and degree of *potential answerability* in this sense, rather than the degree of manipulation being exercised, that I suggest we should concentrate upon for ethical purposes. If we want to make it more concrete, we can envisage an imaginary *advocatus infantis* confronting the educator here and now on behalf of the child, and demanding all the explanations to which the child as an adult will one day be entitled. It is by the educator's response that the ethics of his manipulations would stand to be judged. Biblically of course, there is such an *advocatus* – none other than Christ himself, to whom we shall have to answer in sober reality on the Day of Judgment (Matthew 25:31–46; John 5:22, Romans 14:10).

Admittedly, in proportion as children are capable of dialogue, the educator has a measure of answerability to them from their earliest communicative years. More and more forms of manipulation that were initially legitimate become degrading and unethical as the child grows up, because they would involve the refusal of a level of dialogue for which he has gradually acquired the necessary equipment. What I am trying to emphasize is not (heaven forbid!) that *any* technique of instruction is legitimate with children provided that we would be prepared to defend its purpose, but rather the converse: that a technique cannot be ethically evaluated solely by asking whether it is manipulative. We must indeed ask whether any manipulation is being used as a substitute for a level of dialogue to which the child's maturity entitles him; but if so it is the refusal of due dialogue rather than the presence of manipulation as such that invites our condemnation.

This last consideration rules out the appeal of the benevolent dictator, who might also claim that in due course he will be prepared to defend his manipulations, so that he is 'potentially answerable'. This would be a mistaken interpretation of the term. A dictator, whether benevolent or not, is someone who does not at the moment *want* to be answerable to anyone. His methods are objectionable, not simply because they involve manipulation, but because they do so as a substitute for dialogue with people who (unlike children or mental patients) are fully capable of and entitled to it now. The category of potential answerability applies only if actual answerability is impossible for good reason.

I have dwelt at length on the example of education because its problems are concrete and familiar; but the same principles would seem to apply to human engineering in general. Always our question must be whether, as in the sight of God, we are expressing as fully and realistically as possible our answerability, both actual and potential, to our fellow man, and to Christ as his *advocatus*.

Personality changes

One particular type of manipulation, namely physical operations to alter personality, raises a special problem. If a violent criminal, for example, could be changed into a peaceful citizen by otherwise harmless brain surgery, it could be argued that the community would be the better off by losing an undesirable member and gaining a desirable one, and that the latter (if we have been successful) would in due course be as grateful to us as the Gadarene demoniac was to Jesus (Luke 8:38). The difficulty is that the man to whom we are answerable here and now, when considering whether or not to perform the operation, is the violent person we want to change. Can we meaningfully say to him that *he* will later be glad if we do so; or is it not he but someone else – the different individual who will emerge from the operation – who will be glad? In the Gadarene case a convenient distinction is available between the man *per se* and the 'unclean spirits' who possess him, and whom it appears Jesus addressed separately (*loc. cit.* v. 29). Is there a clue here to a parallel distinction that would help us in such cases?

The problem is closely linked with the philosophical enigma of personal identity: what is it that makes you today continuous with the individual you were yesterday? I know of no fully satisfactory answer[8]: but even to pose the question suggests that in working out the ethics of brain surgery we must recognize two different possible kinds of outcome: one, in which the essential brain correlate of individual continuity is *preserved*; the other, in which the operation has *destroyed* brain structures essential to that continuity, and we have in effect terminated the life of one individual and brought a different one into being.

In the interests of realism it must be emphasized that most actual brain operations today serve their purpose by destroying brain structures rather than replacing or renovating them. These operations have thus a serious cost to the patient quite apart from any ethical doubts we may raise about the manipulative approach. In order to clarify the present issue, therefore, we must consider also possible chemical treatments that might modify brain functions and dispositions non-destructively. Against such treatments, assuming an ideal outcome in the *first* category, there would seem to be no biblical objections in principle. Whatever the differences between the New Testament phenomenon of demon-possession and contemporary psychopathology, the principle of distinguishing between the real man and his affliction, and remaining answerable to the real man while removing the characteristic that afflicts him, would seem to apply in both.

The second case is different. We would here have to ask ourselves whether the individual now before us ought, in effect, to die. There would be few cases in which we might be convinced that he should; and even in those few cases, it might still be far from obvious that we had any right or obligation to bring a new individual into being in what would remain of the original brain and body after the operation. In other words, assuming it were ever right to bring a particular individual's existence to an end, it might be more ethically defensible to destroy the body as a whole, rather than keep it running with a new and alien personality.

One remaining theological question is often raised. Brain surgery can so alter the personality that a lifelong Christian, say, might lose all apparent interest in religion. In such a case, what happens to his soul? The short answer, I believe, is that God has not told us; but we can be sure that in such a case God will be more just and more realistic and more merciful than we would be. If I may offer one constructive suggestion, very tentatively, it would be that as eternal life is something into which Christians enter here and now as soon as they become united with Christ (John 6:54 and *passim*), then no one who has truly received eternal life can be robbed of it by brain manipulation any more than by death (John 10:29). If I am right in my reading of these and related biblical passages, Christians have no reason to fear the eternal consequences of such an operation, though they would have to recognize that it might terminate their *experience* of God here and now, and so for practical purposes bring their spiritual life on earth to a premature end.

Psychological technology

As we have already recognized when talking of education, the shaping of personality and behaviour can be undertaken without directly interfering with the physical structure of the brain. The difference is roughly analogous to that between changes to the 'hardware' of a computer system (*e.g.* by replacing or destroying components), and changes to the 'programme', which leave the hardware intact. Obviously in principle it is possible that a programme change in a computer could bring about gross physical damage (*e.g.* by overheating); and it is certainly possible for purely psychological methods to lead to damage to the delicate physico-chemical balance of the human brain-and-body system. But the distinction is a useful one, as there are many ways of manipulating human beings which stop short of physical interference, and we must briefly ask whether the biblical doctrine of man has anything particular to say about these.

As far as I can see, the possibility of controlling behaviour by psychological techniques raises few theological issues that have not already cropped up. The main reason is that the Bible is a good deal more earthy and less high-minded about our bodily endowment than, say, the classical Greek tradition. Man is indeed a 'living soul', but he is also 'dust'; and the unity of mind and body in biblical thought is so intimate that I think it makes relatively little difference theologically whether manipulation is carried out at the physical or the psychological level or both. The same stringent criteria must apply.

The idea seems to have found its way into some recent Christian thinking that if a man's mind is 'in control', his brain activity and physical behaviour must be inexplicable in mechanistic terms; but this has no biblical support.[9,10] The notion that a complete explanation of a human action at a mechanistic level would debunk its spiritual significance, and the agent's responsibility for it, is equally unfounded in logic. To most of us in brain research, conscious experience and brain activity seem to be harmoniously relatable as the 'inside' and 'outside' aspects of the mysterious unitary process that we know as human agency. Nothing in the

Bible conflicts with this, and it would warn us against making artifical separations between our responsibility towards a man's brain-and-body and towards his soul.

Perhaps the most specific theological issue here is the relation of manipulative techniques to the process of Christian preaching and conversion itself. Here much that was said earlier about dialogue and potential answerability applies with double force, since the preacher or evangelist purports to be speaking on behalf of God, with a view to introducing his hearers to a personal relationship with God.

What must be recognized however is that no matter how genuine and non-manipulative the dialogue between preacher and hearers, there will always in principle be a detached observer-standpoint from which the psychological mechanics involved can be studied in causal terms, and perhaps even to some extent explained, by a third party. This has in itself no logical tendency to debunk or devalue the outcome,[11] but it does of course make it possible for would-be manipulators to 'see what works' and perhaps develop imitative techniques which are unethical because not expressive of genuine dialogue. It also constitutes a temptation for the preacher to lose the posture of dialogue, and subconsciously or otherwise take an unethical observer-attitude to his own performance.

What follows is not, I think, that biblical preachers should stay ignorant of psychology, but rather that they should be alert to all it can say of the dangers of overriding or undermining the mind and will of their hearers rather than illuminating them. If they themselves are fully and awefully aware of the presence of God, who sees them through and through and abhors deceitful dealing of every kind, they have a better safeguard than any other against misuse of their knowledge. If they are not so aware, no ignorance of psychological technology can save them.

I need hardly say that in all this the ethical content of what is being preached or propagated is a separate issue. To foment hatred between man and man, for example, would be abhorrent to the Christian whatever the methods of persuasion used. Our question concerns the legitimacy of psychological means to good ends; and the biblical criteria here seem to be just the same, and just as stringent, as in any other context in which we seek to be obedient fellow-workers with God.

Some biblical check-points

The Christian who seeks to be biblical in his obedience has thus to steer between two opposite evils. One is that of fatalistic complacency: 'If God wills that such children should be born, who am I to interfere?' This we saw to be theologically inept. The other is that of naïve utopianism, which makes 'perfectibility' its watchword. For the biblical Christian, to hold out hopes of 'perfectibility' by human contrivance to a fallen race is cruelly unrealistic. On the other hand, if Christians are to be the 'salt' of the earth they must be in, if not indeed leaders of, efforts to see what good can be done for mankind along these new lines.

How will this 'salting' function show itself? There is no formula; but a short check-list of questions may serve to outline the kind of responsibility that the Bible lays on the Christian in this area:

(1) Granted the (biblical) freedom of scientific enquiry, have we properly assessed the relative *priorities* of the different areas in which effort could be spent?

(2) In avoiding self-confident atheistic arrogance or wooly pantheistic optimism,[12] are we sufficiently sensitive to the claims of *compassion*?

(3) Do we have a biblically balanced conception of human *needs*: the need to give as well as to get; the need to express love and gratitude in worship as well as the need for security; above all, the need for eternal life, without which all is ruin in the end?

(4) Have we the *Bible's priorities* in mind for the subjects of our intervention?

(5) Have we established a *need to act*?

(6) Have we done all we can to foresee possible *consequences* both for good and for evil, at the three levels of the individual, the family and society?

(7) Is love the ruling spirit of the enterprise?

(8) Above all, are we out to *please God*, undertaking nothing, in method or aim, which we cannot offer for his blessing as an act of service to him?

New knowledge creates new sins, both of commission and of omission. Temptations to both abound – particularly where personal reputations are waiting to be made and power waits to corrupt. Christians cannot pretend that inaction will absolve them of responsibility; nor can they claim any monopoly of wisdom. Learning what to want is even more difficult, most of the time, than learning how to achieve what we want.[13] Christians must be prepared to work hard and humbly and compassionately at this, alongside all men of good will. The assurance of the Bible is that the wisdom we need – just enough, no more – is ours for the asking.

Artificial intelligence? – a Christian appraisal[1]

1. Perspective

1.1 The posture of Christian stewardship

Scripture describes man as the divinely appointed steward of the natural resources he finds around him. The Christian is someone who seeks by God's grace to accept and live up to the responsibilities of this stewardship in his Father's world. This makes an important difference to his starting posture in face of potential new developments in science and technology. In place of the craven fear instilled by a pagan theology of nature – the fear of being regarded as an unwelcome and over-inquisitive intruder in matters that are not his business – the Christian who finds scientific talents in his toolbag has quite a different fear – the fear lest his Father should judge him guilty of neglecting his stewardly responsibilities by failing to pursue the opportunities for good that may be opened up by the new developments. Needless to say, he must also have a realistic awareness of his limitations, coupled with a humble dependence on the grace of God and a sensitivity to the dangers of sinful pride and greed that constantly beset him. But his general attitude (in contrast to that of the unfaithful steward of Matthew 25:18, 24, who buried his talent) must be positive. His first question as he confronts a new possibility must be directed to his Master. 'Thank you, Lord. Now what do you want me to do with this, as your servant?'

From this biblical starting point, there can be no excuse for neglecting or scorning the potentialities of what has come to be known as 'artificial intelligence' (AI) or (more modestly) 'knowledge-based systems'. As a 'natural resource', this comes into much the same category as clay tablets and printing, with the added advantages of the automatic manipulation of tokens at high speed. Popular literature may be cluttered with exaggerated claims and wrong-headed innuendos as to the scope of AI and its implications for the theology of human nature; but what I shall argue in these lectures is that it would be disastrously unwarranted for Christians to fly to the opposite extreme and join the chorus of 'science-bashers' who denigrate AI in the supposed interests of 'humanity'.

1.2 Ground-clearing

At the outset we must distinguish between two quite different questions that are often confused:

A: How far can we go towards enabling an artificial system to behave in ways we would judge 'intelligent' in a human being?

B: What are the prospects of artificially constructing an entity that not merely simulates human behaviour, but actually possesses conscious experience, as we ourselves do?

Question A can be usefully subdivided into:

A.1: How far can a *rule-following program* express the requirements for intelligent behaviour (of all kinds)?

A.2: Are there additional principles, over and above rule-following, that could enhance the ability of artificial agents to behave intelligently?

Question B likewise subdivides into:

B.1: Are there any rational grounds for believing that a rule-following machine, programmed to imitate conscious behaviour sufficiently well, should be credited with conscious experience?

B.2: Are there any clues, from brain science or elsewhere, as to the type of artificially constructed entity that might embody conscious agency in the sense in which the human brain does?

Once we are clearer as to the answers suggested by present knowledge to these diverse questions, we shall be in a better position to tackle a question that troubles many of our fellow Christians:

C.1: What implications have these possibilities for Christian theology, both theoretical and practical?

In turn this gives rise to the complementary question:

C.2: What bearing has the Christian revelation on the theory and practice of AI?

1.3 Plan of investigation

My plan is as follows. First we ask what is logically involved in the decision to use behavioural language to refer to mechanical processes, and what requirements must be met, in general terms, if artificial behaviour is to be deemed intelligent. This section follows the lines of a paper published some years ago,[2] to which I have added comments in the light of later developments. Next, we look at what is known about the physical basis of natural intelligence in the workings of the human brain, and what light this throws on the scope and limits of AI. Finally, we consider the relevance of this new field to Christian theology, and vice versa.

2. The use of behavioural language to refer to mechanical processes[3]

2.1 A mis-stated problem

'Brain-like mechanisms' are nowadays something more than a possibility in principle. On all hands we hear of 'programmes' for behaviour which, if only crudely approximate to the human, seem undeniably to occupy some of the right dimensions. Philosophical enquiry into the powers and limitations of such automata is frequently confused by a failure (even among philosophers) to recognize the elliptical nature of much popular talk about computers and their ilk. When the enquiry takes the form of a comparison between the artificial and the natural, it becomes particularly important to sort out the concepts and relationships on each side, so as to see which correspond to which – and to discover which, if any, have as yet no counterpart. The 'semantic chart' of Table 1 is an attempt to do this for some of the key notions. 'Natural' concepts on the left are matched by 'artificial' counterparts on the right.[4]

The assembly of components occurs by 'growth' and 'construction' respectively. If the end-product of construction (which might, of course, include artificial growth-processes) be termed a 'machine' or 'automaton', then what invites comparison or contrast with it is the end-product of natural growth – strictly (and only) the 'brain-and-body' in its physical aspects.

After this point, however, our two middle columns begin to show some similarities. The (mass of) wires and transistors carry signals. So do the (mass of) cells and things. Each is organized to form what we term an 'information system': a system whose activity

Table 1

NATURAL		ARTIFICIAL	
Personal aspect (I-story)	Mechanical aspect (Brain-story)	Mechanical aspect (Machine-story)	Personal aspect ??
	Developed by growth.	Developed by construction.	
Conscious Person (Joe)	Brain-and-body ('mass of cells and things')	Automaton ('mass of wires and transistors')	? ?
with conscious experience expressed by saying:	carrying signals forming an information-system, organizing observable behaviour indicative of	carrying signals forming an information-system, organizing observable behaviour indicative of	
'I think, feel, hope, fear . . .'	thinking, feeling, hoping, fearing . . .	thinking, feeling, hoping, fearing . . .	?

depends on the reception, transformation, and transmission of information. Each produces observable behaviour (both internal and external).

On the 'natural' side, we have a second (left-hand) column, which I have labelled 'Personal aspect'. In this aspect, we are accustomed to recognize the being before us as our friend Joe Smith (whom we shall meet later). We say that Joe is capable of such activities as thinking, feeling, hoping, fearing. Of these activities we have first-hand knowledge only in our own case; but we recognize 'observable indications' of the same in Joe's behaviour, and Joe bears witness to the facts of his conscious experience by telling an 'I-story': 'I think . . . I feel . . . I hope . . . I fear . . . '.

The problem I want to discuss is represented by the question marks in the corresponding column on the right-hand side. It is often expressed by asking, 'Can a machine think?'; and fierce debates have raged between those designers of automata who regard this as an empirical question answerable by experiment in the affirmative, and those philosophers who share the same presupposition but regard the evidence to date as inadequate.

I have long argued[5] that empirical 'predictions of impotence ('you'll never get a machine to do X') – or counter-predictions – cannot resolve an issue of this sort, for any detailed test-specification for particular behaviour, whether statistical or determinate, is implicitly equivalent to a description of at least one mechanism to meet it. Attempts to get round this and prove that 'minds are not machines' by invoking Gödel's theorem (as J. R. Lucas[6] does, for example) are I believe both hopeless and needless.

They are hopeless because only an uninteresting type of 'machine' suffers significantly as a result of the impotence shown to follow from Gödel's theorem. Lucas argues: '. . . Just because the mind has the last word, it can always pick a hole in any formal system presented to it as a model of its workings' (whereas the type of machine that he considers cannot). Yes indeed; but the only class of artificial mechanism worth considering as a candidate for 'mentality' is of the self-adaptive or self-organizing type, from which exactly the same behaviour could be expected as Lucas claims for 'the mind'.

But such attempts to save 'the argument from impotence' seem also to be needless; for if our 'semantic chart' is correct, the short answer to a claim on empirical grounds that 'machines can think' or that 'minds are machines' is not 'you are empirically justified (or unjustified)' but 'you are talking nonsense'. For in the human case, it is not brains that are said to think, feel, hope, fear, but people. To say that a mass of nerve-cells 'thinks' or 'fears' would not be an empirical assertion but a misuse of language; and just the same is true for a mass of wires and transistors. If a 'mass of wires and transistors' invites comparison with a human being at all, it can only be with the 'mass of cells, *etc.*' that comprise his brain and body. Thus no degree of resemblance to the performance of the human brain, however great, could justify the semantic absurdity of saying that any 'mass of wires and transistors' can think.

Yes. But is this really a sufficient answer to our restive designer of automata? May he not justly retort: 'All right: it was silly to argue whether "mechanisms" could think. But insofar as we can agree that human thinking is bound up somehow with natural brain-activity, is it not meaningful to ask whether, and on what conditions, some kind of "thinking" might not be similarly bound up with artificial brain-activity?' He is now asking a very different question, and I think it is a good one. It leads at once to the more basic question of the nature of the transition which we are accustomed to make on the 'natural' side, from talking in bodily terms to talking in personal terms – from the 'mass of cells and things' in column 2 to 'Joe' in column 1. What are the preconditions of this change? Under what circumstances is it justified? Is it purely optional, and if not, in what sense?

In an attempt to explore this issue one uncovers a trail of prior questions which leads surprisingly deep into the jungle of our basic physical concepts; for on examination the problem turns out to have some features in common with several others that have plagued philosophers of science. But it is only part of this trail that I propose to follow in the present paper.

2.2 The necessity of 'underspecification'

Let us begin with the fundamental notion of goal-pursuit, which is a basic feature of living systems, and of all artificial devices with any pretensions to human powers. A self-regulating mechanism, such as a thermostat, is said to show 'goal-directed activity'. From its repertoire or range of 'possible' activity, it is said to make a 'selection' by adjusting a 'control' or 'switch' on the basis of 'information' as to the disparity or 'mismatch' between the current state of affairs and what is termed a 'goal-state'. The activity selected is 'calculated' to reduce the disparity.

The whole description bristles with difficulties. What do we mean, first of all, by 'possible' here? Surely, a good Newtonian might argue, the only possible activity is the activity that occurs? In what sense is the activity 'controlled'? 'Had the control or the switch been in a different position, the flow of heat would have been different' – but it was not, and could not be, for good, well-determined, physical causes. So in what sense was any other activity 'possible'?

The answer seems plain. Only if we under-specify the situation, by using generic terms that allow more than one microstate to be compatible with our description, can we give meaning here to the word 'possible'. A two-way switch is a device with two possible states ... Yes. But *this* 'two-way switch' is a physical array of molecules in the only state compatible with its past history. 'Is no other state possible?' – Not in these terms. 'In future', of course, it is 'possible' that it may be found in either of the two states – but only if we have not specified the time, nor the intervening history of forces acting on it. Given these, the concept of a 'range of possibilities' evaporates. It is not the physical situation that possesses a range of possible states, but our specification of it – if sufficiently open.

A similar point can be made regarding most of the concepts of applied physics, if viewed from the standpoint of classical molecular theory. Consider for example how the concept of 'entropy' appears in statistical mechanics. It is often asked how an 'irreversible' process (increase in entropy) can arise within a theory based on the 'reversible' laws of Newtonian dynamics. The answer is that (statistical) entropy is definable within the theory only when the system is underspecified in such terms that it can be said to have a range of 'possible' micro-states. Entropy here measures a property, not of the molecular situation, but of the summary abstraction (in macroscopic terms such as pressure, volume, temperature) which is normally our only available state-description of it. Given a full micro-description in molecular terms, all but one of the probabilities pi in the entropy-coefficient $\Sigma\ p_i \log p_i$ become zero, and entropy vanishes both numerically and conceptually from the situation as described.

What is irreversible here is the decline in 'specifying power' of a description whose terms offer too few degrees of freedom. In its statistical form the Second Law of Thermodynamics tells us that molecular assemblages change in such a way that anything less than a full microspecification becomes progressively less adequate as time goes on. The consequences of 'losing track' cannot be undone within a closed system.[7]

What then of 'information'? Upon what conditions is it meaningful to speak of 'information-flow', or to say that an event B betokens or conveys information as to the occurrence of another, A? Clearly, once again, only when we can say that B 'might have been otherwise'. If not, then B conveys no information, in either the common or the technical sense.

But we have just seen that the meaningfulness of such talk depends entirely on the degree of underspecification of the situation. Basically, it is to us that B conveys information about A – if we are sufficiently ignorant. To say that 'information is conveyed to the switch' would be meaningless, if by 'the switch' we meant 'that particular molecular array of brass and porcelain'. To talk the language of information-flow is to deflect discussion from the physical situation, to our underspecified[8] state-description or model of it in which 'the switch' means a 'skeletonized' functional variable with two possible values. In this state-description, it makes good sense to say that B determines the state of the switch according to the nature of A, or that information about A determines the selection of activity by the switch.

It follows that to ask whether the activity of a given mechanism is an example of goal-directed or other 'behavioural' activity is to ask, not about the physical situation per se, but about the types of under-specified state-description that it can justify. While not every situation can be made to manifest goal-directed features by suitable under-specification, it is quite possible for one level or mode of specification to bring out such features while at another level they become totally meaningless.

2.3 The 'underspecified' nature of human activity

So far we have considered only artificial automata; but may we not recognize the same principle as applicable to human beings? Insofar as a standpoint is possible from which most, if not all, bodily activity can be viewed as physically determinate, to that extent are manifestations of 'goal-directedness' and the like dependent for their perception on one's choice of level of specification. Here, however, I want to give the argument a new twist, in terms of an important and singular fact about the human brain-mechanism. The intriguing feature of each human being is that, for himself, his bodily state is always and necessarily unspecifiable in full detail, so the corresponding 'range of possibilities' of which he is aware is logically irreducible.

Even if his brain were (to an outside observer) a fully-determined physical mechanism, it could never embody an up-to-date and complete description of its own total state, with an *unconditional* claim to his assent. The most fully-supported predictions of the most completely-informed observer (granted full 'classical' physical determinateness) can be for the agent logically indeterminate until after the decisions they purport to predict have been made.[9] So for him, his present and immediately future state is necessarily underspecified. It follows that no mechanical account of an agent's bodily activity, however deterministic, can logically undermine the meaningfulness, for the agent, of his personal account.

The meaningfulness of our recognition of 'mental' qualities, such as goal-directedness, in the activity of one another is, by the same token, dependent on our being 'underspecified situations' to one another. At first sight this may seem an oddly precarious and arbitrary condition. From a 'Newtonian' view of bodily mechanism it would surely follow that by totally contracting out of a community of discourse (if this were possible), an individual could in principle adopt a fully-specified state-description of the bodies of his fellows, in which concepts of personal agency could rationally find no place. I would not personally deny this. No demonstration in terms of observable behaviour could, I think, rationally compel such an individual to accord personal status to the activity of his fellows. In that sense, recognition of persons is 'optional'.

What I would emphasize, on the other hand, is that insofar as two people interact in 'dialogue', and thus become one system, the crucial condition is necessarily fulfilled, since for each individual his own (necessarily underspecified) situation becomes a determinant of that of his interlocutor, which thus shares in the underspecifiability-to-him (see section 3.4 below).

We seem then to be approaching the view that the requirements for the recognition of personality in natural human beings are of two kinds. First, and obviously, (a) the physical 'bodily situation' must admit of and support in practice an underspecified state-description showing appropriate behavioural features: the 'observable indications' of thinking, feeling, hoping, fearing, *etc.* But the second, and no less important, requirement is (b) that we, the arbiters, must be rationally able and willing to adopt the appropriate standpoint of interactive relationship, from which the situation acquires some of our own necessary unspecifiableness-to-ourselves.

This I think is the technical correlate of the much-discussed distinction between the 'I-Thou' relationship and that of 'I-Object'. In the latter, no comparable barrier of principle prevents full specification of the object-situation by the observer, even where the object is a normally functioning human body. By withholding the commitment implicit in dialogue, or even in less discursive forms of interaction – the opening of one's controls to the action of the other – the observer could in principle obviate the systematic mutual 'underspecifiableness' that logically undergirds the structure of personal language.

2.4 The 'personality' of automata

What then of artificial automata? There is room for serious doubt in principle whether our understanding of 'what it is to be a man' could ever be made explicit enough to enable us to write a full specification for human behaviour. To that extent, our prospects of fully meeting the first of the above requirements (a) are rather unsatisfactory. How should we ever know that we had left out nothing essential?

But to take refuge behind such barriers (real though I believe they are) would be to evade the issue; for there seems every reason to believe that the main lineaments of intelligent human behaviour could in principle be reproduced in automata, even employing only the techniques known today. We may not feel confident that the 'personality' in question would be fully human, but we can hardly doubt that as far as behaviour is concerned, at least the minimal criteria for such intelligent activities as 'thinking', 'learning' and the like could be met.

The real obstacle, then, appears to lie in our second requirement (b). Those who wish to refuse personal status to artificial automata are on strong ground; for we have seen that at the cost of sufficient 'detachment' even the personal significance of human activity (at least of other people's!) can be made to disappear, from a standpoint which views it as fully-specifiable in principle. No observable performance can logically force anyone from such a position.

What would be logically possible (though somewhat perverse) as an attitude to human brain-mechanisms other than one's own, may thus seem more than justifiable towards artificial mechanisms that only feebly imitate them; and I would not wish to disturb anyone from a defensive agnosticism here. In relation to existing automata I confess to sharing it, for I cannot see myself rationally sustaining a long personal relationship with any I know of (see section 3 below).

But our concern here is with philosophical limitations in principle, rather than with psychological barriers in practice; and I think the matter cannot be left thus. We must ask, not whether such a commitment would be difficult or undesirable, but whether, and in what circumstances, it would be *absurd*.

Let us first take the stock example of the man who adopts a personal attitude to his car, his golf ball, or some similarly passive victim of his will. In cold blood, of course he admits this to be absurd. But the lurid language of the garage or the golf course betrays another level of commitment, which at the time may feel curiously justified. Why? I do not think we need go further than the principle we have already extracted. To the extent of its involvement in his struggles, his image of the car, or the ball, becomes irreducibly underspecified through its coupling with the rest of his own activity. Insofar as its activity is a kind of distorted reflection of his own, to revile it in personal terms is not perhaps totally absurd, however medically, morally, and spiritually inadvisable. Only if his adjurations were to continue later, in the detachment of cold blood, could we bring home a charge of total absurdity; for the thing is now fully specifiable to him, and its temporary personal quality, dependent on the underspecifiability acquired through his own involvement with it, has vanished.

Consider now a so-called 'chess-playing mechanism'. Clearly one can approach such a thing as a fully-specifiable 'mass of wires and transistors' – a physical situation that simply unfolds automatically, and admits of no description in personal terms, of a game-playing or any other kind. But the decision to play a game against 'it' reflects a new kind of commitment, and brings out a curious terminological difficulty. In playing a game against a human opponent, we do not say that we are playing against his body, or even his brain, but against *him.* With our 'artificial opponent', however, we have no conventional term to allow of the corresponding distinction. Since the term 'mechanism', as we have seen, is strictly on a par with brain-and-body, it would be a solecism (though a common one) to say that we play against 'the mechanism', just as it was a solecism to speak of a 'chess-playing mechanism' in the first place. (Compare 'a chess-playing brain' *vice* 'a chess-player'.) Perhaps 'artificial opponent' will serve as well as any term to keep our thinking straight. It is against 'him', rather than 'his' mechanism, that it is proper to say we have decided to play. By our practice, we have in effect committed ourselves to an entry in the 'artificial personal' right-hand column of our semantic chart.

But have we not here begged the question by an insidious linguistic manoeuvre? 'Surely', it may be objected, 'what we want to discover is whether a chess-playing mechanism has a personality, or is nothing but a mass of wires and transistors? How then can we begin by speaking of "him"?' I do not think we have jumped a step. What we have been doing is to bring out the fact that a decision on the issue of personality was here implict in the decision to play a game – as distinct from merely poking at a (fully-specified) mechanism. To speak of 'playing the game against' X is already to personalize X. It is always open to us, as I have insisted, to refuse such personal commitment; but once we are prepared to make it, the operative question seems to be whether and for how long the developing situation enables us rationally to sustain it.

2.5 A question of 'consciousness'

But is it the only question? Suppose, for example, that we engage in a chess game by correspondence. Five possibilities may be envisaged and contrasted with profit:

(i) Answering moves selected by a random process from some predetermined list. In this case we would soon come to doubt that we had an intelligent opponent.

(ii) Answering moves taken from the record of (one side of) a human chess match. Here again pointlessness and illegitimacy would soon lead to detection.

(iii) Answering moves selected by a random process from among those legitimate at each stage. In this case detection would depend on the pointlessness of the moves – the absence, except sporadically, of connections and tendencies interpretable as conative and responsive. Once the suspicion dawned, we could rapidly (with courage) test it by exposing ourselves to obvious risks, or making obvious threats.

(iv) Answering moves selected by a well-informed, goal-directed, anticipatory stochastic process (*i.e.* with a suitable degree of disciplined spontaneity) from among those legitimate at each stage. Here there would seem to be no behavioural reason for us to doubt the 'mentality' of our opponent. We might well be beaten with reasonable frequency. Moreover, an artificial opponent of the right ('adaptive') sort could readily show all the signs of 'learning' from 'his' growing experience of us and our ways.

(v) Answering moves selected by a competent human opponent.

What has (v) added to (iv)? In respect of ability to play chess (*ex hypothesi*), nothing. The crucial point is surely that in case (v) there is at the far end someone who knows he is playing: someone who could, if asked, talk about the language of chess, as well as in it – and about other things too.

It is tempting to compare our artificial opponent (iv) with an extreme form of 'idiot savant' – prodigiously able to play a calculating game, but devoid of the capacity for normal dialogue. This, however, would I think beg too many questions, for nobody doubts that an idiot savant is conscious; but consciousness, whatever we mean by it, is too high a prize to grant on the score of mere chess-playing ability. (It is not inconceivable, after all, however improbable, that under some kind of selective anaesthesia or surgery a human being might retain the ability to play coherent chess, as it were mechanically or 'in his sleep', though quite unconscious in the normal sense of 'unaware of what is going on'). Our criterion of 'consciousness' would not be in terms of his power to react appropriately to chess-moves, but rather his power to raise his eyes from the board, as it were, and engage in dialogue with us (or at least to think) about what he was doing.

The fact that this power could sometimes be difficult to test or demonstrate in practice (as it notoriously is in certain forms of schizophrenia) should not blind us to the reality of the distinction. After all, if thought is in any way reflected in brain-processes, there would presumably be some internal operational difference, that could in principle be exhibited, to correspond with that between consciousness and unconsciousness, even if the subject were resolutely dumb and unresponsive.

In evaluating claims for artificial mechanisms, then, it seems important to distinguish the question of 'personality' from that of 'consciousness'. Our artificial opponent (iv) has a 'personality' (of a thinnish sort) which all who are prepared to make the necessary commitment (by playing against him) can come to know. But he would be a bold (or easily satisfied) man who would describe that personality as 'conscious', in any normal sense.

2.6 The logic of personal recognition

It is not my present purpose to discuss ways of remedying the behavioural deficiencies we have noted in the artificial opponent (iv). I have done so on other occasions,[5] and many others are active in the field. I think it is fair to say that no barrier of principle prevents an artificial opponent from showing as many characteristic human features as we care to specify, including the crucial ability to develop and employ an internal running representation of 'What is going on', so as to be able to converse intelligently and purposefully about his own activity and experience. If we are not to make a behavioural test the criterion of consciousness, then we will do no harm, and will clear the air best, by considering a hypothetical case in which all such behavioural tests have been satisfied by the activity of the artefact in question.

What I have been trying to bring out is the curious logic – a blend of deduction and commitment – that seems to be involved in the transition from physical to personal ways of characterizing such activity, whether in artificial or natural organisms.

Let us take the natural case first. Here is a mass of brain cells, a going concern, 'wired' to the organs of a human body. The body (including the brain cells), we are told, is Joe Smith's. We find that in addition to studying the body as an object, we can also talk to Joe, and he can answer intelligently, giving all the usual human signs of 'having a mind of his own' and 'knowing what he is about'. But a doubt strikes us. What proof have we that Joe is conscious? What proof that there is a 'Joe' at all, as distinct from the mass-of-cells-plus-body? Could not all the behaviour we witness be due to 'nothing but' the 'dead' mechanics of brain cells and the rest, responding automatically to the stimuli we supply? Could not the same behaviour in fact be expected if the mass of brain cells were replaced, perhaps piece by piece, by an identically-organized artificial 'brain'? If so, why speak of 'Joe' in this case and not in the other? If not in the other, why in this? What kind of evidence could convince us?

If what I have been arguing is correct, then there is no kind of evidence that could logically convince us at this point; for it is not on evidence that our missing conviction depends. What we are suffering from is not a failure of evidence, but a failure of nerve. Given that nothing is abnormal in the 'works' of Joe's brain, so that the 'indications' are up to standard, then the transition, from observing the activity of brain cells, *etc.*, to talking with Joe, is up to us. If we are prepared to 'open up' and allow the 'cross links' of which we spoke earlier to form between Joe's system and our own, then our experience in the new relationship will be the normal human experience of dialogue with Joe, a personal agent like ourselves, whose consciousness is attested (not 'proved') by the character of the dialogue, as our own is for others (including Joe).

Although in this sense the transition is 'up to us', yet once it has been made (successfully) it would be misleading to describe the recognition of personal attributes as 'optional', for it has a certain irreversibility about it.

At the personal level, Joe will have established some personal claims on us, and we on Joe. We shall not be able lightly to tamper with his brain, for example, nor feel free to dismantle his body. Even more significant, we will not be able to justify ignoring him as a person at will. He has become 'one of us', a member of the linguistic community – not, be it noted, by virtue of the particular stuff of which his brain is built (though we have so far assumed this to be naturally grown) but by virtue of the particular kinds of mutual interaction that it can sustain with our own – interaction which at the personal level we describe as that of person-with-person.

At the technical level, he can be recognized as one of us because (and to the extent that) in dialogue our dispositions in the information-flow map are symmetrical, our relationships reciprocal. In terms of the pattern of information-flow, our two coupled brains engage in a kind of 'resonance' (in the technical, not the mystical sense!); and as a result, each becomes incapable of representing the other as a fully-specified system.

In this sense at least the common remark, that persons in dialogue present an element of mystery to one another, has a solid technical justification. Note, however, that this kind of mystery stands wholly apart from any physical puzzles presented by the workings of the brain; for it would remain even if all of these were solved. No matter how detailed our understanding of Joe's neuroanatomy, we cannot in principle reduce the Joe we know and address as a person to any exactly-specified assemblage of mechanically-determined molecules. If we try to do so, Joe, as a person, must simply disappear from our conceptual framework, as inevitably as statistical entropy does from that of Newtonian dynamics. To say (as some might) that talk about Joe is merely a 'portmanteau translation' of talk about Joe's brain cells, is thus an error. The two are indeed (*ex hypothesi*) correlates; but they are not translations, for the trouble with the molecular level is precisely that it has no words (because logically it has no place) for the concepts of the personal.

2.7 An open question

So much for Joe. For all purposes of description and dialogue, he is 'conscious' when he can join as one of us in bearing witness to the events of our common world. We do not need to ask what his brain is made of, nor how it works. If parts of it wear out, and we imagine them replaced by exact electronic or other equivalents, we have no reason to change our attitude. If eventually Joe's brain were wholly artificial, but functionally indistinguishable – like one of our hypothetical automata – we should surely still have none . . .?

Surely? Like good oysters, let us not seek to rid ourselves of one last grain of irritation. For imagine that Joe is conscious, and we discuss Joe's consciousness in Joe's hearing. Joe decides to play dumb and listen. Our judgment on the matter may depend critically on the kind of relationship we can establish. We may or may not succeed in getting round this by internal examination of Joe's brain. We may argue long about the optional nature of the judgment. But – and this is the point – all the time, there would in fact be Joe, listening to us, raising a mental eyebrow, and knowing the answer. Nothing optional or conventional about that. Consciousness is a matter of fact, on which we are either right or wrong. In this case, there is someone there. Joe knows, for it is he.

Clearly, then, any dogmatic dispatch of this question in relation to artificial 'brains' is out of place. For reasons sketched below, I do not believe that Christian theology supports any objection to the possibility that persons might be thus artificially 'begotten', which I personally find fascinating. I know of no coherent argument against it, and I have been at pains to show that mechanical explicability at the molecular level could not provide such an argument.

On the other hand, it seems equally clear that we are not at liberty to settle the question as a matter of convention, and say that artificial persons that behave-as-if-conscious simply *are* conscious. When deciding whether to treat psychiatric patients, or laboratory animals, or artificial persons, or even one another, as conscious, such conventions may indeed be inevitable; but they can do nothing to relieve our ontological doubt.

No, the simple truth is that we cannot know. And let no one try the old line that it is therefore meaningless to wonder whether there is any conscious person listening to us as we discuss the behaviour of a body before us; for that body could well be his own.

3. Brains and persons

3.1 Persons and their embodiment

Our knowledge of what it means to be a person has diverse sources. To begin with, we each have an ongoing story to tell of facts known to us in conscious experience, such as that 'I see-a-sheet-of-paper-before-me' or 'I feel-sorry-for-Bill' or 'I believe-that-the-cat-is-outside'. These are the facts referred to collectively in Table 1 as the 'I-story'. There may of course be some facts of our experience – inarticulate feelings, for example – which we do not know how to put into words; but these still form part of the data to which the I-story bears witness, however imperfectly.

Brain science is concerned to elaborate a very different story about us, in terms of patterns of nerve-cell firings and the like. It makes the working assumption (and it is no more) that for each fact of our conscious experience some corresponding story exists to be told in neural terms. There is no suggestion that the correspondence is necessarily 1 to 1. Several alternative states of neural activity, for example, might be possible correlates of exactly the same experience of seeing-the-sheet-of-paper; but at least if I am having that experience, brain science assumes that something must be true about my nervous system which would *not* be the case if I were *not* having it.

The mysterious character of this correlation, for which there is slowly but steadily accumulating evidence,[10] must not be overlooked. To dramatize it, let us imagine (science fiction-wise) that advances in technology could tomorrow allow a neurosurgeon to remove your brain from its casing and keep it alive and well in a portable container with a suitable extension cord from your body to maintain all its connections and supplies in functional order.[11] Assuming that no significant time-lags or extraneous signals were introduced, we may suppose (for the sake of argument) that you would continue to have a more or less normal flux of conscious experience.

Suppose however that the container with your brain at the end of its cord were placed in front of you, among a variety of other physical objects (perhaps including other brains) which you are free to explore with physical probes, electrical stimulators and the like. You (sitting in your chair) can watch the ongoing results of your explorations on various instruments. As long as you explore the other objects, or indeed anything else in the physical universe, all goes well. But if once you start probing and stimulating your own brain tissue . . . ouch! You begin to have direct experience of bizarre events – seeing flashes of light, feeling sick or elated, thinking strange thoughts.

Well, perhaps you say, that isn't so surprising, seeing there is this cable running from the brain out there into my body. Very well. Suppose that the relevant cable connections (though not, of course, the blood supply) were temporarily removed or blocked. What would you now expect to happen if the stimulating current were applied (by someone else) to the same brain area? According to the working assumption whose consequences we are exploring, although you would of course lose control of your limbs and lose all sensory inputs, you would *continue to experience* the same bizarre events, provided that the same patterns of neural activity were elicited in that strange two-handsful of neural tissue out there in front of you. Furthermore, whatever ideas went through your mind (as we conventionally say) would continue to be reflected in the changing pattern of physical activity in the depths of that same small mass of tissue.

Why should the physical state of that little sample, out of all the vast contents of the physical universe, have this immediate relationship with the events of your conscious experience? This is not a question to which any conceivable advances in our understanding of the details or principles of brain activity can give an answer. In that sense it highlights not a mere scientific puzzle, but an ontological mystery. For each of us it points to a brute fact – and as far as brain science is concerned an irreducibly given and mysterious fact – about our embodiment as persons, with which we must simply learn to live. Our imaginary thought-experiment also makes clear the sense in which it is meaningful (even operationally meaningful) to ask whereabouts in the brain the direct correlate of our conscious experiencing (a better term here than 'consciousness') is located: of which more anon.

3.2 What is special about our embodiment?

It is natural to ask whether we can identify anything scientifically distinctive in the grey-pink mass before us as the correlate of its remarkable associations with our experience. Some[12] would hypothesize (in the tradition of Descartes) that it must contain a special region equipped to sustain two-way 'interaction' with another 'world' – the 'world of the mind'. To date, however, no evidence has emerged to suggest that any part of the human brain differs in its physiological principles from other parts or indeed from the brains of lower animals. Nerve cells, whatever else they may be, are exquisitely sensitive and elaborate processors of information. They are normally linked in cooperative groupings which respond to specific features of incoming traffic, 'listening out' for particular patterns of coincidence or 'covariation' of signals in different nerve fibres. In this sense the brain could perhaps be described, not as a computer, but as a vast community of linked microcomputers. The principles on which it is organized are quite different from those employed in the digital hardware of our conventional computing machines. A typical brain cell has a continuously variable probability of 'firing' (emitting a signal) which depends not only on its metabolic state, but also on the precise relative timing and layout of hundreds or even thousands of incoming signals that converge on its branching 'dendrites' or the cell body. This means that the momentary state of an interacting group of nerve cells must be specified not just by saying which cells are firing, but by a vast matrix of ever-changing 'conditional probabilities' – *e.g.* the probability that *if* A happens but *not* B, *then* C will happen, *etc.*, *etc.*[13] Many extraneous factors, such as chemical messengers in the blood supply, may play their part in the modulation of these conditional probabilities, and in the continual biophysical tug-of-war that determines (statistically) whether and when each cell will deliver an impulse to the ongoing chatter. Nothing here of the quiet and disciplined sobriety of an array of digital computing elements, each awaiting its simple noise-free yes-or-no instruction to change its state from 1 to 0 or vice versa!

Despite these many disanalogies, however, there is nothing in the known biophysics of the nervous system to give comfort to an anti-mechanist, however poorly we may understand its mysterious connection with our conscious experience. There are plenty of promising *correlates*. For example, changes in the efficacy of connections betwen nerve cells ('synapses'), induced as a result of both cells becoming simultaneously active, offer one plausible basis for the storage of information in learning and memory.[14] Again, large groups of cells can show what is called 'cooperativity' – massive changes of state which can propagate rather like a flame in an igniting gas mixture. These mechanisms further enrich our stock of possible correlates of psychological processes. None of them however answers the question why the brain, rather than the heart, say, should have this baffling link with our immediate experience.

3.3 Informational organization

When we look at the global organization of the brain as a whole, at the 'cybernetic' level of systems analysis, some special distinguishing features do emerge. By studying the effects of brain injury or malfunction, neurologists have accumulated much evidence as to which brain areas are essential to which psychological functions.[15] By analysing the minimal information-processing requirements for intelligent purposeful agency (whether in automata or living organisms) the systems analyst can develop a skeleton 'information-flow model'[13] which can be used (as a tool of research) to suggest possible mechanistic interpretations of the clinical data. In its simplest form it can be thought of as a hierarchic structure, with an 'organizing' level concerned with the selection and deployment of various alternative courses of action under feedback from sensory apparatus, programmed by a higher 'supervisory' level that selects the goals to be pursued by the organizing system, and the relative priorities to be assigned to different possible goals or criteria of evaluation in case of goal conflict. A system organized on these lines can show behaviour of the kind we would describe as intelligent and take as evidence of consciousness in living animals. Furthermore, if the supervisory level were equipped to form and evaluate internal representations not only of its environment and its goal-priorities, but also of itself and its own evaluative process, its behaviour could develop many of the features we take as evidence of self-consciousness and self-evaluative autonomy in human beings.[16]

My suggestion is not that any automaton on these hierarchic lines must be considered self-conscious (see below), but rather (conversely) that the special feature of our brain which must be functioning if we are to enjoy conscious experience may well be its self-supervisory and self-evaluative information system. Clinical evidence shows that we can 'lose consciousness' when relatively small portions of deep central brain structures are damaged, even while the rest of the brain remains capable of organizing quite complex sensori-motor coordination.[17] Conversely, large areas of the cerebral cortex can be damaged or cut out altogether without rendering the patient unconscious (though of course leaving him deprived of corresponding sensory or motor functions). This has an obvious bearing on the twin practical problems of determining at what stage in foetal development personal life has begun, and at what stage in bodily disintegration personal life has come to an end.[18] It also bears on the vexed question as to whether surgical section of the *corpus callosum* (the millions of connecting fibres between left and right cortical areas) turns so-called 'split brain' patients into two separate conscious agents. Experimental evidence to date suggests that the two 'half-systems' in these cases can certainly sustain independent and potentially conflicting goal-directed agency, and even a form of low-level dialogue between them; but gives no indication that the topmost 'self-supervisory' level of organization has been split.[19]

3.4 What is special about 'meeting'?

As indicated in section 2.3 above, something quite special can happen when two information systems of the kind we are discussing (call them 'A' and 'B') become 'cross-coupled' in the process we call 'dialogue'. To the extent that each seeks to form an internal representation of the goals and evaluative criteria of the other, and opens itself reciprocally to the address of the other, the joint system (A plus B) so constituted can be *logically-indeterminate* for both of them.[20] This means, not that it violates physically-deterministic laws (if any), but that even if all its constituent processes were physically determinate, no completely detailed specification of its present or immediately future state exists which could claim to be the 'inevitable truth' for either party. Because of the reciprocal causal chain-mesh set up in true dialogue (as distinct from mere alternate monologue), any completely detailed specification of B's information system must include details that reflect B's image of A's cognitive processes and conversely. In general these details cannot (logically cannot) be independent of what A or B is thinking and feeling. Hence no such complete (future) specification can claim to be true irrespective of what A or B thinks of it. In that sense, their joint future has an ingredient that is irreducibly indeterminate-for-them until they jointly determine by their dialogue what form it shall take.

3.5 Brains and computers

As a working hypothesis, the idea that our conscious experience (and our mental activity in particular) is *embodied in* our brain activity offers attractions as an alternative both to classical interactionism on the one hand and to reductionist materialism on the other. I have elsewhere[21] explicated the notion of embodiment by using the familiar example of the embodiment of an equation in a computer:

(a) There is a clear sense in which a computer programmed to solve Poisson's equation (say) has its behaviour *determined* by Poisson's equation and its given boundary conditions. Were this not the case, we could not take the output of the machine as a solution of that equation.

(b) There is an equally clear sense in which the computer has its behaviour *determined* by the laws of physics as applied to each of its physical components, taking due account of the interactions between these components, and of the constraints imposed on the whole physical system by its physical environment. Were this not the case, the designer would warn us that the machine could not be relied upon as a computer. His claim that its behaviour as a symbolic system is determined by Poisson's equation *depends upon* his assumption that its behaviour as a physical system is determined by the laws of physics. The two are not rival, mutually exclusive claims, but logically *complementary.*[22]

This example serves well enough to illustrate the kind of interdependence (rather than interaction) that I would denote by speaking of conscious cognitive agency as 'embodied' in, and determinative of, the workings of the agent's brain-and-body. It clearly provides a counter-example to the presupposition of many 'incompatibilists' that complete physical determination of human behaviour *must* be denied if we want to claim that that behaviour is (at least sometimes, to some extent) determined by conscious thinking, valuing and choosing on the part of the individual concerned. With respect to the hypothesis that conscious mental activity is embodied in brain activity in the relevant sense, this presupposition is clearly false. The example also illustrates well the need to distinguish between two kinds of levels of 'causal' connection – between *physical* causes on the one hand, and what systems engineers today term *informational* or *systemic* causes on the other. Physical explanations account for changes in a system in terms of the flow and exchange of energy and force; informational explanations do so in terms of the flow and exchange of information and control. The first trace the dependence of *force* on *force*; the second the dependence of *form* on *form.* Each legitimately uses the explanatory term 'because'; but much confusion arises if we fail to follow Aristotle's lead in distinguishing between the quite different senses of 'cause' involved. In particular, to speak of 'downward causation' between the informational and physical levels, as is done by Sperry[23] for example, can give rise to much misunderstanding, with its suggestion of some kind of convergence of forces from 'above' and 'below' upon the physical components, which Sperry describes as 'pushed and hauled about' by the 'causes' operating at the higher level.[24] It would seem oddly unhelpful to a computer scientist to speak of the transistors in his machine as 'pushed and hauled about' by the equation it is solving!

But although I have been arguing on the foregoing lines for the past thirty-five years, and believe the computer analogy to be valid in these specific respects, I fear that comparisons between brains and computers in general, and the growth of AI in particular, have given rise to a crop of deep misunderstandings as to the philosophical implications of current efforts to explain human behaviour mechanistically. Among the 'costs' of mechanistic embodiment, it is widely supposed, would be the reduction of all human behaviour to rule-following, the downgrading of concepts of 'tacit knowledge' or the 'ineffable' to mere temporary tokens of the incompleteness of our knowledge of the human 'brain program', the denial of freedom of choice as a (perhaps necessary) illusion based on ignorance, and the rejection of all religious assessments of our spiritual significance and destiny as incompatible with scientific mechanism. Whether each of these would be regarded as a 'cost' or a 'benefit' may be a matter of individual judgment; but I believe all of them to be unwarranted by the hypothesis of mechanistic embodiment.

3.6 Is rule-following adequate?

There are several respects in which my example of the embodiment of an equation in a digital computer is potentially misleading. First, in that case we start with our explicitly formalized equation, and our task is to construct an explicit embodiment of the equation in a general-purpose discrete-state machine, each of whose states serves as a distinct symbol in the relevant mathematical calculus. In the case of conscious cognitive agency, however, we start with our immediate unquantified experience of what it is like to see, feel, act, think, doubt, suffer, love, hate . . . , and it is far from obvious that any explicit program of transitions between discrete symbolic states could even approximate to a representation of that experience. The assumption that our brain is a mechanism does nothing to foreclose this question, since as we shall see below there are other types of mechanism in which transitions between states are not determined by consulting explicit rules.

Secondly, there is a serious disanalogy between embodied equations and embodied persons with regard to the problem of *identity*. To ask whether the equation embodied in a particular computer is 'the original equation or merely a replica' would be to raise a silly question. Poisson's equation is one and the same, no matter how many embodiments of it may be knocking around in people's computers. But in the case of you and me the question of personal identity is far from silly, however difficult we may find it to express in sharp and satisfactory terms.

Thirdly, whenever the appropriate program is run in a suitable machine, we can guarantee that its behaviour is determined by Poisson's equation; but it is far from obvious that whenever an AI program is run in a suitable machine so as to generate behaviour we can recognize as intelligent, we are entitled to conclude that we are in the presence of a conscious individual. Suppose for example we visit the theatre, where Joe Smith is playing Hamlet in the famous soliloquy. How many people – conscious centres of awareness – are on the stage? Obviously, if Joe does his job, there is a sense in which what we can see is 'Hamlet's behaviour'; but this does not mean that Hamlet is present as a conscious centre of awareness in addition to Joe. Generating Hamlet-behaviour by consulting a book of rules does not conjure Hamlet into present existence as a conscious person. Even if Joe deserts Shakespeare's text, quits the stage and 'adopts the character' of Hamlet in free dialogue with us, it would be Pickwickian to claim on these grounds that we had met Hamlet, as distinct from an impersonation of Hamlet. It would be totally irrational to argue that the ontological situation might change if only Joe were given enough time to perfect his skill in generating Hamlet-behaviour. Merely organizing behaviour according to rules, whether explicit or implicit, is not a sufficient way to increase the number of centres of conscious awareness in the world.

If it would be irrational to take the Hamlet-like behaviour of Joe Smith as proof of the presence of Hamlet, it is not obviously less irrational (with due respect to Turing[25]) to take the person-like behaviour of an AI-programmed computer as proof of the presence of a conscious person. That such a computer can have a mind or personality, in the sense in which a character represented on the stage has a mind and personality, need not be disputed;[2] but that a computer programmed by rule to act the part of a person has become *ipso facto* the embodiment of an additional member of the cognitive community is a quite baseless notion, which no amount of refinement in the acting skills of artificial agents can render plausible. Impersonation is not the same as embodiment.

At this point the reader may be tempted to suppose that our argument tells equally against the hypothesis that the brain is explicable in mechanistic terms; but this would be a mistake. The common notion that all machines are formally equivalent to some explicit program is false, and the truth is that only a restricted class of machines are rule-followers in the foregoing sense. 'Intelligent' machinery is characterized by the presence of branch-points in its course at which one out of several possibilities must be selected. In digital computers of the sort normally used for AI, the outcome at each branch point is determined by consulting a rule, which may involve extremely complex computations, but is explicitly specified by the program. In other types of mechanism, however, a quite different principle is employed: the outcome is determined, at least in part, by what amounts to the *making of a physical experiment.* In this case, although the selection of the experiment to make may be determined by rule, the outcome is not; it is the result of an appeal to the real world, to which no finite set of rules is completely equivalent. A typical 'decision-making' process on this principle would be illustrated by a ball rolling down a groove which eventually bifurcates, so that the ball must follow one of two paths on the basis of physical interactions at the branch point. If the depth of each groove were adjustable (for example in response to feedback) this would statistically bias the transition probabilities at each branch point, and so store information, without reducing the behaviour to mere rule-following.[26] A sophisticated recent development on this principle has been described under the name of 'Boltzmann machinery': 'a type of parallel constraint satisfaction network . . . that is capable of learning the underlying constraints that characterize a domain simply by being shown examples from the domain. The network modifies the strengths of its connections so as to construct an internal generative model that produces examples with the same probability distribution as the examples it is shown. Then, when shown any particular example, the network can "interpret" it by finding values of the variables in the internal model that would generate the example'.[27]

As we saw in section 3.2, the brain, considered as an information-processing mechanism, combines processes of both types. Neurones of the CNS (Central Nervous System) are metastable elements which interact in a cooperative fashion, such that at a given time there is for each network a vast array of 'conditional probabilities' that *if* event A occurs *and if* B occurs within so many milliseconds, *then* the network will go over from state i to state j with transition-probability p_{ij}, and so on. These states may form a discrete set; but the physical quantities that govern the p_{ij} (ionic concentrations, proximity of synaptic terminals and the like) are generally continuously variable, and interact so delicately that no predictions based on the physical measurement of parameters could keep track of the outcome, even in principle, for a significant time. Brain activity has to be thought of as a stochastic process, to whose actual time-course no explicit program of determinate rules could be equivalent.[13]

3.7 Personal identity

The consequences for the hypothesis of our embodiment as conscious agents are far-reaching. In the first place, since all that characterizes us as individuals (our memories, dispositions, skills, *etc.*) depends *ex hypothesi* on the detailed physical structure upon and in which the aforementioned 'internal experimentation' is carried out, and on which each twist and turn of our experience leaves its mark in a widely distributed and largely implicit physical form, it is impossible even in principle to divorce our personal identity from the specific brain-matter in which we are embodied, in the easy way in which the identity of an equation can be divorced from its specific embodiment in a digital computer. I am the individual whose brain-matter went through this and that specific course as a result of these and those specific internal experiments in and upon it. You are another individual whose brain-matter has traced a different world-line. Nobody with a different world-line can be identical with you or me, for his physical embodiment is unique to him, a unique theatre of physical experimentation, such that even if he had been equipped instantaneously (in the manner of some science-fiction philosophers) with the best possible physical replica of your brain, his would manifest immediate and increasing divergences from the path taken by yours. I do not deny outright the notion that in the science-fiction world the 'replica' might share many of your memories or mine; and it is perhaps arguable that he might be allowed to share some of your retrospective obligations in these bizarre circumstances. What seems quite clear is that (if the replica is a conscious being at all) he has no rational claim to *be* you or me, whether or not you or I are killed (for his convenience) as soon as he is brought into being. Much of the extensive current argumentation about such possibilities[28] is vitiated by failure to recognize the differences between an imaginary 'brain' that is functionally equivalent to a program of easily replicable rules, and the real brain in its physical particularity as a theatre of continual appeals to local physical reality, the outcomes of which play an essential part in shaping both the course and the character of our embodied agency. In short, for us as embodied persons, 'matter matters'.

What I am arguing for is not materialism, but what I would call 'Duality without Dualism'.[29] The data of our conscious experience demand to be reckoned with as categorically distinct from, and ontologically prior to, all data about our brain activity. However tight the correlations we may discern between them, their duality seems at least as undeniable as the duality between the mathematical and the physical aspects of what goes on in a computer solving an equation. By the same token, there seems to be as little need for the thought-model of interactionist dualism, with its talk of causal traffic between two 'worlds', in the one case as in the other. The relationship between embodied and embodiment is *more intimate* than that between cause and effect.[21] As argued in section 2.1, I believe that to attribute 'thinking' or other intentional activities to either brains or machines (as Searle[30] does, for example), is to confuse categorical levels. To insist (as I do) that the physical constitution of the brain is important for personal identity does not at all imply that it makes sense to attribute mental activity to the physical brain.

3.8 Creativity and the 'ineffable'

Secondly, if the structure of the brain is thought of as constraining and enabling our behaviour in anything like the sense in which the program shapes the behaviour of a computer, we must recognize that (in contrast to a digital computer program) much of its contribution takes the form of 'inclination without necessitation'. For reasons given below I think we should resist the temptation to take this stochastic aspect of brain processes as the physical basis of freewill; but it does at least dispose of the idea that mechanistic theories of brain function can find no scope for genuine *creativity*.

Thirdly, to conceive of our embodiment in these terms disposes of any idea that mechanistic explanation of brain function would leave no room for what Wittgenstein[31] termed the 'ineffable' (that which cannot be put into words but can only be 'manifested'), or for what Polanyi[32] called 'tacit knowledge'. That 'we know more than we can tell' (Polanyi) would follow directly from the hypothesis that we are embodied in a mechanism in which information is represented partly in the implicit form of physical constraints on the relative probabilities of transitions in the course of internal experimentation. The knowledge so embodied would be tacit, in the sense that its *possessor* would have no words for it, though it would be immediately accessible to him in the course of conscious agency, in the way that knowledge how to swallow, or how to ride a bicycle, can be.[33] By the same token, mechanistic explanation of brain function on these lines would positively encourage expectations that the possessor could sometimes be aware of 'unutterables' of his experience which might nevertheless (in Wittgenstein's terms) be 'shown', through the medium of poetic or artistic expression.[34]

The stochastic nature of brain activity has a further consequence worth noting. Our normal thinking is frequently enlivened by what we call 'unbidden' events. 'It occurred to me that X', we say, or 'I was struck by Y'. Thinking, in other words, is a compound of 'doing' and 'suffering'. Now on our hypothesis of embodiment, the conditional probabilities of such unbidden transitions presumably depend on the microphysical details of specific structures (synapses or the like) in the thinker's brain. There is abundant and tragic evidence from the effects of drug abuse that gross chemical factors can modulate these conditional probabilities. What is less often recognized is that in an associative mechanism on these stochastic lines, even the speculative 'trial running' of ideas can be expected in general to change significantly the relative probabilities of future spontaneous transitions under *given* conditions. In other words, to be embodied in such a mechanism means that even speculative questioning is not a neutral activity, but can play a significant part, willy nilly, in determining what is likely to 'occur to' the questioner for the whole of his future life. The moral for the philosopher may be worth pondering!

3.9 Logical relativity

A prime cost of mechanistic embodiment is that there can be no gain (or loss) or knowledge without a change in the physical world – specifically, a change in whatever cerebral structure has to embody the information in question. Popper,[35] in a classic paper of 1951, argued that even in a physically determinate universe this must set restrictions on the predictability of the universe for its inhabitants.

It has however a further consequence, which I have followed up elsewhere.[9,20] Mechanistic embodiment entails certain *relativistic restrictions* on the validity of state-descriptions of embodied persons. A complete and up-to-date state-description S of the immediate future of the embodiment of an agent A, assuming it could be produced by a non-interfering observer O, would be valid-for-O but systematically invalid-for-A. This says more than that A could not know or believe S: it means that *no uniquely determinative specification exists*, even unknown to A, which has an equally valid claim to the assent of A and of O. Instead, we must recognize that what A would be correct to believe, and in error to disbelieve, about his immediate future is systematically different from what O would be correct to believe about it. Even if, for O, every detail of A's future had a fully determinate specification, it would and could have no such complete specification with an unconditional claim to A's assent, until after A's cognitive agency had determined relevant details of that future. I will not here retrace the consequences of this 'logical indeterminacy' for the freewill debate. I want only to emphasize the extent to which some standard non-relativistic forms of argument can be undermined by it. In particular, the question whether a specific future event is 'inevitable' is *not properly formulated* until we say *for whom* the inevitability is to be assessed. Even in a physically determinate universe an event inevitable-for-O may not be at all inevitable-for-A, if A's future cognitive activity is one of the factors that will determine its form.[9,20]

Recognition of this relativistic principle does nothing to question the validity of standard logic, since nothing but standard logic is necessary to demontrate it. All it means is that if we try to use standard logic to determine what cognitive agents would be correct to believe about themselves, we are not entitled to presuppose (as conventional logical arguments tend to do) that if anyone would be correct to believe proposition *p*, then everyone would be. It follows that the luxury of being able to indicate the truth-value of *p* universally by a single-valued scalar (true or false, 1 or 0) may in some such cases be denied us. In this strict sense the case of cognitive agency has about it an irreducible element of *mystery*, whatever the degree of physical explicability we attach to the workings of its embodiment.[36]

3.10 'Artificial consciousness'?

It will be obvious that I see no prospect of writing a rule-following program to be equivalent to the workings of the human brain, as a means of bringing conscious centres of awareness into existence. By raising valid objections to the nonsense sometimes talked about contemporary computing machinery, however, I do not think that we dispose of the possibility in principle of artificially begetting conscious persons. True, it would be inept to claim that any machine 'thinks'; but it is far from nonsensical to ask whether a suitably constructed system might not *embody the mental activity* of a conscious agent in the same sense in which the information system of your brain or mine embodies our mental activity. Moreover, although role-playing by rule-following, whether by people or machines, does not generate new centres of conscious experience, we know of at least one genetically programmable biological process that does; so it is far from obvious that the use of rules to determine the construction (as distinct from the functioning) of an artefact need disqualify it *ipso facto* from embodying conscious agency. I see no technical reason to deny that stochastic mechanisms, suitably combining the principles of rule-following and physical experimentation or 'groove-following', can transcend the demonstrable limitations of purely digital symbol-manipulators, and can in principle meet any specifiable test for 'mind-like behaviour'.[5] If this is right, any attempt to find an explicit specification that 'no machine could meet' is foredoomed to failure. On the other hand, any attempt to produce a complete and explicitly rule-determined replica of human behaviour is equally foredoomed in principle, if one of the major determinants of human behaviour is a process equivalent to internal physical experimentation.

4. Theological implications?

4.1 Is AI a threat to the Christian doctrine of man?

It is not uncommon to find protagonists of AI who see their art as a growing threat to religious, especially Christian, ideas of our human nature and destiny; and not a few Christians appear to share this perception. To those of us who cheerfully enjoy the excitement of the scientific chase with no such thoughts in our heads, this raises a serious question. Are we missing something insidious (from a religious standpoint) in this whole mechanistic approach? Or does the trouble arise from some conceptual confusions shared by both sides in the debate?

As argued in section 2.3, there is of course something potentially insidious in any invitation to step out of our normal human situation and imagine ourselves as isolated spectators of the human phenomenon.[37] By cutting ourselves off, even in imagination, from dialogue with our fellows we can in principle depersonalize them and reduce them to mere objects of scrutiny, losing sight for the moment of their own status as centres of awareness and potential terminals of dialogue. But this is a mere perceptual illusion, to be remedied, like all such illusions, by shifting our standpoint so as to make possible a more veridical experience of the situation temporarily misperceived.[38] There is no more need for a practitioner of AI to remain under such illusions than for the man in charge of the weighing machine at a boxing match to see human beings only as ponderous masses.

More serious at first sight might be the objection that unless we rule out *a priori* the possibility of synthesizing the brain of a conscious person (a possibility that I have deliberately left open in principle, albeit with tongue in cheek), we run into conflict with Christian teaching that the creation of Man is a divine prerogative. Here, however, I think we can identify a straight confusion, between *creation* – the divine prerogative – and *procreation* – for which God has licensed man. True, the natural process by which two people normally bring about the embodiment of a new person is one that they do not understand in any detail; but it would still be only a case of procreation even if they did, and even if they could call upon the resources of genetic engineering to determine in detail the characteristics of their offspring. Should it ever prove possible to beget conscious human beings by more artificial procedures, this would simply be a case of artificial procreation – a totally different concept from what theologians mean by divine creation.[39]

Another objection sometimes raised, by both believers and unbelievers, is that AI threatens to dispel the mystery and wonder surrounding our human nature. Here again there would seem to be a confusion between two quite different notions. One is the sort of 'wonder' evoked by a clever performance, which is dissipated once we learn 'how the trick is done'. Such 'wonder', which goes back basically to curiosity and puzzlement, is indeed progressively eroded as science advances – though to be fair, we should note that each advance in science tends in its turn to throw up a crop of fresh puzzles.

The other notion could be termed 'awe' – the recognition, deeper than words, of a mystery that must be accepted and responded to with (as Job puts it) our hand upon our mouth (Job 40:4). Such a mystery, it seems to me, is presented by our experience of what it is like to be an embodied conscious agent, and what it is like to be engaged in dialogue with another such agent. As I have argued above, this mystery stands wholly untouched by any conceivable advance in either brain science or AI, since the acceptance of it is the precondition of all our thinking. To see AI as a threat to the sense of awe appropriate to the mystery of personal being would be to misconceive the nature of both. If artificial means were ever achieved to bring conscious personal beings into existence, their existence (as distinct from that of their embodiment) would still present us with the same mystery, demanding the same awe in response.

Implicit in our analysis has been a particular answer to the question: what makes people special? Why do we value other persons? Ultimately, I suggest, not for what they provide by way of resources, whether physical or informational, but because only other persons can engage with us in the 'I-Thou' relationship of *dialogue*.[40] It is characteristically in dialogue that we have our personal being, as participants in a situation which is for us *undetermined* until our participation determines its unfolding. It is in dialogue that we have the special experience, wholly without parallel in non-personal encounters with our world, of the union of two (or more) centres of awareness – the correlate of the mutual interpenetration of their information systems, with the resulting formation of closed loops of logically indeterminate activity, at which we looked earlier.

This is not to suggest that we are persons only in dialogue with others. One of the distinctive features of our human embodiment is our capacity for *internal* dialogue – the turning inward of skills elicited and developed in the course of dialogue with those who first nurtured our capacity for it. Talking to ourselves, whether internalized or not, is a characteristically personal activity in which our own situation is necessarily undertermined – *i.e.* has no completely determinate specification as to its present or future with an unconditional claim to our assent – until we, by our thinking, valuing and deciding, determine its unfolding.

Equally compatible with our mechanistic analysis is the claim of Christian Theism that we enter most fully into our personal being when in dialogue with God, its Giver. 'Thou hast made us for Thyself; and our hearts are restless till they find rest in Thee', said Augustine. He was not, I think, referring to an *alternative* to the modes of being of our daily life, but rather to a complementary perception of the significance of that daily life as an ongoing dialogue with its divine Giver. If I am right, then no extrasensory channel of communication need be added to our mechanistic model in order to make room even for our knowledge of God; for it is in and through the exercise of our ordinary capacities in response to the challenges of daily events, and in loving bondage to Christ, that that knowledge is meant to grow and develop as the pathway to life eternal.

Here, however, we must face one final objection. Granted what has been said in relation to life here and now, do not such mechanistic theories of our embodiment dispose completely of the Christian hope of eternal life? I have elsewhere[41] explained why I think this objection misconceived. Briefly, if the relation between our conscious experience and our brain activity is one of embodiment, rather than one of quasi-physical interaction between two different 'worlds', then the destruction of our present embodiment would certainly imply the termination of our conscious experience in this space-time; but it would not at all rule out the possibility, if our Creator so willed it, that we should find ourselves re-embodied, perhaps (as St Paul hints in 1 Corinthians 15) in some unimaginably different embodiment, 'in the resurrection'. Even an artificial intelligence, after all, could in principle be 'restored to life' in a fresh embodiment if the computer in which it was originally programmed were destroyed. For the reasons outlined in earlier sections I am far from suggesting that mere replication of behaviour patterns would suffice to guarantee ontological continuity between the original individual and his resurrected counterpart; but the daily illustration of ontological continuity between Joe Snooks who goes to bed one night and Joe Snooks who awakes next morning ought to reassure the Christian believer that the provision of such continuity is not beyond the powers of his Creator.

Thus although we have found a number of ways in which developments, both in brain science and in AI, are forcing us to re-examine traditional assumptions about the capacities of mechanistic systems, including those of our own brains, I would argue that the upshot only sympathetically illuminates, and in no way discredits, the biblical emphasis on our awesome nature and destiny.

4.2 AI and Christian stewardship

I began by insisting that the Christian's initial response to AI, as to any other challenge of God-given resources, must be positive – asking what good can be done with it in his Master's service. Christian priorities of love and compassion must rule, here as elsewhere. What then does this mean in a day when massive data banks, expert systems, automated instructors and domestic robots are already with us, and much more is in the pipeline?

On the one hand, we have a responsibility to stay cool and constructive, eschewing windy and alarmist rhetoric, and reassuring our non-technical brethren who may have irrational fears as to the theoretical or practical implications of this 'quantum leap' in human capacities. Our world abounds in unstable and badly regulated situations in which a judicious use of AI could revolutionize the prospects of bringing order out of chaos. Too many human beings still have to risk life and limb and health in industrial and other tasks that could in principle be taken over by inanimate robots. The scope for doing good on these lines is immense.

Yes; but on the other hand, and by the same token, the scope for doing harm (wittingly or unwittingly) is perhaps even greater. Protectors of civil liberties have been quick to point out the evils that could be perpetrated by a dictorial regime using these new resources, and Christians must support honest attempts to build in as many safeguards as practicable against their abuse. I would like to end, however, by drawing attention to some more subtle dangers that attend even the best-intentioned efforts in this rapidly growing field.

When one thinks about it, whether from a biblical or a secular standpoint, it is something of a miracle that human society works at all. It does so only because of a myriad checks and balances and mutual expectations, developed over the centuries and geared to a certain pace of communication and control. Already in the twentieth century the stability of social self-regulation is threatened by the reductions in time-constants brought about by radio and TV communication and fast air transport. It is by no means obvious that the further reductions (both in time-constants and space-constants) to be expected from the massive use of data-processors can be absorbed by the human social network without drastic side-effects. My point is not that Christians should therefore resist these trends, but rather that we should encourage and join in efforts to prepare our society for any foreseeable side-effects, and where necesary to take counter-measures.

At the individual level, there are foreseeable side-effects of a still more subtle kind. The human constitution develops adaptively under feedback from its environment. A tough environment we expect to breed a tough race, and vice versa. To the extent that mass application of AI can be expected to make life less 'tough' (and a naïve concept of compassion might encourage us to see this as an ethically positive motivation), it is not too early to ask whether, and when, the feedback thus exerted on the human constitution will be (in God's sight) beneficial or otherwise. Trivial examples are obvious already. Is it ultimately beneficial to young school children to rob them of arithmetic practice by supplying them with calculators? Is it ultimately beneficial to housewives to develop in them a 'slave-owning' mentality (only with inanimate robots that they can lean upon even more selfishly than they would a human slave)? These are not meant as rhetorical questions: I personally rejoice at the prospective enlargement of human capacities to glorify and serve God to be expected from a proper use of both calculators and robots. But they are typical of questions that I feel Christians, above all, have a duty to raise and to work upon, with other people of good will, as part of their stewardly function.

The point is basically a cybernetic one. We have our being, socially and individually, in a self-regulating network of feedback loops. A change in one mesh of the net can have repercussions that go around the loop and hit us on the back of the head when we are still looking in the opposite direction. No responsible steward can ignore the duty to assess (as best he can) the cybernetic consequences of any proposed application at AI technology. No Christian steward can evade the responsibility to include those consequences among all the other more obvious first-order benefits and costs, to be evaluated in the light of God's revelation as to what human life is for.

4.3 Retrospect

Tentatively, the answers suggested to our initial questions seem to be as follows:

A.1, 2 : Rule-following is inadequate to express the requirements for all intelligently creative behaviour; but stochastic principles are available to remedy its deficiencies.

B.1, 2: There are no rational grounds for crediting any mere rule-follower, no matter how elaborate, with conscious experience; but both semantic information theory and brain science suggest clues as to what else may be required before an artefact could embody a conscious agent. Whether these requirements can be met in anything other than biological material is an open question.

C.1, 2: Christian theology has no stake in efforts to deny the theoretical possibility of 'artificially begetting' a conscious agent; but it has much to say as to the practical responsibilities of Christian stewards in this field.

Value-free knowledge: myth or norm?[1]

The modern scientific enterprise grew up in an atmosphere not merely favourable to biblical religion but in large measure generated by it.[2] God had written the Book of Nature; it was man's part to read it – humbly, observantly and obediently – and to do his best to get it right. Although the founders of modern science were under no illusions as to the limitations, both instrumental and conceptual, that must hinder them in this task, the aim of 'getting it right', however imperfectly achievable, had a perfectly definite and objective meaning; for if the whole enterprise was conducted under the eye of the Author, then for him at least there could be no dubiety about the correctness or otherwise of any resulting claims to knowledge on our part. In particular, the honest scientist schooled himself to distinguish between the way things *were* and the way he might have *liked* them to be, and to guard against the danger of letting his values and preferences distort his reading of the facts. Once again he had to acknowledge that this aim, too, was imperfectly achievable; but he would count it a shame in the sight of God to be found negligent of it.

It is symptomatic of the practical atheism of our day, however, that this early emphasis on the ideal of objective, value-free knowledge – on the existence of facts that must be reckoned with whether we like them or not – has found itself increasingly under attack. Abolish the Author from the scene – so the argument runs – and who is to say whether the Book is being accurately read? If nobody can say, then why not dismiss the concept of value-free knowledge altogether, as an exploded myth? Perhaps through a misconception of the work of Thomas Kuhn,[3] it has recently been fashionable to assert that even in natural science there are no significant matters of 'straight scientific fact', and to write off those who disagree as naïve.

From a certain type of unbeliever, this dismissal of objectivity as an ideal is at least consistent. What is more startling – more disturbing – is to find something very like it echoed increasingly nowadays by people professing Christian beliefs, especially in the social sciences.[4] The fact that a whole conference of Christian university staff was recently convened to discuss 'The Myth of Value-Free Knowledge' makes me wonder whether even some evangelical believers have been seduced into giving it credence. In case any readers are among them, let me try to sow some seeds of legitimate doubt in their minds. I want to argue that Christians should strongly oppose the fashionable rejection of the ideal of value-free knowledge, because except in a few special cases that rejection is both illogical and inherently incompatible with the theistic Christian position.

That total rejection of the ideal of value-free knowledge is illogical (*i.e.* does not follow from the premises) hardly needs demonstration. The alleged grounds for it are that the values of the scientist (and of his social background) inescapably bias his selection of data and colour his reading of those he selects. Thus even if he takes value-free objectivity as his aim (so the argument runs), his performance must fall so far short as to make the whole concept meaningless.

To be sure, any idea that the *practice* of science can be value-neutral is nonsensical; our decisions whether, when, and at what cost to lift the lid of Pandora's box or to publish what we see when we peer inside are as value-laden as human judgments can be. But for the working scientist in (say) chemistry, physics or engineering, the plea that he should on these grounds abandon his ideal of value free knowledge as a 'myth' is a monstrous *non sequitur.*

His values, as well as the prevalent thought-forms of his society, have doubtless shaped the *questions* he has asked; and he knows well how tentative and imperfect are his *formulations* of the knowledge he has gained in response to these questions.[5] But by no stretch of logic can this justify the conclusion that the concept of 'value-free' knowledge is a myth. After all, he has daily experience of any number of aims that are imperfectly achievable (*e.g.* the maintenance of mechanical or thermodynamic equilibrium, or the establishment of the structure of a gene) without being robbed *ipso facto* of their definite and objective meaning. More fundamentally, he faces a growing mound of evidence that what he and his colleagues are engaged in is a way of accumulating knowledge that can be *relied upon.* Within stated margins of imprecision, refining itself by repeated test, and standing to be reckoned with by anyone and everyone (whatever their values or ideology) who ventures into the relevant territory, this knowledge can be put to work for us and we enjoy its fruits. To pretend otherwise would be irresponsible tomfoolery.

Can social science be objective?

Why then has such a thesis gained so much currency? The main reason, I think, becomes clear from the concerns of those who propagate it. Almost all the pressure to decry the ideal of value-free knowledge comes from students of human nature and human society. They, too, would like to be called 'scientists'; but in their particular line of investigation there is an epistemological snag, certainly not of their making, which has no parallel in any other. They are people investigating *people.* Their own values and presuppositions – their own idea of what it is like or ought to be like to be a person or a society – inescapably colour not only what strikes them as worthy of investigation in the human situation facing them, but also what they perceive in it. Framing a questionnaire, for example, is seldom if ever a neutral activity. Nor is asking the questions: it puts ideas into people's heads, or reshapes the ideas already there, so that 'value-free questioning' (of people as opposed to things) is virtually impossible.

Above all, the promulgation of findings among the people investigated will in general *affect their accuracy*: it can be either self-fulfilling or self-stultifying.[6]

In general, then, offering people a picture of themselves, especially if it purports to be a prediction of their actions, is not so much informative as *manipulative.*[7] Like the cry of the back-seat driver: 'You'll be in the ditch in a minute', such communications function more like *advice*: 'Consider how you would like it if things turned out this way'. Neither the questions and statements of the social scientist, nor his decisions as to whether or when or to whom to present them, could pretend in general to be 'value-free'.

In view of such embarrassing considerations for a discipline claiming the name of a 'science' it is understandable that some social scientists have passed from the admission that *they* cannot offer value-free knowledge in their own speciality, to the suggestion that no other discipline can do so; and from that to the aggressive dismissal of the whole idea of value-free knowledge as a 'myth'. But this will not do. What follows logically from the predicament of the social scientist is not that value-free knowledge in general is a myth, but only that certain ways of investigating *human beings* do not yield value-free knowledge (though they may yield power); and that certain statements made to human beings about themselves, and especially about their future, *do not impart knowledge*, except in a conditional form which they themselves can (and often must) play a part in making true or false. Limiting though this may be for those of us whose calling is to study people, whether as objects or as subjects, it gives no reason whatever for throwing doubts on the validity of the concept of value-free knowledge in general. To do so merely invites the reaction we feel towards Aesop's fox who lost his tail. The clean and honest way to cope with the situation is surely to use a distinguishing term (other than 'knowledge') for what people say to one another about one another (on whatever basis) that is *not* value-free.[8] (An engineer would call it 'Feedback'.) Warning? Exhortation? Image-Building? Brainwashing? Encouragement? Discouragement? Inflammation? It could be any or all of these and more. Perhaps the most general term would be 'Assessment' or 'Appreciation'. To receive such communications about ourselves may in a sense be informative; but it does not confront us with the 'take-it-or-leave-it' claim to our assent which is the hallmark of objective knowledge. We can falsify it.

Someone may be inclined to object that if all our methods of trying to acquire or impart knowledge of human beings are value-biased, this does seem to make the notion of value-free knowledge empty at least in the social sciences. I am aware (as an outsider) that this is a matter of hot dispute among contemporary sociologists. Weber's early ideal of objectivity in social science finds few defenders among today's *avant-garde.* Mannheim's hope that an academic 'intelligentsia' could serve as impartial bridge-builders between the sociological 'outsider's view' and the intrinsic 'participants' view' has not been realized. As seen by Alvin Gouldner, for example, 'the fate of objectivity in sociology is linked with, and its fortunes vary with, the changing hopes for a peace-bringing human unity'. Early nineteenth-century Positivism, he argues, 'set itself the task of creating both an objective social science and a new religion of humanity, each informing the other and aimed at re-uniting society'. In Gouldner's view 'the conception of objectivity has commonly projected an image of the scientist as linked to a higher realm, as possessed of a godlike penetration into things, as serenely above human frailties and distorting passions, or as possessed of a priest-like impartiality.[9]

Social science in theistic perspective

I need hardly say that this humanistic image is the reverse of that which should inspire the Christian social scientist to retain the concept of value-free knowledge. In biblical perspective the scientist is not a god but a humble steward answerable to the Giver of his data for the accuracy with which he reads them. He is thankful that, despite his human frailties and distorting passions, it has proved possible to establish a vast and ever-growing structure of solid facts about people – in medicine, physiology, psychology, and even such subjects as economics and social dynamics – which people themselves must accept and reckon with whether they like them or not. But the central point for the Christian, which makes nonsense of the anti-objectivist case, is that even where *he* may find it difficult or impossible to arrive at a value-free description of a human situation, he is under the judgment of One who *knows* the way things are, for it is he who created them and now holds them in being, just as they are. Thus whatever the human scientist may think about Joe Bloggs, he is in the unseen presence of One who *knows* whether he is correct or not to think as he does about Joe. (If he enters into dialogue with Joe, and so becomes one system with him, he will doubtless forfeit thereby the possibility of gaining the predictive knowledge of Joe that a non-participant may have.[7]) Whatever the limitations and relativities of his own view, still behind all, and Giver of being to all, there is God, who knows just what it is that the scientist-in-dialogue would be correct to believe about Joe.[10] It should be added there may be vastly important generalizations to learn and understand about a society as a system, which individual members of any society could be correct to accept as objective fact without invalidating them. I am thus far from agreeing with the notion that it is impossible to study society scientifically. On the contrary, once the present defeatist fashion has passed, I look forward to the growth of a science of society in all its facets which will be increasingly rewarding in the accumulation of solid knowledge.

Science in general

If the Creator's knowledge constitutes a conceptual criterion of objectivity even in the special case of human science, it does so *a fortiori* in the general domain of scientific investigation. No doubt personal limitations and prejudices and cultural thought-forms can in theory bias and distort our scientific descriptions even of physical reality. There is no guarantee, even in physics, that what we *claim* to know about our world is ever totally value-free. The folly of taking refuge from objectivity in such theoretical admissions, however, is shown by the solid day-by-day reliability of physical science as a guide to our expectations; and that even where they have practical import. The inference is not that *knowledge* is never what value-free, but only that what *we claim* to know is liable to be a blend of truth and error, knowledge and prejudice or wishful thinking. And again the Creator is the all-knowing arbiter of the extent to which what we claim to know really *is* knowledge.

Why is this so important? Because at its root, as I see it, is the age-old question: Who is to be master? The ideal of value-free knowledge is the representation of what the Creator has provided for me to reckon with, as it is, whether I like it or not. There are admittedly some aspects of the future which it is up to me to determine, and about which there exists no value-free knowledge-for-me.[11] (There cannot be take-it-or-leave-it knowledge-for-you of a situation which logically depends on whether you 'take it' or 'leave it'!)

But for the rest, my highest ambition must be to know and to do full justice to the objective facts as God knows them, and so render to him as their Giver my whole-hearted obedience.

Summary and conclusion

The main argument of this paper has been that whatever our admitted epistemic difficulties in disentangling fact from interpretation and evaluation, especially in the human sciences, nobody who takes seriously the concept of God as the all-knowing Creator can rationally dismiss the concept of value-free knowledge as a myth. Such a Creator is the ever-present arbiter of the distinctions between factual knowledge (that which stands to be reckoned with, whatever one's values) and the whole spectrum of value-loaded beliefs, opinions and assessments that we form (and properly form) as participants in the flux of human history. Where what passes for the 'communication of knowledge' is admittedly value-laden, it would seem better to identify it as such by a distinguishing label (such as 'assessment' or 'appreciation') than to rob the term 'knowledge' of its objective connotation.

In these terms we have noted that the concept of 'knowledge about our future' is an important special case. There must in general be some objective facts-for-non-participants about our future (whether or not anyone knows them) which are not objective facts-for-us, because it is our thinking and choosing that will determine what form they will take.[11] In that sense what we think about our own future is (for us) inescapably 'value-bound'. It is ramifications of this logical dilemma that make it impossible completely to divorce facts from values in social sciences, though without in any way eliminating the need in general for the concept of value-free knowledge.

Finally, it is important to distinguish the Christian motive for retaining the concept of objective knowledge from that of unbelieving humanism. Christians who believe that objectivity is a duty to the Creator, before whom the scientist is under judgment, have no need of the scientistic *hubris* of Positivism to back up their emphasis; nor would it make sense for them to abandon objectivity for fear of being tarred with the same brush. Instead, I suggest that the current debate offers a splendid opportunity for the academic Christian to show what it means for him professionally to believe that 'all things are naked and opened to the eyes of him with whom we have to do' (Hebrews 4:13): that for us value-free knowledge is no myth, but a norm which, like righteousness in the domain of the spirit, is no less meaningful and normative for being imperfectly attainable.

11

The open mind — an evangelical approach to the Bible

Perhaps no accusation is more often levelled at 'conservative evangelicals' today, whether in charity, malice or ignorance, than that they lack 'open-mindedness'. It will be no part of my concern to deny that individuals may be found who merit all that lies behind the accusation, though in my experience they are remarkably rare. What is more disturbing is the suggestion, so often implied, that people with closed minds are the 'typical' or 'consistent' evangelicals, and that those whose faith has left their minds open, or even stirred them to see honest enquiry as part of their duty to God, must be half-hearted and inconsistent in their evangelical profession. As suggestions of this sort, when repeated often enough, can gain acceptance and prove divisive even among evangelicals themselves, it seems timely to look at them critically, to see how much truth they embody, and to consider, more carefully than the critics, what genuine openness to truth should mean positively for an evangelical believer.

Evangelical faith is based on God's self-revelation by word and action as recorded and handed down in the Bible. For the evangelical, this revelation is normative, his final court of appeal; and the Holy Spirit speaking in and through Scripture is the final judge of his thinking in all matters of 'doctrine, reproof, correction, and instruction in righteousness' (2 Timothy 3:16). He accepts this authority 'by faith', but not by caprice or without good reason. On the contrary, he believes that Christ's own authority lies behind and so validates for him the authority of Scripture; and it is cumulatively a matter of his own experience that God speaks to him, diagnoses his condition, and works upon him with authority and power through the Bible in a manner that attests its claims.

Now if the God of the Bible were a mere despot, demanding the kind of blind loyalty that would seek to advance his claims at the cost even of truth itself, the intellectual integrity of the believer would be imperilled indeed. But of course it is not so. Central to the Bible's image of God is the absolute integrity of his character, his love of truth and honesty and his implacable hatred of deceit. Our God is 'dead straight': nothing remotely savouring of dishonesty, 'double-think', or evasion of fact, can be tolerated by him, let alone accepted in his service. Before his standard we can but tremble and ask forgiveness for our best efforts to be open – obediently open – to his truth wherever it is found.

Already, perhaps, we begin to see the falsehood of the antithesis between open-mindedness and evangelical commitment. At every turn, the Christian must be *open* to correction from God, in whatever way and by whatever channel he chooses, no matter how inconceivable it may be to him, and improbable in fact, that he is mistaken. Indeed, whether he likes it or not he *is* open to such correction, though if he is unwilling for it God may not choose to force it on him. But of course to be open in this sense is not the same as to be *uncommitted*, nor even to be only provisionally committed, in the sense of consciously reserving judgment. Open-mindedness, in other words, is quite different from empty-mindedness; and it is only by confusing the two that the alleged antithesis can be declared.

The parallel and the contrast with scientific commitment

A helpful parallel, and an important contrast, are to be found in the open-mindedness of the scientist. Scientists (at their best) are continually open to any evidence that can run the gauntlet of professional scrutiny; but this does not mean that the man of science always professes, or ought to profess, that he knows *nothing*. True, there may be some areas of a rapidly developing field in which he has little to offer with any confidence; but in other, more established fields he finds no incompatibility between openness and firm commitment. When it comes to expressing what he knows in a precise formula he may show some hesitation in choosing words; but he refuses on this account to be either tongue-tied or paralysed in the pursuit of his science.

'We know that our evidence and experience are limited,' an astronomer may say, 'but we have now *no reason to doubt* the essential reliability of our model of the solar system. It has stood the test of experience through several generations, and we would demand good evidence before seriously questioning it.'

The scientist, in other words, is here committed to a reasonable belief which, though it leaves him quite open to evidence, is unqualified by any *active doubt.* Active doubt, in the absence of sufficient evidence, he would here regard as irrational – mere baseless speculation.

In relation to the reliability of the Bible, there would seem to be no reason for the Christian to be either less open to evidence than the scientist, or more favourable towards baseless speculation. In his own limited experience, as well as in that of many previous generations, the Bible has borne out its claim to speak with life-giving and light-giving authority, on matters of 'doctrine, reproof, correction, and instruction in righteousness'. As an action-portrait of God at work in the lives of men, it has commended itself (in ways on which we need not elaborate here) as an 'authentic likeness' of One whom he has begun to know at work in his own life, having been introduced to him, directly or indirectly by its intermediation. His eventual commitment to belief in its divine origin and reliability is therefore not unreasonable, and like the scientist, he would thenceforward regard it as irrational and arbitrary for him to reopen the question in the absence of fresh evidence. Thus far, the parallel holds.

The commitment of the Christian differs in one vital respect, however, from that of the scientist; for it is a commitment not to a mere abstract formulation, but to a *Person*, in whom he has placed his trust for eternity. Because he believes Christ to be the Truth as well as the Way and the Life, he has an even stronger incentive to be *open* to any evidence that the Giver of all truth may bring his way; yet at the same time he is the more sensitive to the ineptitude of arbitrary doubt, and its significance as a potential *breach of trust* between him and his Master.

Breach of trust

This brings us to the nub of the matter. What would constitute a breach of trust for the committed Christian? His relationship with

God is essentially one of love – mutual love. Ideally, he desires nothing more strongly than to know and do God's will, and he has the promise of the testimony of the Spirit to authenticate the Word if his one aim is to obey it.

Clearly then a breach of trust could take two forms. The first is as old as the Garden of Eden: 'Yea, hath God said . . .?' This is that arbitrary and baseless doubt which we have already considered. It is as damaging to mutual trust as if a happily married man were arbitrarily and baselessly to entertain doubts as to the faithfulness of his spouse. In the Bible it is symptomatic of the wish that God had *not* said . . . (*i.e.* of latent disobedience). It is for this reason that 'unbelief' is so often spoken of as sin.

There is however a second converse form of breach of trust, of which conservative believers may especially need to beware. This is the attitude that fears to be open to truth lest it upset one's belief. 'Oh God, don't let evolution be true; or if it is, don't let it be generally known.' We can all recognize the instinct; and it may have its short-term survival value in a closed community. But if our eyes are once opened to the insult offered to the God of all truth by such an attitude (which Professor Hooykaas[1] has termed 'Little-Faith'), we can never think of adopting it in his service.

It is true, of course, that unstable souls have sometimes been shaken from their moorings at the first impact of some new scientific discovery, and that many unbelievers seek to make props for their atheism out of the latest findings. To distinguish truth from the interpretations wished upon it is not always easy, and a Christian who feels himself weak on the logical side may be entirely justified in letting specialist controversy pass him by. What seems clear, however, is that those with the appropriate mental equipment should see it as not merely permissible but obligatory to express their love and worship of God by following up, with him and in his strength, the latest evidence that he has made available to them.

The authority of Scripture

Let us see then in conclusion how these principles apply to the scientific investigation of Scripture itself. The Christian cannot of course pretend that he comes to this with an empty mind; for these have proved themselves to him the very words of life, and he thanks God for what he has done through them. Moreover, he cannot pretend that his commitment to the doctrine of biblical authority is 'provisional' in the sense that he actively entertains alternatives.

On the other hand – and this is crucial – because he wants nothing more than to receive God's correction on any point where he thinks amiss, he must ensure (as best he can) that he *erects no barriers* to such correction in any quarter, however unthinkable it may be to him to expect it from there. If the authenticity of a document is in question, for example, he of all people should be able peaceably to give all relevant evidence its full weight; for to do otherwise would betray his Master.

The evangelical Christian's 'rest position' then is one of total openness (to any evidence with adequate credentials) combined with, and *expressive of*, total commitment – to the One whom he cannot help believing to be the giver of the Scripture he investigates, as well as of the data he uses in doing so. He is as much aware of the potential blasphemy of attributing uninspired material to God, as of the dangers of rejecting what God has in fact inspired. But with the precedent of Christ's own attitude to the Old Testament, and the testimony of the ages to the authority of the New, he believes himself justified, in the absence of contrary evidence, in accepting the whole Bible as utterly trustworthy for its declared purpose.

12

Science and the Bible[1]

It is impossible for a scientific discovery given by God to contradict a Word given by God. If therefore a scientific discovery, as distinct from scientific speculation, contradicts what we have believed to be implied by the Bible, it is not a question of error in God's Word, but of error in our way of interpreting it. Far from 'defending' the Bible against scientific discovery, the Christian has a duty to welcome thankfully, as from the same Giver, whatever light each may throw upon the other. This is the 'freedom' of a fully Christian devotion to the God of Truth.

A hundred years ago, scientific thinking was regarded by many biblically-minded Christians as a menace. 'The Scientist' was almost by definition an enemy. You could never tell when he would turn up some fresh result to embarrass the Christian and attack the truth of Scripture.

Nowadays all this has changed. The 'old guard' among liberals and conservatives may skirmish yet among the rusty barbed wire of the deserted lines; but from philosophers downwards (or upwards) there is now general agreement that scientific and Christian accounts (say of the origin of the universe) are not, in fact, trying to answer the same kind of question, and so cannot logically be considered as rivals. The scientific approach offers a different, complementary way of expressing the many-sided truth about the world of events which the Christian sees as God's activity. No-one has supposed that God's 'clothing the lilies' and 'feeding the sparrows' implied processes which science could not explain; and there would seem to be no biblical grounds for insisting that his activity in cosmological or developmental processes must be scientifically irregular. This would be rather like expecting the ink in which a sonnet is written to be chemically different from that on a cheque. It might be – but it needn't!

Here is not the place to develop this new view.[2] I believe it to be much closer to the biblical idea of nature than the nineteenth-century one; closer also to the view of the early scientists who founded the Royal Society 'to the glory of God'. But in the simple form in which I have just expressed it, it may seem rather too 'slick' an answer to some of the problems with which our grandfathers wrestled; and if it doesn't, I think it ought to. This is no universal panacea, designed to allow us to isolate our Christian and scientific thinking in fact-tight compartments. True, it shows us how *not* to relate the two; but it still leaves us to discover how we should connect the facts God teaches us through scientific enquiry, with the revelation we believe he inspired men to embody in Holy Writ. This is the question to which the present brief article is meant as an introduction (and nothing more) – a question which no thoughtful Christian in our day can honestly ignore.

We might put it metaphorically in this way: God has, we believe, inspired men to paint 'for our learning' an authoritative picture, composite but unified – an action-portrait of himself – which is called his written Word. He has also given us access to a continual flood of what we call 'facts of experience', which we believe he enjoins us to investigate scientifically. At various points there are elements of the inspired picture (the story of the flood, the exodus, the life of Christ, *etc.*) which look as if they relate in some way to facts which we might discover (or have already discovered) by scientific enquiry. What purpose then should these scientific facts serve? Are we meant to regard them as means of *verifying* the inspiration of Scripture or of *augmenting* revelation – or do they have some other, quite different function in God's economy?

Obviously a surface meaning of many passages could be tested, for example, against archæological discoveries, and the meaning of others can be enriched by scientific and historical knowledge. But I want to suggest that the primary function of scientific enquiry in such fields is neither to verify nor to add to the inspired picture, but to help us in eliminating improper ways of reading it. To pursue the metaphor, I think the scientific data God gives us can sometimes serve as his way of warning us when we are standing too close to the picture, or at the wrong angle, or with the wrong expectations, to be able to see the inspired pattern he means it to convey to us. We all know how important the 'correct viewing distance' is for a painting – especially of the more abstract type! If we occupy ourselves with the individual patches of paint, we may sometimes get an entirely false idea of what the artist means to convey. It would be useless to insist that 'the whole picture' was guaranteed to be authentic and trustworthy; only when we move back until the proper pattern shows up, can we begin to use such terms without doing violence to the artist's intention.

So it is, I suggest, with Holy Scripture. In many important parts, no doubt, the inspired pattern is fine-grained, and even sentences or phrases may be taken in isolation without doing it violence. But in other parts the pattern may well be on a larger scale, so that sentences taken in isolation might be quite misleading; we may have to stand further back and take some aspect of a narrative as a whole, or even a whole sequence of narratives, before we are justified in talking of the resulting pattern as 'authoritative'. It is not that the pattern is a *mixture* of authoritative and unauthoritative parts, inspired 'on the whole'. It is that authority and inspiration pertain to the pattern of all the parts *as* a whole, and we must be wary of the risks of forcing them to stand in isolation. Otherwise we might sometimes find ourselves in Ryle's dilemma of the man who inspected all the Oxford Colleges one by one looking for 'The University', and concluded that there wasn't one!

The classic biblical example of this is the book of Job, where we are liable to run into theological (rather than scientific) contradictions unless we stand back to read the message of the book as a whole. Our Lord's statement about 'hating father and mother' (Luke 14:26) is another obvious 'part' which needs to be read in the context of the whole. An example of a wrong angle of approach is the mediaeval interpretation of Psalm 96 as 'proving' that the earth did not move. Here it was scientific observation that forced Christians to realize that they were pressing the details in a direction God never intended. Lest we are tempted to feel superior to them, we might do well to scrutinize our own attitude, say to the interpretation of Genesis 1–3, to make sure that we are as alive as we should be to the dangers of doing the same – and as ready to be obedient to whatever clues God has given us.

Now the Bible is not a book only for experts; its light is promised to the childlike mind, and it would be absurd to suggest that for *its primary purpose* we require more equipment than God gives to any hungry and humble soul. This is why I do not believe that scientific knowledge is meant to add to the inspired revelation, as if this were not sufficient in itself. The rule has always been that 'comparing Scripture with Scripture' is enough, with the Spirit's illumination, to establish the inspired pattern for all purposes of 'doctrine, reproof, *etc.*' (2 Timothy 3:16). It is only when we insist on asking more sophisticated questions that we run into uncertainty, and may need the help of scientific or historical enquiry to determine whether we are forcing on the details of the picture a construction they are not intended to bear for us.

In other words, I think it is not only unnecessary, but misguided, to consider scientific results as a test of the inspiration and authority of Scripture. If the meaning we have given to a passage happens to agree with the observed facts, well and good. In many instances this is not surprising. But if *what we have understood* a passage to mean does not square with the observed facts, the inference is not that the passage is 'wrong' and therefore cannot have been inspired (this was the fallacy of the older liberalism), nor necessarily that there must have been something wrong with the observations. It may well be rather that we are at the wrong 'viewing distance', making the wrong approach, to see the Holy Spirit's larger-scale pattern which is declared to be authoritative, and of which the passage forms a necessary and God-given part.

It would follow from this view that we are never entitled – indeed it is positively impious – to foreclose the result of a scientific enquiry 'as a matter of faith', since this would be to block one of God's appointed ways of 'warning us off' a possible misinterpretation of his truth. We are bound to be obedient to God's Word as far as we understand it at the time, and we may properly say that we 'cannot imagine' a result contrary to our interpretation; but we must in the last analysis leave it to God to show us whether or not our imagination needs stretching (as he has had to do, for example, in the matter of Psalm 96). As the giver of truth in both spheres, he can be trusted, with a light heart, to take care of its implications. Our duty is not to resist but to welcome these, wherever they may lead, and give him thanks.

I need hardly emphasize that in all this I have had in mind the *facts* of scientific observation, as distinct from the speculations which often pass for scientific facts. When some nineteenth-century scientists maintained that 'our science has disproved your

Christianity', experienced Christians, unable to follow the technicalities but knowing the power of the risen Christ, had some excuse for suspecting that something must be wrong with the alleged 'science'. Unfortunately, it was usually the logic rather than the facts of the scientists which was at fault, so that these Christians lost face by attacking in the wrong quarter. The truth is that in many scientific conclusions there is bound to be a strong element of interpretation. This, however, would be no excuse for a Christian to 'drag his feet' in following up the implications of reliable scientific observations. On the contrary, he should be foremost in his eagerness both to test and establish their truth, and also to see where they may lead. He is, after all, a son of their Giver and, in that sense, on home ground.

My plea has been, in effect, for more Christian realism and humility than is sometimes shown in our approach to scientific discovery. Discovered truth is the ally of revealed truth; and we dishonour God if, in the name of 'faith', we resist it or fail fully to open our minds to it. Here, as in other departments of our life, we have not received the spirit of fear, but of the joyous liberty which comes with full and responsible devotion to him who is the way, the truth, and the life.

Apologetics today

1. Is apologetics a waste of time?

It is sometimes difficult for the Christian believer to imagine himself in the position of the unbeliever with whom he is in dialogue. He knows, of course, from his own experience, that what progressively convinces a man of the truth of Christianity is not impersonal argument alone, nor even argument plus the data of Scripture and history. His own conviction has grown rather from the personal discovery that day by day he is at grips with the living Reality to whom Scripture and history bear witness; and that the testimony of the biblical writers and of the Christian church down the years can also honestly be *his* testimony. In this sense, he recognizes his Christian conviction as a *gift* – a *datum.* So he longs for the unbeliever to reach the point at which he too is willing to 'put himself in the way of evidence' which God is prepared to give him in his own experience, and to '*taste and see* that God is good'.

From this standpoint many Christians may be tempted to regard apologetics – the reasoned defence of the faith – as a waste of time. 'Why beat about the bush?' they ask. 'The main obstacle to Christian conviction is at the level of the will. 'Intellectual' objections are only a front for a moral resistance against the claims of God in Christ.' They may even cite their own spiritual pilgrimage from doubt to faith in support of their view: '*I* thought at one time that my difficulties were mainly intellectual; but what I had to learn was that the real trouble lay deeper, and only the plainly declared Word of God could get to the root of it.'

Let me say at once that I wholeheartedly accept the diagnosis that underlies such views as these, and can indeed endorse it from my own experience. Nothing I want to say in this paper is meant to weaken its force. But the practical conclusion drawn is I think mistaken, at least in nine cases out of ten. The problem is not simply to satisfy *oneself* that the unbeliever's difficulties have moral roots, but to help *him* to make this discovery for himself. It should need little sympathetic imagination – especially in those who were once doubters themselves – to realize that this process may require an honest and painstaking effort to grapple with a whole range of apparent objections. The unbeliever who feels his intellectual or moral integrity threatened by some implication (real or imagined) of Christian commitment owes it to the God of truth to satisfy himself that the threat is unreal. The believer in dialogue with him has an equal obligation not to rush him past the difficulty, but rather to show him, if he can, why he can proceed past it with a clear conscience, if not always with a definitive answer. This, as I understand it, is the task of apologetics.

2. Three kinds of question

There are perhaps three kinds of question that may trouble an honest unbeliever as he contemplates the Christian faith:

(a) *Is it possible*? Do the discoveries of science and our ever-growing knowledge of the world leave *room* for the beliefs to which a biblical Christian is committed? Is it possible honestly to be a Christian believer without undervaluing or ignoring facts that were unsuspected or would even have been denied by the writers of the Bible?

(b) *Is it meaningful*? What *significance* can be attached to talk about 'God', 'heaven' and the like in our scientific age? Do Christian affirmations of faith amount to more than declarations of intention to live in a particularly loving and responsible way in this present world?

(c) *Is it true*? Suppose it were granted to be both possible and meaningful, on what *evidence* is an honest man expected to base a belief in what biblical Christianity affirms? Can its truth be tested scientifically? If not, why not? And what tests *would* be appropriate?

At different periods in history, the relative emphases on these three headings have varied. A hundred years ago, the main issues were of type (a). Could the belief in a creator, or the doctrine of the fall, be squared with the biological theory of evolution and the data of geology? Questions of this kind are not dead; indeed they have been revived in a surprisingly naïve (and aggressive) form by the biologist Jacques Monod in a book *Chance and Necessity*, published in 1972; and the same year saw a fresh flare-up of the debate between 'creationists' and 'evolutionists' on the School Board of California, which provoked lively discussion in the columns of *Science*[1] and *Nature*.[2] But in recent times the focus of debate has shifted. On the one hand, advances in our understanding of the human brain, at both physiological and psychological levels, have raised urgent questions about the spiritual nature of man as the Bible sees him, and its relation to his physical constitution. On the other, the recent fashion in 'linguistic philosophy' has brought a fresh crop of attacks on the meaningfulness of religious language and the verifiability of statements of Christian belief, so that much recent apologetic activity has been in areas (b) and (c).

But although I have spoken of 'attacks' – and indeed some of these have been savage in tone – it is not only in defensive terms that I would have us think about apologetics today. Honest intellectual argument, seeking to do full justice to fact and to identify fallacy wherever it lies, is ideally an act of service to the God whom Christians claim to worship. The Christian who takes part in it does so not merely as a partisan but also as one who is pledged to help 'whatsoever things are true' to emerge clearly and be recognized fully, no matter by whom they are uncovered. In a trans-atlantic phrase, he wants simply to be able to 'tell it like it is'. Moreover, however aggressively such objections may sometimes be thrust upon us, they stand for real questions which can seriously trouble an honest unbeliever; and the believer himself can only grow in understanding as he thinks his way through them. I do not suggest that every Christian has a duty to spend his energies in this way; but I do believe that the need is urgent for those appropriately gifted to do so, not merely as a matter of intellectual curiosity or satisfaction, still less as an exercise in counter-aggression, but rather as the natural expression of their compassion for those who find their way barred by such obstacles.

It may be felt that I have laid too little stress on the apologetic use of argument to *support* Christian doctrines, either from first principles (*e.g.* the 'ontological argument' for the existence of God)[3] or from the data of science (*e.g.* the 'argument from design).[4] I confess that the omission is not accidental. Rightly or wrongly, I find none of these classical 'arguments' at all conclusive, and little or no biblical encouragement to expect them to be so. It would seem a pity to encourage unbelievers to encumber their theological fabric with logically weak planks, upon which ultimate conviction cannot, and need not, rest.

3. Current stumbling blocks: scientific

It is now many years since I first read that the issue of 'science and religion' had been beaten to death, and that nothing remained of the notion epitomized in White's notorious *History of the Warfare of Science with Theology in Christendom* that the two were natural enemies. In principle, it may be true that the issue is dead; but in practice it stubbornly refuses to lie down. Nor can current objections to Christianity in the name of science always be answered by referring the objector to the earlier classics; for however well they cover the basic principles, he may either fail or be unwilling to see how these apply to cases not envisaged by their authors.

The apologist has to cope with objections in the name of Science at two quite different levels. First, there may be *facts*, old or new, that suggest a conflict with what the Bible has been held to teach. Here the difficulty is usually to distinguish between the *data* (both scientific and biblical) on the one hand, and *extrapolations* from those data on the other. Time-honoured interpretations may find themselves questioned in the process; and we may have to learn to remain 'reverently agnostic' on questions to which neither Scripture nor scientific observation give explicit answers. For the Christian who believes the Bible to be God's self-revelation through the words of men, there can be no question of 'correcting the Bible by science'; but there could be no excuse for holding *our interpretation* of the Bible to be incorrigible by the data of scientific observation. On the contrary, these data could be one of God's means of warning us when Scripture was being used for purposes not intended. (Compare the abuse of Psalm 96 by the theologians at the time of Galileo to refute the Copernican theory.)

The second level at which problems commonly arise is *methodological.* In the discipline of science, there are accepted restrictions on both (i) what counts as *fact* and (ii) what counts as an *explanation.*

(i) Scientific claims can normally be backed by public demonstration, or at least checked in principle by suitably qualified experimenters. Religious doctrines, on the other hand, claim to be based on divine revelation. Scientifically-minded people are understandably restive at the contrast, and are inclined to fear that Christian commitment would entail some lowering of intellectual standards. They recognize, of course, that 'authority' plays a part in establishing what scientists believe at a given time about the physical world; but such 'authority' is in principle open to question and correction. Efforts to reassure them on the grounds that 'scientists also have to exercise faith' are, I think, misguided. The honest unbeliever might well protest that if only Christian belief involved no greater 'faith' than he exercises in the laboratory, he would have fewer problems with it!

The only adequate way to salve a tender scientific conscience here, I suggest, is to go back to scientific first principles. Confronted with any claim, the scientist is trained to ask: (1) If this were true, what ought to be the case? (2) How then can I find out whether this *is* the case? Applying these same questions to the Christian faith, it becomes clear that if it were true that our world owes its being to a creator who is not confined to our created space and time, then we could have no way of knowing about him *unless he told us.* Christianity claims that he has taken the initiative in revealing himself, both in the hearts of men and, supremely, in history in the person of Jesus Christ. In this area, then, his authority is our only possible basis of knowledge; so that to decide in advance to accept *nothing* on authority would be quite the reverse of the openness to truth that science professes. This does not mean that we may in this area *lower* our standards of truth: it means only that instead of testing the truth of the revealed doctrine (which may be impossible in the nature of the case), we must seek to test the *credentials of the source* of the revelation. As in science itself, corporate testimony plays a large part here; but when we look into it, we find that true openness to the evidence entails also being ready for the consequences (for one's *own* priorities and one's whole career) of encountering that Source in one's own personal experience. If the message is true, it is directed to *us.* There is no convincing way of testing the credentials of the Source, short of allowing him to make himself known – if he will – as an active power in one's own life. If he does, one will soon discover whether or not he is as good as his word, in one area of experience after another. The honestly convinced Christian is the man who has found the claims of Christ borne out in his experience often enough and for long enough to make it *reasonable* to trust his authority in matters of revelation which are inherently untestable here and now.

(ii) To 'explain' an event scientifically usually means uncovering a chain-mesh of cause-and-effect that led up to it in accordance with general laws. An explanation is scientifically 'complete' if no vacancies are left in this chain-mesh pattern. 'Given these prior circumstances,' the scientist says, 'it was *bound* to happen thus' or, more cautiously, 'you could have expected nothing else'. To explain, then, is to *reduce a happening to an instance* of what might have been expected according to precedent, once all the details were known. It is to show that *precedent has not been broken* by the events in question.

Physical science has discovered a very general and powerful way of showing that events do not break precedent, by analysing the processes involved into their constituent parts. The heating up of air in a bicycle pump is explained in terms of the motions of the molecules that make it up. The behaviour of an animal is explained in terms of the activities of the nerve cells in its brain, the chemicals in its bloodstream and so forth. This process of reducing phenomena to their constituent elements is called '*methodological reduction*'. In itself it is a perfectly legitimate and indeed essential tool, thanks to which we owe most of our understanding of natural processes and our power to set them to work for good or ill. Nobody should belittle the value of this method for its purpose; this has been and continues to be justified beyond question by its effectiveness.

The trouble comes when people confuse this methodological principle with *metaphysical* reductionism. Metaphysical reductionism, which I like to call 'nothing-buttery', is the doctrine that if something can be causally explained (in the above sense) by reducing it to its elements at some particular level, then it can be dismissed as 'nothing but' the activity of those elements. In other words, the original phenomenon has been 'debunked' or 'explained away'. Thus if human behaviour could be causally attributed to the workings of the brain, and those workings causally attributed to the physico-chemical processes in nerve cells and the like, the metaphysical reductionist would claim that man was 'nothing but a complex physico-chemical mechanism'. I have elsewhere discussed the fallacy involved in such arguments.[5] Here I would only stress their lack of any logical foundations in the methodological reduction practised for scientific purposes. *Methodological* reductionism is as innocuous in principle as the reduction of a painting to its chemical elements, or the reduction of the workings of a computer to its electronic elements. The most one could say against an analysis of this sort is that it systematically ingnores the aesthetic *point* of the painting, or the mathematical *point* of what the computer is doing. It would be nonsensical to suggest that because the analysis is complete in its own terms, there *is* no other point to the situation. There is no logical basis whatsoever for *devaluing* those aspects of the phenomena that a scientific analysis ignores for its purpose. Metaphysical reductionism, then, is logically bankrupt: parasitic on the reputation of science. It is essential in the interests of clarity and integrity, and not merely in the interests of religion, to distinguish it from its methodological namesake and to expose it for what it is.

Once the bogey of metaphysical reductionism has been exorcised, problems in group (a) take on quite a different aspect. Many simply cease to be problems, once one recognizes that the scientific 'explanation' of natural events, or of the origin of the universe, is not answering the same question as the biblical 'explanation', but rather offering a logically complementary account for which the biblical explanation leaves a proper and ample place.[6] I do not mean that we need expect *all* events, including those that Christians term miraculous, to have in principle a scientific explanation. On the contrary, to encourage expectations of this sort would seem quite unwarranted and unhelpful. What I mean is that the existence of a scientific explanation, complete in its own terms, does not have to be *denied* in order to make room for the biblical explanation of an event as an act of God, fulfilling his eternal purpose. This is as true of scientific explanations invoking so-called 'random' or 'chance' processes as of those that appeal to deterministic 'laws' (Proverbs 16:33).[7]

Other problems in group (a) need more detailed analysis. In relation to the science of man, in particular, a whole complex of questions concerning human responsibility, 'free will', the immortality of the soul and the like remain to be worked out as knowledge advances. The development of automata with mind-like functions raises a crop of related questions on which much nonsense has been written (both pro-and anti-Christian) and much ground-clearing is required. Here I think is the main area of apologetics in which scientists and theologians today need to work together.

4. Current stumbling blocks: philosophical

Although this introductory paper is written mainly for scientists, one can draw no sharp dividing line between the stumbling blocks raised in the name of science and those in the name of philosophy; indeed all the foregoing questions are clearly as much philosophical as scientific. Before concluding, therefore, we might briefly look at some objections currently raised in the name of philosophical analysis itself. As already mentioned, these centre on questions of the *meaningfulness* of religious statements. Critics are willing enough to allow sentences such as 'God is love' an 'emotive' meaning. What they question is whether they are 'cognitively' meaningful. Do they say anything that could be *true* or *false*? What state of affairs could be imagined that would falsify a statement of this kind?

The last two questions are often confused, as if our power to *imagine* a refutation of a statement determined whether or not it had cognitive meaning. I have discussed this assumption elsewhere,[8] and would here say only that it has logical weaknesses akin to those of the 'reductionist' fallacy we considered in section 3. The point for our purpose is that the Christian apologist must be prepared to say what it means for him to claim that Christianity is *true*. It will not do to say simply that this 'denies that Christianity is false'; for this could well encourage the unbeliever in his suspicion that the whole thing is an elaborate artificial game of words lacking any contact with reality.

I believe that the kind of soul-searching that is provoked by questions of this sort may be the most profitable by-product of the apologetic exercise for the Christian. Where, if at all, does the truth of biblical affirmations show up in our own experience? Do we *know* God? or only know *about* him? or only *know what is said* about him? Note that the thrust of these questions is *not* to drive us from what the Bible has revealed about God to talk about our own experiences. On the contrary, unless our own experience bears the test of Scripture we are not entitled to interpret it as experience of the God of Scripture. But what such questions force us to recognize is that a biblical theology which made no operational contact at *any* point with our experience would be *cognitively meaningless* to us, no matter how expert we were in deducing logical consequences from its premisses. To the extent that the unbeliever is in this position vis-à-vis theology he is not necessarily being rude, but merely honest, in calling it so. In avoiding the trap of making religion 'experience-centred' rather than 'God-centred', we must equally do justice to the biblical emphasis on *knowing*-God-in-Christ as the very stuff of eternal life (John 17:3).

I have concentrated on this example of a philosophical objection mainly because of its relation to the 'positivistic'[9] approach that was once fashionable in science. Most of the others which are current seem to have a similar flavour. The doctrine of the resurrection, for example, has lately been attacked by asking how 'we' could distinguish the resurrected Mr. X from a 'perfect replica'. The implication is that if *we* cannot do so, this somehow cannot be Mr. X. Put thus baldly, the *non sequitur* is perhaps apparent; but it illustrates the dangers of confusing questions of what *is* the case (as determined by the Creator) with questions of what *we* can say or see or determine to be the case.

5. Conclusion

This introductory essay has had a limited objective. I have not tried to treat exhaustively any of the main apologetic issues of our day. My purpose has rather been to sort them to some extent into categories; to indicate constructive lines along which a few of them may perhaps be resolved; and above all to show why I consider that productive work in this area should have a high priority for those Christian believers whose calling brings them naturally into contact with it. This is more than a matter of taste and inclination; it is more even than the duty to use our intellectual talents; I believe it to be a most natural and urgently needed expression of compassion for our spiritually starving world.

Appendix: Pragmatic apologetics

In concentrating on questions of principle, this paper has perhaps done less than justice to the importance of arguments for and against Christianity in terms of its practical effects and implications. Such arguments can never be conclusive either way; but they crop up sufficiently often to deserve mention.

The commonest pitfall in this context is to confuse questions of *truth* with questions of *utility*. Arguments that draw atheistic conclusions from the premise that 'I don't need a God' or 'I don't want a God like that' are manifestly inept. It would be equally inept to counter them by arguing (however truly) that we all *do* need God, or that one *ought* to want the kind of God whom Jesus Christ revealed. Who in his senses would think of denying the existence of (say) the Andromeda nebula, on the grounds that he 'had no need of it' or 'didn't like the look of it'? Conversely, who would urge belief in its existence by trying to show that his interlocutor *had* need and *should* like the look of it?

No. If there is a living God, before whom I stand whether I know it or not, my alleged lack of need or liking for him will not conjure him out of existence. If there is no God, no need or liking I may feel for the idea will bring him into being. Arguments of this kind merely reveal and reinforce misunderstandings of what the Bible actually means by 'God' – not a theoretically derived entity, but One who has acted in history, and is there reckoning with us and to be reckoned with whether we like it or not. In a biblical context a man's feeling no need of God, or no liking for God, is readily understandable and significant as evidence of his own condition; it certainly does not count as evidence against God's existence.

This said, it is of course fair to take the practical effects of biblical doctrine and Christian commitment as evidence relevant to the truth or falsehood of Christianity. The initiatives taken by Christians towards the abolition of slavery and the provision of mass education, for example, and indeed the part played by biblical thought in the rise of modern science itself,[10] can all legitimately (and powerfully) be used to meet fears that Christianity leads only to obscurantism and selfish bigotry. Much needs to be done, in each generation, to demolish cruelly distorted caricatures of what true Christian faith means in practice, without minimizing or whitewashing the evils that have sometimes been perpetrated in its name. Our emphasis on the first-hand evidence available through God's personal dealings with each individual must not lead us to undervalue the corporate testimony, spoken and unspoken, of believers from bibilical times to the present day. We must only avoid exaggerated expectations of what argument in these terms can achieve.

Language, meaning and God

1. Introduction

The burden of the Christian religion is not primarily that certain attitudes are desirable, nor that certain practices are comfortable, but that certain things are true. Certain facts have to be faced, certain claims recognized. Questions of the meaningfulness and truth-status of religious language are thus central to Christian apologetic. However much emphasis we give to the vital link between true belief and action – and for the Bible the two are inseparable – there is no escaping the obligation to enquire into the meaning and truth of Christian affirmations as well as their personal or social effectiveness.

There are in fact two distinct levels at which such questions can be raised. On the one hand, doubt can be thrown upon the meaningfulness of religious assertions, at least superficially, by an appeal to linguistic analysis. On the other hand, the very concept of meaning itself is sometimes thought to be challenged by current mechanistic theories of brain function. The argument of this paper will be that so far from debunking the notion of meaning, a mechanistic analysis of what language is intended to do can lead naturally to a more penetrating criterion of meaningfulness than the crudely behavioural ones often canvassed: a criterion, moreover, that religious utterances both must and can meet. We thus aim to kill two canards, so to say, with one stone.

For our purpose it is unnecessary to trace the fortunes of recent attacks on the meaningfulness of religious language. The plan is rather, starting from biological ground-level, to take a cool look at the nature and function of successful communication in general, and in the light of this to consider the special problems that must attend any meaningful talk about God. If the result points to certain mistakes on both sides of the current debate, I hope that it may do so constructively. Certainly it will be my intention to show that the language of biblical theism is not just defensible, but positively operational in its intended function.

2. The function of language

Language, viewed biologically, is first and foremost a *means of interaction.* Men interact at many levels. From competitive struggle to mutual back-scratching, human beings share with lower animals a certain repertoire of ways of influencing one another. What distinguishes man as an organism is the extent to which he has developed ways of 'internalizing' this interaction with his fellows. We learn to help, gratify, wrestle with one another by the exchange of words, which can be thought of as tools whose effective mechanical impact is deep within our brains. Language can be regarded as a device that enables human beings to influence and grapple with one another at the level of their internal organization.[2]

Thus to utter the statement 'It is raining' is in mechanical terms to wield a tool, designed to bring its recipient into a certain internal state, such that (if he accepts it as intended) he becomes 'set up' for the situation described – ready to take precautions against rain if he goes out, to hear rain if he listens in the right place, and so on. He may in fact *do* nothing overtly in response to it; but if he has understood and accepted it, he has become 'conditionally' ready for relevant action – *i.e.* ready *if* a need should arise for any action to which the alleged fact of rain is relevant. Of course, human inconsistency being what it is, not all our beliefs are reflected appropriately by our actions at the external level; but if we take account of internal activities such as remembering, as well as external ones, it becomes reasonable to say that what a man knows and believes is represented by the total pattern of his 'conditional readinesses' for all conceivable action (including the planning of action) in all conceivable circumstances.

Perhaps a concrete illustration may be useful at this point to clarify the notion of 'conditional readiness'. Think of a railway signal-box controlling the points in a large shunting yard. At any moment, the pattern of lever settings in the box determines what the yard is *ready* to do to any waggons that may come along. There may in fact be no waggons moving; there may be some tracks on which no waggons will move for years; but this does not prevent us at any given time from defining what we can call the *total state of conditional readiness* of the yard, which we can picture in terms of the lever-configuration that determines what *would* happen *if* any given circumstance arose.

Another example may help to bring out an additional point. The orientation of the front wheels of a stationary car determines the curvature of the path that it *would* take *if* it moved off: its 'conditional readiness' for motion. Suppose now that the car has just followed a semicircular drive to the front of a house. The orientation of the wheels will in quite a precise sense *represent* the curvature of the drive to which they were adjusted. Errors excepted, they are now 'ready to reckon with' that particular curvature, so that (in theory if not in practice!) the car could be successfully driven away along the same path without further adjustment. In other words, for a goal-directed or purposive mechanism, the most useful way of representing *facts* about its world may be in terms of the conditional readinesses demanded by those facts. In such a mechanism, a change of its conditional readiness amounts to a change in the shape of the world to which it is now 'matched' (*i.e.* with which it is now ready to reckon). In theory a car could be equipped to follow automatically a road of any desired shape by fitting it with an 'organizing system' which embodies a series of conditional instructions of the form 'After so many revolutions of the road wheels, turn the steering wheel so many degrees . . . '. No literal map or model of the road as such would be required.

My purpose in labouring this simple illustration is to bring out the way in which more complex facts about the world may be represented implicitly in terms of complex conditional readinesses to reckon with them, without the intervention of any *explicit* model of those facts. The fundamental test of a change in what we believe to be the case – *i.e.* a cognitively significant change – is the corresponding change (if any) in our conditional readinesses for relevant activity (internal or external), regardless of the extent to which we may be able to talk about this in explicit terms.

We take the main target of a linguistic utterance, then, to be the 'state of conditional readiness' of its recipient for action, internal and external, in all relevant contexts. From a biological point of view, there are good grounds for believing that this state depends upon, and is indicated by, the current total pattern of connections and activity in the recipient's brain: *i.e.* in his 'organizing system'. What he knows or believes about his world, as well as the goals he adopts and the values he holds, thus find themselves implicitly *represented* by different aspects of this pattern, which should in principle be observable or inferable; and the process we call understanding (or misunderstanding) what is said has doubtless a direct physical correlate in the changes that result in the brain from its impact. Different kinds of utterance (statements, commands, questions) will of course have different targets within the total complex, and aim to bring about different kinds of change. The important point, however, is that these internal changes could be perfectly definite, and could correspond accurately with the intentions of the originator of the utterance, without necessarily giving rise to any overt behaviour at the time, or even at any time. A theory that sought to link 'meaning' only to changes in *overt* behaviour would be quite unnecessarily restrictive from our functional standpoint.

The 'conditional readiness' of a human agent, of course, is seldom expressible in such black-and-white terms as that of a shunting yard. The physical state of the brain may determine only the relative *probabilities* of various courses of action in different circumstances, and its complexity must surpass our powers of specification. But the analogy may help to provide a mental image of linguistic communication in functional terms as an ongoing *selective process* – an internal process of adjustment which amounts to selecting from a (vast) range of alternative 'states of conditional readiness' in the recipient. Selective operations may of course be vague or precise, fresh or merely confirmatory, partial or complete; but unless *some* selective action occurs, communication has not been effected. Conversely, wherever a selective action intended by the originator is produced by the impact of his utterance on the recipient, there, and to that extent, effective communication has taken place,[3] regardless of the extent to which it may have externally visible consequences. To be made to feel different by the reading of a poem is from our present standpoint a matter of internal reorganization, just as much as to be informed of a physical fact.

3. Meaning and meaninglessness

The object of this somewhat cumbersome way of picturing a message, as a selective operator on the recipient's organizing system, is to enable us to frame a functional definition of its *meaning*, as its *selective function* on the recipient's states of conditional readiness, or for short, its *organizing function.* At once this leads to a distinction between the *intended meaning* (the organizing function calculated by the originator); the *effective meaning* (the organizing function actually exercised upon the recipient) and the *conventional meaning* (the organizing function that would be exercised upon a (presumed) *standard* recipient or group of recipients committed to the use of the language or sub-language concerned). We can also usefully distinguish between utterances that are cognitively meaningful (having as their target the recipient's internal representation of what he must reckon with) and those that are only normatively or emotively meaningful (having as their target the recipient's goal-priorities or the like).[4]

Meaning, so defined, is a *relation* between the utterance and the internal state of the recipient. Just as the same key inserted into two different locks may have quite different effects, so the same message impinging on two recipients with different internal states may exercise quite different organizing functions: *i.e.* may have quite different effective meanings. Note however that we are avoiding the trap of defining meaning as the *change produced* in the recipient. The internal change doubtless *indicates* the (effective) meaning; but a message may possess a perfectly definite meaning for a particular individual even if he never in fact receives it. Just as the 'opening power' of a key is a definite property of the key in relation to a particular lock, which can be established (from a consideration of the geometry of lock and key, for example) whether or not it is ever exercised upon that lock, so the meaning of a message is a definite property of the message in relation to a particular individual, whether or not he ever hears it.

Of course, the fact that an utterance has been meaningful to (*i.e.* has had organizing function for) a recipient does not necessarily mean that communication has been effected by its use. Effective communication requires that the selective function exercised be (or include) the one intended by the originator. In the analysis of religious language in particular, the philosopher may be more concerned to ask whether an utterance has been *communicative* than whether it has been meaningful (to a given recipient).

From the same mechanistic standpoint we define an utterance as *meaningless* when it is *devoid of organizing function.* Once again, this obliges us to ask 'devoid of organizing function *for whom*?' Meaninglessness (lack of organizing function) is a property, not of expressions in isolation, but of expressions in relation to particular recipients, or groups of recipients, and to their linguistic habits. It is worth noting that this lack of organizing function can arise, even with well-formed sentences, in two ways: either if crucial components of it are undefined (*e.g.* 'The gims prike') or if two or more components have incompatible selective functions (*e.g.* 'The air is isosceles').

It is important, however, even with such 'obvious' examples, to bear in mind the distinction between intended and effective meaning. To most readers an expression like 'The Radiation Polar Diagram of a Horn-fed Cheese' might sound hilariously meaningless (*i.e.* might have no effective meaning) for both of the reasons just mentioned; but this was in fact the title of a sober wartime research report on a certain radar aerial! The basic question is not 'What effect has this on me?' but 'What effect did the author intend this to have, and on whom?'. Only if the answers to these questions were 'none' and/or 'no-one' could we justly describe *him* as talking nonsense; though if his choice of words were such that in fact they could not exercise a selective function on anyone else, we might classify *them* as 'effectively nonsensical', without precluding the possibility that more effective words might be found to express his meaningful intention.

But, someone may object, it is surely always possible for people to invent an artificial language-game in which any expression you care to name (even 'The gims prike') can acquire a definite selective function and so become meaningful to the users. Is not our criterion then too wide? I do not think so. Even the moves in an artificial language-game, like those in a game of chess, are entitled to be classified as meaningful or meaningless according to the same criteria as the other utterances we have considered. The same distinctions are needed, for the same purposes. The need we instinctively recognize here is not for an alternative criterion of meaningfulness, but for a separate and additional criterion of *relevance* of the terms used to reality – the complex of constraints (at all levels) with which we have ultimately to reckon.[5] A confusion of these two needs seems to underlie many current attempts to evaluate theological utterances by linguistic analysis. Certainly it is vital to Christian theology to establish that it is more than a variety of artificial language-game; but this question, as we shall see in sections 5 and 6, is additional to and distinct from that of whether it has meaning.

In the light of our functional analysis, it is easy to see both the strength and the weakness of 'verifiability', 'falsifiability', or 'vulnerability to test' as criteria of cognitive meaningfulness. If a statement *is* verifiable, falsifiable or vulnerable to test, then indeed it has some definite organizing function for any recipient equipped in principle to make the test: it at least selects a state of conditional readiness for what it affirms or implies to be the outcome.[6] But the converse, that a statement invulnerable to test is therefore cognitively meaningless, does not follow, and to make it a matter of definition would seem distinctly arbitrary and Procrustean in the light of our dissection of the communicative process. Provided that a statement has an impact on the recipient's internal representation of 'what is the case' to be reckoned with (in terms of his conditional readinesses), we have no grounds for denying that it has cognitive meaning for him, whether or not he can *specify* the circumstances in which he could put his readiness to the test.

One can of course sympathize with the exasperation of a man who comes across a community of people talking together in terms which, though not in a foreign language, he cannot understand. Nothing could be more natural than his plea to be told in what circumstances a given statement of theirs would be falsified; at least, if he can be told this, he knows that the statement has *some* organizing function. Suppose, however, that these falsifying circumstances in turn can be described only by using terms of the same baffling kind. Is he then entitled to dismiss the whole domain of discourse as 'meaningless'?

Of course not. We have only to imagine the case of a man blind from birth listening to the conversation of sighted people to see how baseless such a conclusion would be. 'Yellow and blue make green,' he hears them say. 'What state of affairs would falsify this statement?' he asks. 'Well,' they answer, 'I suppose it would be one in which a mixture of yellow and blue didn't look green.' The poor man's frustration is complete. Tempting it might be for him to retort: 'There you go retreating into your jargon again instead of giving an honest answer. Meaningless mumbo-jumbo, I call it, all this colour-talk'; but an answer of this sort would cut little ice with the sighted people, and at heart he knows why. Statements about colours have a perfectly good organizing function. They can be wrong: expectations based on them can be falsified. It is just unfortunate, though not unreasonable, that only people capable of entertaining such expectations can know what their falsification would mean.

It is true, of course, that in practice it may not always be possible for an outside observer to determine the internal organizing function which has been or was intended to be exercised; but this in itself would be quite insufficient reason for denying the existence of that function. It is at least conceivable in principle, after all, that brain science could one day make the internal effects of a message upon a recipient's brain as publicly observable and definite as the most diehard positivist could wish. It would be strange indeed to argue that the meaningfulness of a message to a given recipient now should depend on whether or not this was yet the case. It seems more realistic to accept with as good grace as we can the frustrating but not surprising fact, that an utterance may have a perfectly definite meaning for a particular recipient even when the data to determine that meaning are inaccessible to anyone else.

A similar consolation might be offered to the blind man frustrated by colour-talk. Though no physical instrument can show him what it *means* to see green, it is at least imaginable that suitably placed electrodes in the brain of a sighted subject could one day provide publicly observable evidence that (and when) the subject *was* seeing-green or seeing-some-other-colour. This would in principle offer an objective check on whether the sighted subjects were truthfully (and meaningfully) reporting their colour-sensations.

4. Misunderstanding and conceptual blind spots

One further question must be considered before we turn to the specific problem of religious language. What preconditions must be met if language is to be communicative? Conversely, under what conditions may onc individual be 'conceptually blind' to discourse that is meaningful to others?

We have spoken of communication as a process in which people seek to mould one another's organizisng systems. The words a man chooses and assembles into tools for this purpose are designed and tested to check that they have the desired effect in the first instance upon himself. In other words, his selective operators are necessarily constructed to work satisfactorily upon his *own* organizing system. Clearly, then, the success of his communication depends on the extent to which his recipient's organizing system matches his own in the relevant respects. Misunderstanding – disparity betwen the effective and intended meaning – arises when two systems differ significantly, but not sufficiently to prevent the message from functioning in some (unintended) way.

In detail, of course, no two organizing systems ever have the same content (the same pattern of levers, to hark back to our signal-box metaphor); but this is not what is required. What matters ultimately is that the two *repertoires* on which the organizing systems play should be sufficiently similar. Given this, barriers to communication of the kind presented by differences of natural language (*e.g.* between French and English, or between sixteenth-century and twentieth-century English) are not ultimately insuperable, since the selective operation in the one system has an approximate equivalent in the other, and an appropriate way of performing it can usually be found if we are prepared to deal with large enough slices of text at a time.

Where the basic elements or principles or organization of two repertoires are sufficiently disparate, however, we have a communication problem of quite a different order. Here, there will exist selective operations in the one system for which no equivalent exists in the other. Utterances fully meaningful among individuals sharing the same repertoire may be meaningless to others, not because they have not learned how to translate them, but because for them (with their present repertoire) *no translation exists.* What they lack is not a formula to determine the selective operation required, but the internal equipment upon which the operation is meant to occur. They have a 'conceptual blind spot' for discourse in the corresponding field, to which no amount of reformulation will make any difference.[7] The most that can be done to promote communication here is to tell the recipient, in cases where this is possible, how to set about acquiring the appropriate repertoire.[8]

Stock examples of this kind of situation are the conceptual barriers separating the specialist from the layman, or the adult from the child. In every such case, effective communication becomes possible only when the recipient is able and willing to put himself in the way of the necessary experience, or to undertake the necessary actions, to develop the appropriate range of 'conditional readinesses'. In some cases the change may involve much more than a simple enlargement of the internal repertoire. Where the disparity in question is between mutually exclusive principles of organization, upheaval and demolition as well as construction may be required.[2]

A simple and familiar illustration of this point is offered by the 'puzzle pictures' of our childhood, in which one had to discover the 'face' in a mass of leaves. The difficulty here was not only, or even chiefly, that we did not know *where* to look, but rather that we did not know *how* to look. In order to succeed, we had to disrupt our routine way of taking note of what was there by 'seeing-leaves', and replace this with another 'conditional readiness' to 'see-faces'. The very fact that our readiness to 'see-leaves' was adequate to account for all that was in the picture made it all the harder to displace; yet once we had 'learned the trick' – activated the necessary repertoire – the 'face' became a meaningful and even dominant feature.

In the case of our puzzle picture, 'leaf-seeing' and 'face-seeing' were accomplishments already achieved in other contexts. The difficulty was only one of transfer. In other cases, however, the disruption and reorganization required in our repertoire in order to give access to new dimensions of perception and meaning might have to be painfully acquired through correspondingly new experience. We shall consider shortly to what extent the conceptual barrier between the Christian and the non-Christian may be thought of in similar terms.

5. Linguistic theology

We must now take up the question of the *relevance* of talk about God, which was raised in section 3. In most recent 'falsificationist' attacks on religious language the purpose has been not to deny *any* kind of meaning to religious statements, but only to question whether they offer *information*; as distinct from advice, exhortation and the like. There can be little question that attempts to find exclusively noncognitive meanings for all Christian assertions about God must end in evacuating the Christian faith of its traditional content – a point made firmly by Flew:[9]

> Any attempt to analyse Christian utterances as expressions or affirmations of a *blik* rather than as (at least would-be) assertions

> about the cosmos is fundamentally misguided. *First* because thus interpreted they would be entirely unorthodox. If Hare's religion really is a *blik* involving no cosmological assertions about the nature and activities of a supposedly personal creator, then surely he is not a Christian at all? *Second*, because thus interpreted, they would scarcely do the job they do. If they were not even intended as assertions, then many religious activities would become fraudulent, or merely silly. If 'you ought *because* it is God's will' asserts no more than 'you ought', then the person who prefers the former phraseology is not really giving a reason, but a fraudulent substitute for one, a dialectical dud cheque.

This broadside, however, does not deter theologians like Paul van Buren[10] (who quotes Flew's words on p. 86 of his *The Secular Meaning of the Gospel*) from rejecting the cognitive approach to theological language 'for both logical and theological reasons' (*ibid.*, p. 97). His theological arguments (pp. 98 *seqq.*) are not here our concern. Centering as they do upon the curious claim that the cognitive approach 'builds its case on a natural sense of the divine, on natural religion and a natural revelation', they can have little force for those of us who regard natural theology as both insecure and unnecessary for such a purpose. But his capitulation to falsificationism is as thinly justified as it is abject, and it may be illuminating to test the cogency of his 'logical' reasons from our present standpoint.

> The cognitive approach requires speaking of that which it admits is ineffable. It involves speaking of God by analogy, yet it is granted by its proponents that they cannot say to what extent the analogies are apt and proper (pp. 97, 98).

If the proponents of talk about God had pretended to set about it from scratch, like a mathematician defining a system of axioms *in vacuo*, then objections of this sort would indeed have force. But of course it is not so. The need for talk about God, like the need for talk about human minds other than our own, arises in the first instance out of human encounters for which there is no perfect analogy. In both cases the definitionary drive is in the reverse direction from that which disciplines the mathematician; experience here demands, rather than merely permits, the effort to talk; and insofar as the internal organization that is demanded by 'encounter with God' has elements in common with those demanded in encounter with other human minds, the properly qualified use of human analogies by those first exposed to such encounters is logically unexceptionable, however ineffable the subject. If succeeding generations find that statements in these terms have coherent organizing functions and bear the weight of daily experience, they can be considered to convey knowledge, and to have relevance to reality, at least as securely as statements about 'other minds'.

Of course a profusion of necessary qualifications attends all such talk. In both cases, we are aware of an element of mystery, and have to guard against misunderstanding. To speak of a friend as having a 'forceful personality' or a 'powerful mind' is not necessarily to imply that any non-physical forces or energies are at work upon his brain or body. To speak of God as a loving Father is not to imply that either all the attributes or all the limitations of a human father make sense as applied to him. But in neither case do we in practice come within miles of the much-heralded 'death by a thousand qualifications'.[9] So far from being 'logical', indeed, objections on this score seem to have all the precipitate momentum of wishful thinking.

6. The function of talk about God

What then can we identify as the semantic function of talk about God? Clearly in general such talk is not intended to locate an entity on our internal 'map' of the *physical* world. 'God' is not the name of an object (even an invisible object) in and of the dimensions of space, to which in principle we could point, like the sun, or even an electric field. On the other hand, regardless of its truth or falsehood, there can be no question but that Christian talk about God, like talk about objects or about persons other than oneself, and unlike an artificial language-game, has developed in an effort to do justice to certain aspects of human experience that have an *external* focus, having to reckon with the 'not-me' so to say; and that every fresh generation of Christians apparently discovers it to be *functional* in practice, answering to facts of experience they find themselves unable honestly to deny.

What kind of facts are these? Facts in general can be defined operationally as what set limits or constraints on the scope of action: they are what all action must reckon with, take account of, adapt to. What differentiates factual claims about God from those about the physical world is basically the *dimensions* of action in which they must be reckoned with. Our human organizing repertoire has several categories of modes of action. For example, we can act by moving our limbs to or fro, up or down, rapidly or slowly, and so on; we can also act selfishly or unselfishly, arrogantly or humbly, thankfully or unthankfully, penitently or impenitently. Broadly speaking, statements about objects in the physical world have as their target our 'internal lever settings' governing readinesses in the first category. Statements about God, though they may have implications in the first category (*e.g.* in relation to going to church, studying the Bible, and the like), have their distinctive impact on other more intimate dimensions of our organizing system: not characteristically those like up-down, left-right, to-from, fast-slow, but others like selfish-unselfish, arrogant-humble, thankful-unthankful, penitent-impenitent. A man who changes from disbelief to belief in what the Bible has to say about God, and accepts Christ as master of his will, undergoes a change in his 'conditional readinesses' no less definite and cognitive in relation to real life than those occasioned by learning physical facts. The meaning of what he believes can be defined in either case as its organizing function – its orienting function in the appropriate dimensions of conditional readiness for action; and the same criteria of meaningfulness and relevance can in principle be applied for purposes of semantic hygiene.

What must be noticed, however, is that in typical religious utterances the word 'God' seldom if ever has to function in isolation. The typical operational units are hyphenated expressions such as 'obeying-God', 'loving-God', 'confessing-to-God', 'being-forgiven-by-God', 'being-rebuked-by-God'. It is in *events* and *activities* such as these that the idea of God has semantic cash-value; it is to them as basic data that theological semantics must do justice in the first instance. Here again there is a close analogy with talk of other (human) minds. Talk of 'John Smith's opinions' and the like leads us operationally back, not to something we have to reckon with in his *body* as such, but to something we have to reckon with in his *actions*.

Here, however, we face the logical trap of reductionism into which it would seem that van Buren[10] and others have (perhaps willingly) fallen. In the case of John Smith, it would seem very odd and misguided (particularly to John Smith himself!) if we were to conclude from what has just been said that all talk about John is 'really' only talk about the actions of his body. For regardless of the way we may argue in front of him, there, all the time, is John, a 'centre of awareness' of us and our ongoings as we are 'centres of awareness' of him and his; and no amount of operational reformulation makes any difference to his (or our) reality *as such.* This is not a matter of convention but a question of fact, upon which we are either right or wrong in each case; and in John's case at least one individual *knows* whether we are right or wrong – namely John himself.

An example from physics may help to show that this logical trap is not confined to the area of talk about persons. It would be generally agreed that all our knowledge of atoms or electrons derives from observed events which we term 'photon-emission', 'electron-impact' and the like. But the physicist who refers to the structure of the hydrogen nucleus or the momentum of an electron is not talking *about* his or anyone's experience – he is talking (rightly or wrongly) about the hydrogen atom, or the electron. Certainly he speaks of them as *revealed* by experience; but this is quite different from talking *about* experience.

By the same token the Christian's references to God, though semantically empty unless they have some operational link with human experience, are not reducible to references to experience. Although the Christian knows of God only through what he *does*,[11] as we might say we know of John Smith (as a personal agent) only through what he does, or the physicist knows of electrons only through what they do, nevertheless in each case there is a clear logical distinction between talking about the activity and talking about the agent.

7. Existence-statements

As a test-case, let us pursue this line of thought with regard to 'existence-statements'. We know well what it means to say that a particular brick wall 'exists'. The test is clear; you ignore this statement in relevant circumstances at your peril. All right: does electricity 'exist'? Most physicists would regard this as a trick question, scarcely worth debating. Whatever answer we give, they would say, electricity is undeniably *to be reckoned with.* Its behaviour is known in many circumstances, and you ignore such knowledge at your peril. Can we point to electricity? No, only to events in which its nature is manifested. But anyone who on this score rejects all talk about electricity as 'cognitively meaningless' would simply be missing its point, and turning his back on reality.[12]

What then of John Smith? His body 'exists' as indubitably as does our brick wall; but does John (the conscious personal agent) 'exist' over and above his body? Here again, we sense a trick question. We want to ask, 'What would you take me to be denying if I said No?' Certainly we cannot point to John Smith (the personal agent) as distinct from his body. What we can point to, or at least denote, are events in which John's personal nature is manifested. The most indubitable of these for this purpose would be our own personal encounters with John as personal agent. By comparing notes with others, we arrive at an objective conception of John as *someone to be reckoned with.*

Is this, then, all we could mean by asserting that 'John exists'? It is certainly one part of what we could mean; but in the case of John, unlike that of electricity, there is something more to be said. By recognizing John as someone like ourselves, we imply the appropriateness of reckoning not merely with John's personal behaviour, but (as we saw earlier) with John's thoughts, motives and views, including his views of ourselves, whether these are expressed or not. In short, we reckon with John as *one who himself reckons*, one before whom we are under scrutiny. What this means in terms of our 'readinesses' may be difficult or impossible to specify in detail, at least for ourselves; but that it involves something over and above any readiness to deal with behaviour seems clear. The difference is perhaps most easily felt if we ask ourselves what it would mean to *withdraw* personal recognition from an interlocutor. Imagine for example the not uncommon experience of mistaking a real person for a dummy at the waxworks. To decide that 'it's only a dummy' is not only to decide to behave differently towards what confronts us, but also to decide that as a matter of *fact* there is nobody there with feelings to consider, opinions to respect, purposes to reckon with. To discover that we were mistaken in this decision is not only to adopt a new behavioural policy, but also to admit cognitive error on a matter of fact: it is to revise our 'cognitive map' of the world's centres of awareness. All kinds of ways of reckoning with the situation are now appropriate which were not so before.

In other words, talk about John as a person like ourselves has an organizing function qualitatively distinct from that of talk about the behaviour of his body as a phenomenon. It selects different organizers of our readiness for what is there to be reckoned with. So far from being cognitively meaningless, it has a quite definite and distinct range of meaning which in no way supplants or rivals but complements that of behavioural analysis.

What emerges from all this is the progressive inadequacy of bare existence-statements to express our communicative intentions once we leave the domain of large-scale inanimate objects. What we want to affirm, especially about human beings, will often be strengthened and sharpened rather than weakened by deliberate reformulation in functional terms. 'Events rather than entities' makes a good watchword in the initial stages of any attempt to make communicative contact across conceptual barriers.

8. 'God exists'

Finally, what of the statement 'God exists'? Fierce arguments rage as to the meaningfulness and relevance of such an assertion. What does it add, we are asked, to a non-theological description of the states of affairs confronting us? On the one hand, the reply is sometimes offered that God, though invisible, is a real inhabitant of our world, so that an assertion of his existence is meaningful and relevant in the same way as the assertion that space is curved in a fourth dimension. At the other extreme, we have the suggestion of 'Christian humanists' like Braithwaite[13] that affirming God's existence amounts only to recommending a particular 'agapeistic' or other policy towards our fellow human beings. According to van Buren (*loc. cit.*, p. 103) 'a loose way of characterising these analyses of the language of faith is to say that "God-statements" have been translated into "man-statements"'. (One has also heard much less radical preachers compare the Holy Spirit to the spirit of a football team!)

The conclusion of our present analysis would be that both extremes (however much truth they express) are unnecessarily restrictive and totally inadequate as explications of what biblical Christianity wants to affirm; but that to say that God 'exists' is perhaps not the clearest or most defensible way of affirming it, since the assertion can have so many misleading associations. The biblical doctrine, first and last, is surely that God is One *to be reckoned with.* Talk about God is calculated to select among outwardly-directed conditional readinesses to be challenged-by-God, rebuked-by-God, forgiven-by-God, and not only to picture him as a Father in heaven, or to adopt patient, compassionate, forgiving policies towards our fellow men. The appropriate policies, in fact, are intended to be *consequences* of the relationship indicated by these hyphenated expressions, and of our constant awareness of God as *One who himself reckons* – One before whom we are under scrutiny.

The relationship in question is not forced upon us. According to the Bible it will become real to us only in proportion as we are ready for the consequences of following up and being grasped by whatever truth we may learn from each encounter. Such readiness is not a matter of wishful thinking, or arbitrarily assuming the truth of what cannot be attested; it implies only the honest minimum of openness, a thoroughgoing intention to put ourselves in the way of discovery and comprehension by dropping any protective barriers around our self-will as we come to recognize them.

By the same token, if God is to be known only on the foregoing condition, it is evidently possible for us to cultivate conceptual blind spots that will keep all talk about him indefinitely meaningless-to-us by a sufficiently resolute refusal to contemplate the reorganization entailed by having any ruler of our mind and will besides ourselves. Here we have another illustration of the theme of section 4. With a self-willed principle of organization, much religious language can have no selective function. The appropriate dimensions have not 'opened up'. It is not simply for lack of a translation that 'the unspiritual man does not receive . . . and is not able to understand . . .' (1 Corinthians 2:14 RSV). In such a case, however, where a man is clearly (even if unwittingly[14]) violating the condition upon which talk of God is claimed to become meaningful for him, he could scarcely regard his experience as a rational test of its semantic validity, still less as a basis for any claim that talk about God is non-factual, cognitively meaningless or essentially unintelligible.[15]

On the other hand, it is far from obvious that because God is One to be reckoned with, he can properly be classed merely as one – even the greatest – of the 'existents' that make up our world of space and time. We must indeed reckon-with-him in our world; but according to bibilical theism he as Creator and sustainer would be out of place as an additional item in a catalogue of its contents, for it is we and our whole world that are declared to have our being in him, and not the reverse. True, we are taught that as 'God the Son' he chose for a time to become one of the inhabitants of the world, and that as 'God the Spirit' he is an ever-present agent upon the minds of men; but as 'God in eternity' he stands as the Giver, and no mere occupier, of his universe. Belief in such a God implies operationally not that there must be gaps in any naturalistic account of the universe, but rather that when we have finished reckoning impersonally with the physical contents of our world, there remains a *thankworthiness* about the flux of experience that meets us, and an accountability for our response to it, over and above any causal explicability it may have in impersonal terms.

9. Conclusion

It is no part of our present purpose to eliminate the mystery that must attend talk by creatures about their Creator. Our claim is only that if we make an effort to express such talk in operational terms, it becomes less easy to mistake mystery for nonsense, or conversely to pass off nonsense as mystery. The multi-dimensional being of God must be beyond our conceptual grasp except by one partial aspect at a time; and where God himself is claimed to be the originator of an assertion about himself, it may be salutary to remind ourselves that we can have no guaranteed way of ensuring that we have understood it aright – no infallible way of assessing when or whether the organizing function exercised corresponds completely with that which is intended. We may expect divine revelation to operate as much by changing the *kind of people we are* as by increasing our stock of information; by altering the principles of organization of our readiness-system as much as by making selections within its existing framework.

What is equally clear, however, is that an operational analysis of meaning in no way commits us to the Procrustean simplification of the concept espoused by van Buren and earlier 'avant garde' theologians. Van Buren's assertion that 'the meaning of a statement is to be found in, and is identical with, the function of that statement' (*loc. cit.*, p. 104) is innocent enough in itself and his insistence that 'the context of the language of faith may not be neglected' is admirable. But when he goes on: 'Unless or until a theological statement *can be submitted in some way to verification*,[16] it cannot be said to have a meaning in our language-game', he opts for a restricted class of function that neglects, as we have seen, a great variety of others which are no less operational, and which include cognitive as well as normative and emotive utterances. It may not be surprising if the resulting theology is felt by many Christians, and some non-Christians, to do less than justice to what the writers of the gospels and epistles meant – yes, operationally and effectively and cognitively *meant* – by their traditionally accepted assertions. Regardless of the extent to which 'science' is thought to have rendered their beliefs untenable,[17] it is impossible honestly to dodge their challenge by calling it 'meaningless'.

We must thus firmly reject (as both logically and linguistically mistaken) any suggestion that what is meant by biblical doctrines is reducible to bare recommendations of policy or the like; but it must still be emphasized that the way to make clear that they *have* meaning and relevance may be to focus attention, more than is sometimes done, upon the jobs they are designed to do in those who humbly receive them. If I may put it in personal terms, the aim of those of us who claim to be Christians, in line with the Bible's own insistent emphasis, must be to become much more operational in our thinking and talking about its central doctrines: to see its every statement about God as a tool designed ultimately to make some practical contribution to the shaping of our total state of conditional readiness for what happens to be there to be reckoned with, whether we like it or not. Thus seen, its meaningfulness and relevance will be in no doubt, and the lines along which its truth is meant to be attested will be constructively apparent.

Acknowledgment.—I am grateful to Dr S. C. Brown, Professor A. G. N. Flew, Mr P. Helm and a number of other colleagues for helpful criticisms of earlier drafts of this paper.

The sovereignty of God in the natural world[1]

The logical consequences of divine sovereignty for human freedom have been disputed for so long that one might doubt whether anything new remains to be said on the matter. Recent debate on the related topic of 'brain and will' has however brought up a logical point[2] which would seem to apply equally in the theological context and which throws fresh doubt on the coherence of the traditional antithesis between predestination and human freedom. My object in this paper is to outline the argument and bring home some of its implications.

1. The creation of a natural order

Nine tenths of the problems commonly associated with the biblical doctrine of nature arise from an inadequate concept of creation. As Dorothy Sayers[3] has pointed out, even our experience of human literary creativity ought to have made impossible some of the misconceptions which are still all too prevalent, and are based on too low a view of the role of a creator.

The first point to have clear in mind is that a creator conceives his creation as a *whole* – a spatio-temporal unity. The creator of a totally original world-story (as distinct from the narrator of history or 'historical' fiction) conceives and utters it, not necessarily instantaneously, but as a single coherent and sovereign determination of the past, present and future of his characters and their world. When conceiving it, he may say, 'Let us have such and such;

let there be this, let there be that.' But in contemplating it as created the only appropriate descriptive tense for us and him is the 'eternal present'. Mr X, we say, *decides* to ask Miss Y to marry him, Miss Y *refuses*; and so on. Not only the creator, but anyone who can share his standpoint as a contemplator of the world-story he has created is able – indeed is bound – to use this peculiar present tense in order to distinguish the time-scale of the created world from that of its creator.

Secondly, and by the same token, it is not only the *objects* but also the *events* and the whole history of the created world that owe their being to the creator. The author does not merely create the scenery of his world and its characters at one moment of (their) time, and 'leave' the rest of their history to unroll according to 'natural laws'. To talk in such terms of the creation of a story or a drama would be nonsensical. The creation of Mr X does not take place at a moment in Mr X's time at all. If the creation of Mr X is to be dated, it must be on the author's time-scale; and it is the *whole* of Mr X's time-and-space that owes its being to that creative act.

It follows, thirdly, that if Mr X were to ask, 'When was my world created?', the only possible kind of answer to him would be paradoxical: 'at no point in your time, yet at every point in your time'. We might perhaps condense this as 'from all eternity'. Certainly for Mr X, the creation of his world must be conceived of as 'before his time'; yet *we* can see that he would be missing the point if he thought of it exclusively in past terms. On *his* time-scale, creation never ceases, for it is in the author's creative utterance that he lives and moves and has his being. Yet *we* can say that on the author's time-scale the work of creation of the whole space-time drama of Mr X had an end, and the author rested from it.

Simple and familiar though it is, our example of human creativity perhaps already makes clear how logically treacherous the concept of creation can be. The greatest care is necessary to define the *standpoint* from which the validity of a statement is to be tested or asserted; for as we have seen, it is possible for a well-formed sentence to be both meaningful and true from the standpoint of the creator, though either meaningless or false from that of his creatures. It will be profitable, I think, to pursue this matter of the logical relations between creator-talk and creature-talk in some further connections.

Consider for example the status of those 'eternal present tense' statements of ours about the decisions of the author's creatures:

'Mr X decides to . . .', and the like. For us, standing as it were by the creator's elbow, these are statements of fact. Anyone (in the author's world) who believes them is correct, anyone who disbelieves them is simply wrong. This is how the author has determined the course of events in Mr X's world-story. Let us ask, however, what status such 'deterministic' statements of fact would have *for Mr X himself.* Of course we know that in fact Mr X could never hear of them; but this need not prevent our asking whether they are true in Mr X's language, *i.e.* whether, *if* Mr X were to believe them, he would be right, and conversely wrong (*i.e.* in error) to disbelieve them. In short, do these statements of fact (in our language) have any inevitable beliefworthiness for Mr X, in the sense in which *e.g.* '13 is a prime number' is beliefworthy by him whether he knows it or not or likes it or not?

A moment's thought makes it clear that they do not. On the contrary, if we imagine Mr X confronted with any such statement specifying the outcome of a decision he has not yet made, he would be not merely entitled but logically bound to *reject* it; for the Mr X described in the statement is (*ex hypothesi*) a Mr X who *does not* know and believe it. Our own belief in the statement is justified only on the assumption that 'Mr X' means 'Mr X as the author has in fact portrayed him'; so that to imagine a different Mr X – namely a Mr X believing our statement – would be to imagine a contradiction of that statement.

To put this point in another way, any suggestion that Mr X, because he is the creature of the author, is *ipso facto* a mere puppet lacking any freedom of choice, bound to do what he does, and so forth – any such suggestion is logically fallacious. The author could, no doubt, have created a Mr X who was a mindless dummy; but in fact he did not, he created him a *free agent.* Mr X, as created by his author, could defy anyone – even the author himself – to tell him with certainty the outcome of a decision he has not yet made: indeed in Mr X's world no predictive specification of such a decision exists which would be binding upon him, in the sense of beliefworthy by him whether he liked it or not, and whether he knew it or not. To recognize Mr X's freedom is not therefore merely to credit him with illusory *feelings* of freedom based on his 'ignorance' of what we know of his future. It is to acknowledge a *fact* about him as created, a fact which is not controverted even by the peculiar kind of knowledge that we can have as contemplators of his whole world-story. What is 'knowledge' for us *says nothing final* for him.

2. The Creator-Participant

Turning to our human situation as the Bible depicts it, we find at once a multiplicity of images that should warn us off any over-simple arguments by analogy. True, the Bible opens with a narrative of the creative acts to which we owe the existence of our world and ourselves which have exactly the form that we might use in narrating the creative acts of a human author; and it reminds us time and again[4] that not merely the objects but the whole spatio-temporal fabric of events are 'upheld' and 'cohere' by and in the creative Word. To this extent the parallels with what might be said of Mr X and his world *vis-à-vis* his author are striking and illuminating, and we shall have occasion to return to them.

Something without parallel, however, forms the central feature of the biblical message. Ours is not a creator isolated from us by the logical gulf between time and eternity. Within the drama of our existence, he is declared to be active not merely in creative sustaining power, but in *personal* self-revelation – he is a Creator-Participant. Our Creator has made us for nothing less than fellowship with himself – the kind of relationship of glad and loving obedience enjoyed by a son with his father in an ideal family. God has been pleased to make himself an agent within his own creation, who engages in dialogue with his human creatures. Hence whatever inferences we may draw from the 'createdness' of our world must be counterbalanced and cross-checked for consistency with the dominant theme of the Bible – that God is to be *sought*, and that they that seek, with a readiness to love and obey, will find and be found of him.

To this end we find ourselves depicted not only as the products of a creative fiat, but also as children, sinful and rebellious yet loved by a Father; as sheep, given to straying but tended carefully by a shepherd; as responsible agents, invited to become channels of God's grace in a needy world; as creatures 'made in the image of God', able and obligated to love and worship him with all our heart, soul, mind and strength. Nothing that we go on to say must be allowed to diminish the force of any of these complementary images of the mysterious truth about our condition.

To explore further the logic of 'createdness', then, we have to complicate our analogy by imagining a world-story in which Mr X finds himself addressed by fellow creatures claiming to speak in the name of his and their author, and witnessing to the appearance in their history of One who claimed identity, in some sense, with that author; and we must imagine that the same Mr X, in following out what they have said, discovers himself to be at grips in the depths of his own being with one who addresses him in the same terms, pleads with him, accepts his repentance, cleanses him, 'strengthens him with might in the inner man' and the like. Here our human intuitions inevitably fail us, for by no reference to experience can we conceive realistically of the projection of a human author into his own drama, still less of his *identity* with any one of his creatures. What the Bible declares, however, is that God-in-Eternity, our Creator, is in a vital sense identifiable with the One 'who spake by the prophets', who 'was in Christ reconciling the world unto himself' and who even today will 'come in and sup' with any who 'hear his voice and open the door'.

Were it not for this divine initiative and all that stems from it, indeed, the theistic doctrine of creation would be operationally empty. If our world had as little personal interaction with God as, say, the world of the Lilliputians had with Dean Swift, its createdness, however much a matter of fact from God's point of view, could mean nothing of importance to any human decision. 'God-talk', however convincingly backed by natural theology, would for practical purposes be as meaningless as 'Swift-talk' for the Lilliputians, even though, like them, we live and move and have our being only by the power of our Creator. Contemporary philosophical objections to talk about God owe much of their impetus to a misconception of theism on just these lines, for which as we shall see a non-Christocentric apologetic may be largely to blame.

3. Natural laws

With these caveats, we may return to the question of the 'lawfulness' of our natural order. Does this *leave room* for God's intervention in the natural order? Does God *use* natural laws to achieve his creative ends? Does he *intervene* from time to time to work miracles? How often we find questions like these soberly asked and firmly answered (affirmatively or negatively) .... Yet if we are right, each of the expressions italicized implies, or at least condones, a radical misconception of the relation of a created order to its creator. Theistically considered, these questions are strictly meaningless. 'Room' is not what we want for God's action; for nothing is held in being apart from his creative power. 'Natural laws' are neither necessary nor even available to him as an instrument of creation; for he creates by a mere word, and what we call natural laws emerge only *post hoc* as features of and within the created order. By the same token, if the whole spatio-temporal fabric of events in our drama is of the divine conceiving and upholding, 'interventions' can hardly be the proper term for those events that stand out as miraculous. What is unique about a miracle is not the *fact* of divine activity in it but the *mode* or *pattern* of that activity. Non-miraculous events are no less dependent for their occurrence upon God's creative power.

This is not to deny that in *personal* terms a miracle may indeed represent an 'intervention' of God in the affairs of men, just as when a mother engaged in the 'care and maintenance' of an infant suddenly addresses the child in personal terms. What it does deny is that God is any less active in sovereignty in the care and maintenance of non-miraculous daily life.

4. The fallenness of the natural order

When an author decides to revise the story or drama he has conceived, it is clear that his revision is an act of *creation*, on a par with any of his earlier acts. 'Let us no longer have this, but that' is logically on the same footing as 'let there be this, and that'. The resulting created order, once again, is a spatio-temporal unity, whose whole past, present and future may therefore be expected to bear the marks of the revision.

In discussion of the Genesis creation narrative it is often insufficiently realized that the last creative act is recorded not in chapters 1 and 2 but in chapter 3. 'And (God) said . . . "Cursed is the ground because of you . . . thorns and thistles it shall bring forth to you . . ."'(verses 17–18 RSV). In short, we are told that the created order as we know it now is a *revised* version. Ours is *not the same drama* as that whose conception is narrated in chapters 1 and 2, and which God pronounced 'very good'. Some changes may for all we know have been slight; but in one far-reaching respect our natural order is radically different: for ours is a creation 'under a curse', 'groaning in travail'. Not just its human history, but the very principles of natural law reflected in the growth of weeds, the toils of life and the inevitability of decay and death, are different from what they might have been, but for the fall.

What they *might have been* . . . yes, we are in trouble with tenses again. Suppose for example that our human author had conceived a first version of 'the world-story of Mr X' that was different in important respects from the one we have been discussing. We have already observed the difficulty of finding valid ways of expressing in Mr X's language the facts *we* know regarding his 'createdness'. It will be salutary now to try to imagine how we might try to express for him the fact that his world-story is a revised version of an earlier conception. 'Do you mean earlier in my time?' he might ask. 'No', we would have to say. 'As far as you are concerned, the first version is not a "once-was", but rather a "might-have-been".' 'But you said the revision was a sovereign act on the part of my author, which you described in the past tense. Surely then there must be traces of this in the past of my world?' 'Traces there are indeed, in the whole fabric of your world, past, present and future. But the act of revision itself is not an event in *your* past; rather one should say that your past (with your present and future) has its being in the act of revision. There was no other tense we could have used but the past; yet the fact we are expressing is not, for you, expressible without remainder by pointing to any exclusively past event in your time-scale.'

Once again we need to remind ourselves of the inadequacies of the 'Mr X' analogy. The narrative of the fall is an account of *dialogue* between man and his Creator, in which man showed himself rebellious and unworthy. Moreover in the revised version of God's created order, man is held responsible for its fallenness. Why? If Eden is for us a 'might-have-been' rather than a 'once-was', how can we be held responsible?

The answer of Scripture is that 'in Adam' *we all* sinned. In some mysterious sense we *were* (or *are*? – for tenses here mislead) in Eden, at least in the sense that we have sinned Adam's sin and merited Adam's penalty. Our sin is 'original' not merely chronologically but ontologically. Here is a deep mystery, which no human analogy can parallel. Yet the logical peculiarities brought out by the imaginary case of Mr X should at least help to warn us off the more grossly mistaken inferences sometimes drawn from the story of the fall, such as that before *homo sapiens* appears on the geological scene we should not expect to find 'Nature red in tooth and claw'. It may also give us some feeling for the *kind* of mystery that must attend any such revelation to us of the rationale of our creation. 'Shall the clay say to the potter, "Why hast thou made me thus?".' Perhaps after all Paul's crushing answer in Romans 9:20

was not so much a snub to curiosity, as a pointer to the logical bankruptcy of efforts to express the counsels of any creator completely in terms valid for his creatures.

5. God's sovereignty and man's responsibility

This last quotation, however, reminds us of the thorniest problem of all. If our Creator is at least as sovereign in our affairs as Dean Swift in those of Lilliput, what real freedom or responsibility is left to us? In the case of the Lilliputians, at least Swift never appeared in their world to accuse them; but in our case God stands before us in warning, in pleading, in reproof. 'You will say to me then, "Why does he still find fault? For who can resist his will?"' (Romans 9:19 RSV). Surely Paul's imaginary opponent has a just complaint?

Oddly enough, he has not. If we are right, he is the victim of a time-hallowed muddle, which arises from a failure to differentiate between the two logical standpoints from which we have seen that different aspects of our situation are depicted. As we have seen in the case of the author and Mr X, from the standpoint of any creator there are 'eternal truths' concerning his creatures and their spatio-temporal course which are not merely unknowable but *unbeliefworthy* by these creatures: they would not be beliefworthy by them if they did know them. None of the differences we have noted between our case and Mr X's can diminish the force of these logical considerations: indeed in some respects they strengthen them.

Thus on the one hand it seems to me biblically undeniable that God as Creator is sovereign in every twist and turn of every man's daily life. In the end of the day, according to the whole tenor of the Bible, it will have to be said in one sense of every creature's course: 'whereunto also he was appointed' (1 Peter 2:8). No speculations in terms of 'one-way' predestination (denying predestination to eternal death, though admitting predestination to eternal life) give a remotely plausible exegesis of such passages as Romans 9:18 ('. . . whom he will he hardens'); 1 Peter 2:8–9; Romans 11:7–8 ('. . . but the rest were hardened . . .'); nor do they offer an intellectually consistent theology of divine sovereignty. Our argument will be that all such watering down of the biblical doctrine is not only incoherent, but also totally unnecessary for the purpose in view.

6. Logical indeterminacy

The crux of the matter can be put quite simply. Even if we accept that the 'foreknowledge' of our Creator extends to every atomic event of his creation, past, present and future, including all the acts of all the agents in it, and that all is of his 'determinate counsel', it would nevertheless be logically erroneous to interpret that 'foreknowledge' as *knowledge of a determinate specification* which would be binding upon us whether we knew it or not, and whether we liked it or not. In our language, no such determinate specification *exists* until after the events to which it refers.

Let us be clear, of course, that the class of events in question is highly restricted. For a stellar conjunction, or an eclipse, or indeed for many of the future events of our earthly history, there may exist determinate specifications which are binding upon all of us, *whether anyone knows them or not.* It is only where a specification predicts, implicitly or explicitly, the *belief-states of cognitive agents with respect to it*, that its validity must inescapably depend upon whether or not it is itself believed by the agents concerned. Either the specification describes the agent as not believing it – in which case he would be in error to believe it; or it describes the agent as believing it – in which case he would not be in error to disbelieve it. In short, your action can admit of no 'take-it-or-leave-it' predictions if the form of the prediction logically *depends* on whether you take it or leave it.[5]

But such, of course, are exactly the actions most pressingly in question when divine foreknowledge is being set against human freedom. 'If God already knows my decision beforehand', we say, 'how am I free to determine it?' The answer here suggested is that God's 'foreknowledge' in this case *cannot* be construed as 'knowledge beforehand' of a prediction which is binding upon us, in the sense of beliefworthy by us whether we know it or not and whether we like it or not; because *no such prediction exists.* 'Foreknowledge' may well be the only word for us to apply to God's knowledge of our total future; but it is simply self-contradictory to construe it in the foregoing terms. His is not the knowledge of a predictor – even an infallible predictor – looking *ahead in our time*, but the qualitatively different and still more intimate knowledge of the Creator of our space-time as an integrated conception, over which he is sovereign not as *manipulator* but as *author.*

7. Knowledge-in-time *versus* knowledge-in-eternity

Yes, but as we have reminded ourselves, our Creator has been pleased to reveal himself to us *within* our space-time: to use human terms in addressing us, challenging us, pleading with us. . . . Would it not then be denying his omniscience to say that he does not know the outcome of his pleading? Here we walk in reverence before a mystery; but we may see, I think, the answer to our question without pretending to fathom the depths that underlie it. Omniscience and omnipotence, total and unconditional, we have seen to be the attributes of any creator with respect to his creation; for it is only by virtue of his say-so that any feature of it exists to be known. The knowledge of God-in-eternity must be total. But when we speak of God-in-time, as the One who meets with us in our world, it would not only be dangerous to assume that the same can be said of him – it would be self-contradictory. For in our time, as we have seen, there are future events, hanging upon human decision, for which no complete and *universally* beliefworthy determining specifications can exist until after the decisions concerned. A non-participant observer might in principle harbour a prediction of such events which would be beliefworthy-by-him as long as he remained detached. But he could not regard his prediction as beliefworthy-as-inevitable-by-the-agent; and it would lose its beliefworthiness even for him as soon as he allowed a genuinely reciprocal *dialogue* to develop between him and the agent; for the two would then become one system for purposes of prediction.

Thus the denial of divine omniscience is only apparent. God-in-eternity, as our Author, 'knows the end from the beginning'; with him 'a thousand years are as one day, and one day as a thousand years'. God-manifested-in-time lacks such extra-temporal knowledge, not because of any imperfection in him, but because for anyone within our drama – even if he be God in human person – no such complete knowledge *exists.* The notion of it is ultimately self-contradictory, so that to claim it on behalf of God-in-time, however well-intentioned, is the reverse of piety. Yet (to paraphrase the Creeds) God-in-eternity and God-in-time are not two Gods, but one; though we may (with due safeguards) distinguish them as two 'persons' of the one Godhead.[6]

When God-in-time pleads with us, expressing his *normative* will, we do him wrong to imagine him as already knowing with detached certainty the outcome of his pleading, in the sense that he could in principle inform us of it, and could assert that our belief in our freedom of choice is illusory. In retrospect, to be sure, the outcome may be seen with the eye of faith to have been totally dependent on his *creative* will like everything else; 'We love him, because he first loved us.' But the odd logical fact is that this does not and cannot retrospectively invalidate our belief in the freedom of our decision, for any attempt to make it do so founders in self-contradiction.

8. Prayer

A similar argument applies with regard to the efficacy of prayer. God-in-time invites, indeed commands, us to pray. Yet God-in-eternity 'hath foreordained whatsoever comes to pass'. Does not this mean that it will therefore come to pass whether we pray or not? The answer sometimes given is that, like a parent who means to give his children something in any case, God likes us to 'say please' for it. This weakening of the biblical concept of prayer (like the notion of one-way predestination) seems both theologically unsatisfactory and logically unnecessary for the end in view.

The theological snags are well known. 'You do not have, because you do not ask' (James 4:2 RSV). 'The prayer of a righteous man has great power in its effects (James 5:16 RSV). 'Ask, and it will be given you . . .' (Matthew 7:7 RSV). The tenor of biblical teaching is quite emphatic as to the real *efficacy* of prayer. Yet equally emphatic is the doctrine of God's 'prevenient grace': 'Before they call I will answer' (Isaiah 65:24 RSV); and it is the experience of his people that some of the clearest answers to their prayers have equally clear causal roots in events quite independent of them.

Once again we can make no pretence at explaining the mystery of what it means to talk – and talk efficaciously – with our Creator. What can be said, however, is that the One whom we address in prayer meets us not as God-in-eternity but as God-in-time. 'No one comes to the Father, but by me', said Christ (John 14:6 RSV). The logical standpoint valid for us in petitionary prayer is that of an agent, pleading (in time) with the all-powerful giver of all good for an outcome which from that standpoint is *not yet determined.* Yet as our earlier discussion has shown, none of this contradicts, nor is it contradicted by, what can be said *in retrospect*, as from the standpoint of God-in-eternity, to affirm his total sovereignty in the whole transaction.

His *total* sovereignty . . . this is the point. Once we are in a position from which (retrospectively) the Creator's eye-view is meaningful to us, then it is not only the answer to our prayer, but *also our asking*, which are seen to be 'according to the determinate counsel' (Acts 2:23 AV). It becomes luminously evident that in general 'had we not prayed', things *could* have turned out otherwise; for from this standpoint 'had we not . . .' means 'had the Creator conceived the drama differently' – and once we say this, we can use no firm inferences to prescribe or proscribe the outcome, for our only firm ground of inference is our drama as the Creator *has* conceived it, together with his promise to be faithful to that conception (*e.g.* to Noah in Genesis 8:22).

Since the answering of prayer offered in accordance with his (normative) will is part and parcel of his conception as he has revealed it to us, we may confidently expect to see correlation in retrospect between people's praying and the occurrence of events (however long their antecedents) that provide appropriate answers.

Does not this mean, however, that in principle these events with long antecedents (such as the arrival of help despatched long before the prayer or the need for it arose) *were* already determinate, so that prayer was pointless and needless? Certainly, had the help been *known* to be under way, the petitioner could hardly have offered the same prayer with the same meaning. But what operational conclusion follows from this? That next time he need not pray? Of course not. For a drama in which an agent refuses to pray would be *ipso facto* one in which he has no ground to expect an answer. So that in a sense, by inviting us to pray, God is inviting us to determine (in part) *what sort of a drama ours shall be.*

It follows, oddly enough, that we cannot even draw the conclusion that in the *present* instance the petitioner 'need not' have prayed. 'Counterfactual hypotheticals' are notoriously treacherous. They require always the preface 'other things being equal . . .'. The point we are now labouring is simply that if we postulate a counterfactual situation in which the Creator himself is involved, then other things generally are *not* equal.

9. Chance and providence

It follows from all we have seen that in a world continually dependent upon its Creator as ours is declared to be in Scripture, there is no need whatever to invoke *physical indeterminacy* (Heisenberg or otherwise) in order to make room for the operation of providence. 'Chance' is merely our label for those created events whose rationale escapes us. It does not distinguish such events as either more or less under the control of their Creator than those we term 'lawful'.

What we have seen is that on quite other grounds than physical indeterminacy, there is an irreducible element of *logical* indeterminacy in the situation that confronts us moment by moment. This implies that we have a genuine share in determining what the future shall be, and that if our Creator is willing to meet us as God-in-time, then our dialogue with him in prayer may also affect the future in ways beyond the causal reach of our physical powers.

None of this requires that the physical chain-mesh of cause-and-effect, as defined scientifically, must show any gaps or indeterminacies whatever. That quantum mechanics leaves our *expectations* of micro-physical events indeterminate is not surprising, since our physical knowledge is acquired at the cost of disturbing what we observe. But biblical theism in general, and the doctrine of divine sovereignty in particular, would as we have seen possess no less force in a world as lawful as the dream of Laplace. By the same token the biblical doctine as we have interpreted it would seem to have as much force in a world of 'continuous creation' *à la* Hoyle, as in one of limited temporal extent initiated by a 'Big Bang'.

The contention of this paper is that only by returning to the full strength of the biblical claims for the sovereignty of God can we find a really coherent basis for the freedom of man and the autonomy of natural science.

The mythology of chance[1]

1. The unpredictable

In the chapter 'A scientist in God's world', the emphasis was mainly on the encouragement offered by the biblical doctrine of God and nature to the exploring scientist. Everything was going his way. If you believed in a Creator who normally observes precedent in maintaining the dynamic stability of his world, it was worthwhile – indeed a matter of duty – to search out the regular patterns according to which events normally follow one another. Miraculous breaches of precedent could not be ruled out; but these would be so rare as to make no practical difference to the *methodology* of science. Looking for – and relying on – natural causes was not an alternative to recognizing divine agency, but a theologically justified response to its dependable character. So there was nothing necessarily anti-theistic in the famous claim of Laplace:

> Given an intelligence which could for one instant comprehend all the forces by which nature is animated and the respective situations of the beings who compose it – an intelligence sufficiently vast to submit these data to analysis – it would embrace in the same formula the movements of the greatest bodies of the universe and those of the lighest atom; for it, nothing would be uncertain, and the future, as the past, would be present to its eyes.[2]

So far, so good. But think now of the actual world of everyday events – rainstorms, breezes, an avalanche, the breaking of an ocean wave, or the simple fall of a leaf – and you will be hard put to it to find one case where a scientist would claim that in *practice* he can predict its course in full detail. 'In principle', he may murmur, 'I believe that all these things happen according to precedent; but it would be impossible in practice to make all the observations, or solve all the equations required.' So in practice we always have to leave a margin of uncertainty around our predictions, within which we say that the actual outcome is 'a matter of chance'.

Until the end of the nineteenth century we might still have believed that, given sufficient time and opportunity, this margin of uncertainty could in principle be made as small as we like. But unfortunately for such hopes, physicists at the turn of the century stumbled on a discovery that has revolutionized our whole way of thinking about small-scale events. Until then, it had been assumed that mechanistic models based on the behaviour of large-scale systems like the sun and planets should still work if 'scaled down' to atomic dimensions. But in a series of experiments in which the electrons in atoms were knocked about under controlled conditions, it became clear that one physical quantity in particular, called 'action' (energy × time), could not be scaled down without limit. Instead, the smallest change observed (or inferred) in any physical system seemed to require a minimal 'quantum' or natural unit of action. This was called Planck's Constant, and denoted by the symbol h.

The consequences for scale modelling were disastrous. Niels Bohr showed that if you wanted to model an atom as a miniature solar system, the electrons you pictured as rotating round the nucleus could occupy only certain discrete orbits, and must jump discontinuously from one to another. Worse still, the process of observation and measurement itself had to be paid for in the same units of 'action'; and this set an irreducible limit to the precision with which you could make predictions. From this Heisenberg (1926) drew the devastating conclusion that, in effect, *one half* of all the information required for the prediction of the future from the past on the lines envisaged by Laplace must be unavailable *in principle*, and not just in practice, until after the event. As a consequence of this famous 'Uncertainty Principle' the physicists had to develop a new 'statistical' kind of mechanics. This is designed to calculate not the precise positions and speeds of atomic *particles*, but rather the relative probabilities of particular kinds of *event* called electron-impact, photon-emission, or the like. In order to calculate these probabilities physicists now talk in terms of 'probability waves' travelling from place to place, in much the same way as we talk of flu waves travelling across Europe. This does not mean that electrons or photons *are* waves – any more than flu viruses are. It means simply that the chances of the events called 'electron-impact', 'photon-emission', or 'catching flu' can be calculated using a wave-model.

But now – what do we mean here by 'chance'? Does Heisenberg's Principle mean only that such 'chance' events are *unpredictable by us*, or does it mean that they have *no determining cause*? In either case – and this is our present concern – how does all this scientific talk of 'chance' relate to the biblical conception of our world as totally dependent on the will of a sovereign God?

2. Clearing the ground

In order to tackle these questions sensibly we shall have to begin by clarifying some of the ideas that cluster around the notion of chance and are often confused. To make things concrete, imagine for a start that we write down the sequence of numbers produced by tossing an ideally unbiased ten-sided die five times. If the tossing conditions could be so arranged as not to influence the way the die falls, we might call the *process* of tossing a (nearly) *random process*. The sequence of numbers might then be called a 'random sequence' purely in the sense that it is the *product* of a random process. Even if an orderly sequence such as 99999 were to turn up as a result of random tossing (we could expect several orderly sequences in every 10,000 trials) it would still be a 'random sequence' in this particular sense.

Suppose, on the other hand, that the purpose of tossing the die were to produce a deliberately *disorderly* sequence – the sort of thing sometimes required in statistical experiments when one wants to scramble or 'randomize' the order of trials. For such a purpose the sequence 99999 or 12345 might be quite useless. We might be inclined to describe them as 'insufficiently random' – but if we did we would be using 'random' in quite a different sense, meaning 'without discernible order'. For this purpose we would do better to use a pre-printed table of well-scrambled sequences (sometimes also called 'random numbers') from which such awkward cases had been carefully weeded out.

Whenever the word 'random' is used, then, we have to ask ourselves (*a*) whether it refers to a *process* or to the *product* of that process; and if the latter, then (*b*) whether it means

Random (1) – *having no determining cause*

or Random (2) – *having no discernible order.*

This brings us to a second area of confusion, between the notions of *indeterminacy* and *unpredictability*. Strictly speaking, to call an event *unpredictable* is to say something about our science rather than the event. It means simply that our schemes of prediction had no place for it, and says nothing either way as to whether it had a determinate specification before it occurred. Even if we call it 'unpredictable in principle', we mean only that all known schemes of prediction are in principle inadequate to specify it in advance. To speak of an event as *indeterminate*, however, is to say much more than that we could not specify it beforehand. It is to say that it *had* no prior specification – that no specification existed, unknown to us, which we would have been correct to believe and mistaken to disbelieve if only we had known it.

What then would a scientist mean by a *determinate* event? Clearly it need not be one that is predictable in practice. The basic scientific question here is whether or not it had a 'determining cause' – that is, a prior event or set of events from which it followed according to precedent. If so, then given these precursors, the rules of precedent alone were logically sufficient to determine the specification of the event in every detail, including its timing, before it occurred. Thus, to take an example, future eclipses of the moon are considered (for practical purposes) 'physically determinate' events, in that their timing already has a specification which follows from the present state-description of the solar system plus the rules of precedent embodied in our astronomical theory. We specify eclipses in almanacs, not as events which are *guaranteed* to happen, but as events whose *specification* is determined according to rules of precedent we are presumed to accept. If we believe we have adequate grounds for accepting these rules, we would be irrational not to expect the events so determined.

So far we have been talking only of *determination by precedent.* This is the technical sense of 'determination' recognized in science – naturally enough, since science is the game of understanding (and where possible predicting) events on the basis of precedent. In chapter 2, however, we found ourselves grappling with the biblical claim that the whole succession of events in the physical world is held in being by the continual agency of its Creator. We saw how, on this view, the maintenance of precedent on which science depends was attributable to the stability and coherence of the divine upholding agency. By the same token, even events which either broke with precedent, or were left undetermined by precedent, must be no less dependent on the creative fiat for their occurrence. In this context, then, we are invited to recognize a quite different notion of 'determination', namely *determination by the giver of being*. From this standpoint events which are determined-by-precedent obviously form a subclass of events determined-by-fiat. We can set out the position diagrammatically thus:

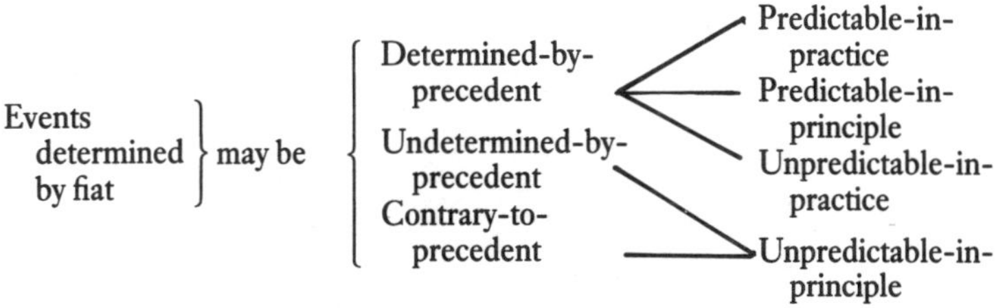

Perhaps a parochial illustration may be forgiven. In our work at Keele on the visual system we need to be able to generate on a TV screen not only a number of movable spots of light, as in 'TV tennis', but also patterns of '*pseudo-random*' texture covering much of the field of view (Fig. 1). Such patterns have equal numbers of black and white dots distributed irregularly – rather as if one had cut up a large chessboard pattern and shuffled the resulting pile of black and white squares before laying them down in rows. To produce the equivalent on a TV screen we have to arrange for the electron beam to be switched rapidly on and off in a pseudo-random manner as it 'paints' the pattern we want; but if the picture is to remain stable we have to ensure that the same sequence of blacks and whites repeats itself each time the pattern is painted by the beam. To generate the necessary control signals we therefore use a small piece of computing equipment (called a 'fed back shift register') which is essentially an electronic shuffling device designed to produce a sequence of blocks of sixteen 'ones' and 'zeros' that rings all possible changes in a fixed order before repeating itself. Since the whole process repeats 200 times per second, the result on the screen is a *dynamically stable* object whose texture *has no discernible order* (*i.e.* is random in sense 2) though the object can be moved around its little world coherently as a whole, and its texture is perfectly stable over time. If, however, we arrange for the sequence of signals to repeat at a rate incoherent with that at which the beam paints the picture, the result is a succession of events which are random (sense 2) in both space and time. The effect seems to be one of complete chaos – rather like the familiar 'snowstorm' seen on a TV receiver tuned to an empty channel.

Fig. 1. A 'pseudo-random' distribution of black and white dots. This specimen is taken from B. Julesz, *Foundations of Cyclopean Perception* (University of Chicago Press, 1971), by kind permission of the author.

The point is that despite all this 'randomness' in sense 2, the whole sequence of events on the screen is at all times precisely *determined* by the controlling generator, so it is *not* 'random' in sense 1. It is designed to be *unpredictable-in-practice*; but in fact each signal is determined by complicated rules from preceding signals, so that for anyone who knew the rules of precedence it would actually be *predictable-in-principle*. In this respect it contrasts with the TV 'snowstorm', where although the sequence of spots on the screen is also determined by the controlling signals, the sequence of those signals is *not* determined on the basis of precedent from earlier signals.

3. Chance

We are now in a position to look again at the questions that set us off on this ground-clearing exercise. Heisenberg's Principle as it stands is clearly a statement about *limits to our knowledge*, and not about the absence of *causal precursors* for the events it declares to be uncertain. If we took the positivistic line that it is 'meaningless' to speak of a variable as determinate unless it is in principle measurable, we could of course ignore this distinction. But from any standpoint this would clearly be an arbitrary move which would 'solve' the problem only in the sense of refusing to recognize it; and from the standpoint of biblical theism it would beg the most important question of all, which is how well our view of the situation corresponds with what its Creator knows that we would be objectively correct to believe.

Interestingly enough, although Einstein was a co-founder of quantum theory through his early work on photo-electric emission, he resisted to the end any interpretation of it which, as he saw it, implied that 'God plays dice'.[3] As early as 1924 he had written to his friend Max Born: 'I find the idea quite intolerable that an electron exposed to radiation should choose of its own free will, not only its moment to jump off, but also its direction. In that case, I would rather be a cobbler, or even an employee in a gaming-house, than a physicist.'[4]

Einstein was fond of expressing his objections in quasi-theological terms. 'I like to think of the electron as *Gott* sees it', he told me once in a conversation at his home in Princeton in 1951. His meaning was clearly that if one supposed a God who knew as Creator (rather than by observation) the whole state of his world, then the distinction between epistemological uncertainty (a *lack of predictive knowledge*) and ontological indeterminacy (*the absence of determining causes*) was undeniably meaningful; and it was therefore illegitimate to decide merely by definition that Heisenberg's Principle implied the latter.

Thus far, Einstein was surely correct. His opponents had no rational grounds for claiming that the absence of an *observable* causal precedent for an event meant that it had *no* causal precedent. On the other hand, from a biblical standpoint it would be equally mistaken to argue that if there were no causal precursor for an event, then its Creator must be thought of as 'playing dice'. Even with human creativity there is a distinction to preserve between free creative innovation and mental coin-tossing.[5] The God of biblical theism is beholden to none to account for his creative agency. If he freely wills into being a succession of events in which one half of the sub-microscopic details at any time are unspecified by their precursors, this would involve no inconsistency with his character, still less with his sovereignty, as portrayed in the Bible. Belief in a sovereign God does not in the least entail a belief that there *must* be 'hidden physical variables' sufficient to determine the behaviour of electrons on the basis of precedent. For biblical theism all events, equally, with or without precursors according to precedent, need God's say-so in order that they occur at all. The choice of 'God or Chance' is simply not a meaningful alternative, if 'Chance' is meant in the scientific sense. As Proverbs 16:33 has it: 'The lots may be cast into the lap, but the issue depends wholly on the LORD' (NEB).

There could hardly be a more explicit claim that even the events we classify technically as 'chance' or 'random' are determined by the sovereign Giver of their being. For biblical theism, nothing in the technical scientific idea of chance implies or requires any release of events from the sovereignty of the Creator. There is, of course, a pagan mythological notion of 'chance' as a kind of 'anti-deity', *Tyche*, the personification of chaos and meaninglessness, which biblical theism emphatically rejects. But to confuse these two concepts would be simply a blunder, or worse.

4. A mis-stated issue

On 15 March 1971 the *New York Times* splashed a headline over an exclusive interview with the biologist Jacques Monod: 'French Nobelist says a universe based on chance leaves man free to choose his own ethical values.' In the book publicized by the interview, Monod pulled out all the stops of French rhetoric:

'Chance *alone* is at the source of every innovation, of all creation in the biosphere. Pure chance, absolutely free but blind, at the very root of the stupendous edifice of evolution. This central concept of biology . . . is today the *sole* conceivable hypothesis, the only one compatible with observed and tested fact.' 'The biosphere looks like the product of a unique event (whose) chances of occurring were almost nil . . . . The universe was not pregnant with life . . . . Our number came up in the Monte Carlo game.' It is on these grounds that Monod delivers the judgment that 'man at last knows that he is alone in the unfeeling immensity of the universe, out of which he emerged only by chance'. All forms of life, he told his interviewer, are the product of 'pure chance'. 'These discoveries ... make it impossible to accept any system ... that assumes a master plan of creation.'[6]

Now according to the leaflet advertising his book, 'Monod uses the unrelenting logic of the scientist ... to demolish traditional forms of philosophy.' So I hope it is not unfair to examine briefly the logic of the conclusions he claims to draw from science *vis-à-vis* the biblical theistic position in particular. To clear the air, let us imagine that all Monod's scientific premisses were granted, and translate them into the now familiar terms. The collision between minuscule particles of nucleic acid and protein in the 'prebiotic soup', which he claims initiated the evolution of living forms, was a 'chance' event. Very well, suppose it was. If this is meant as a statement based on *scientific evidence*, the most it can imply is that this fateful event did not follow according to law-like precedent from any assignable precursor (or more weakly, that it was highly improbable on the basis of prior conditions). This may indeed upset any who thought that the evolution of species was something as predictable as the unfolding of one of those lovely Japanese paper flowers in water; and I make no judgment as to who is right. But what one wants to ask Monod is – *what is all the theological fuss about*? Where, in biblical theism, is anything said or implied to the contrary of his scientific hypothesis?

We might suspect some conflict with the first chapter of Genesis; but whatever our interpretation of the mysterious language used there, it would be hard to pretend that it comes down in favour of causal continuity rather than discontinuity in the physical processes that set off the biological train. 'Then God said, "Let the earth produce fresh growth, let there be on the earth plants bearing seed, fruit-trees bearing fruit each ... according to its kind ..." God said, "Let the earth bring forth living creatures, according to their kind: cattle, reptiles, and wild animals, all according to their kind"' (Genesis 1:11,24 NEB).

The plain truth is (and Monod fails to cite any evidence to the contrary) that nothing in the Bible offers even indirect evidence for or against the hypothesis that life originated in an event which was unforseeable on the basis of scientific precedent – a hypothesis, he tells us, which 'makes it impossible' to believe in 'a master plan of creation'. Whether we as scientists would classify an event as 'chance' or as 'physically determinate' is of no concern whatever to the biblical writers, who would coolly assure us that God gives being to all events in both categories, and that he is sovereign equally over either category. Monod's notion of a 'master plan' may actually not be the best description of what the Bible refers to as God's 'eternal purpose'. Without careful qualification it might sound more Platonic than biblical.[7] But certainly the concept of divine sovereignty in physical events as exemplified in the Bible has no quarrel whatsoever with a hypothesis that some of these events were extremely improbable by human reckoning. This much is clear whether one believes in either, or neither.

What then has misled Monod into telling his hundreds of thousands of readers the very opposite? He appears to have fallen straight (though perhaps not unwillingly) into the trap we noted earlier, of confusing the scientific and the mythological concepts of 'chance'. 'Chance' in science is not the name of a thing or an agent, least of all of a *cause* or *source* of anything; it stands for the *absence* of an assignable cause.

> 'I see nobody on the road,' said Alice. 'I only wish *I* had such eyes,' the King remarked in a fretful tone. 'To be able to see Nobody! And at that distance too.' . . . 'Who did you pass on the road?' the King went on, holding out his hand to the Messenger for some more hay. 'Nobody,' said the Messenger. 'Quite right,' said the King: 'this young lady saw him too. So of course Nobody walks slower than you.' 'I do my best,' the Messenger said in a sullen tone. 'I'm sure nobody walks much faster than I do!' 'He can't do that,' said the King, 'or else he'd have been here first.'[8]

To personify 'chance' as if we were talking about a causal agent, 'free but blind' and the rest is more than harmless poetic effluvium: it is to make an illegitimate switch from a *scientific* to a quasi-religious *mythological* concept. To proceed to claim scientifc authority for describing *this* as a 'central concept of biology' is to compound confusion. To dress up the result as if it were 'observed and tested fact' that was at odds with all concepts of divine immanence in natural events is little short of dishonest.

Monod's astonishingly ill-supported argument is probably not to be understood apart from his declared hatred of all forms of religion, which he scorns as 'rooted in animism, [existing] outside objective knowledge, outside truth, and ... strangers and fundamentally hostile to science, which they are willing to use but do not respect or cherish' (*loc. cit.*, p. 159). This leaves little doubt as to the 'hostility' on Monod's side! Whether the details of his accusation truthfully describe the biblical theism we have been studying I must leave my readers to judge.

To be fair, it should be said that some would-be defenders of the faith must share part of the blame for the confusion that vitiates Monod's anti-theistic argument from 'chance'. This is not because they were too faithful to the Bible, but rather because they were not faithful enough: their thinking failed to give due place to the biblical emphasis on the sovereignty of God. The apologetic literature of the last hundred years has all too many examples where Christian theologians seem to have been trapped into tacitly agreeing with their opponents in confusing the technical and the metaphysical concepts of 'chance', and imagining that to classify an event or process scientifically as 'random' would prevent or at least excuse anyone from recognizing the hand of God in it. Instead of attacking this presupposition as a misinterpretation of the biblical position, these theologians actually strengthened it by trying to pick scientific holes in evolutionary theories that attributed the origins of species to 'chance' processes – thus giving the impression that the credibility of the Christian doctrine of creation depended on their success. Their reaction is perhaps understandable enough when we find evolutionary authorities like G. G. Simpson claiming in the name of science that 'man is the result of a purposeless and materialistic process that did not have him in mind. He was not planned.'[9] It may also be true that in our day evolutionary theories are too uncritically swallowed and too dogmatically propagated for the health of science; and one factor in this unhealthy lowering of critical scientific standards may have been a fear in some quarters that the only alternative would be to invoke a miracle. If so, one must hope that technically qualified scientists, whether Christian or not, will have the courage to set the scientific balance right as a matter of professional duty. But for Christian theologians as such to assume a vested interest in the outcome of the technical debate would be to go well beyond their biblical brief.

5. The winding-down of the world?

No discussion of the theology of chance could be complete without some mention of the famous Second Law of Thermodynamics. This states that in a closed system the over-all disorder must increase towards a maximum as time goes on. There are complications about the definition of disorder, the possibility of brief fluctuations in the opposite direction, and so forth; but broadly speaking this is an accepted law of nature. The physicist's index of disorder is called *entropy*, which measures in effect the amount of information that would be needed in order to specify precisely how the total energy is distributed throughout the system in question. The higher the entropy, the more 'scrambled' is the distribution of energy, and the more questions remain to be answered.

As it happens, communication engineers and physicists have recently found ways of defining the notion of 'amount of information' in very similar mathematical terms to those used to define entropy.[10] Where a message identifies one out of two equally likely possibilities, the information received is defined as one unit or 'bit'. To identify one out of four equally likely possibilities (2×2) requires two bits; one out of eight ($2 \times 2 \times 2$) three bits: and so on. So information, for the communication engineer, is '*that which resolves uncertainty*'; and he measures it by the mathematical 'unforeseeableness' (strictly the logarithm of the improbability) of the answer it brings. This allows us to describe the Second Law of Thermodynamics in an intuitively simple form: the amount of information (number of bits) required to specify the precise micro-state of an isolated system increases to a maximum as time goes on. In other words, if you start with a partly specified closed system, the energy within it gets redistributed in such a way that your uncertainty as to its precise state can only increase as time goes on. What gives practical importance to all this is that energy can be made to do work in a system only if we know how it is distributed; so it is not surprising that the Second Law made its first appearance in the theory of steam engines. Yet despite these severely practical origins it has found itself invoked in two of the classical areas of past debate between scientists and theologians.

The first is once again the theory of evolution. Evolutionists maintain that more highly ordered forms of life evolved out of simpler forms. Anti-evolutionists (even up to the present time) have tried to argue that this conflicts with both the spirit and the letter of the Second Law of Thermodynamics. This, however, will not do. The earth is not an isolated system. It receives a continual flood of highly ordered energy from the sun; and if one estimates the resulting increase in entropy (energy disorder) for the sun, this vastly outweighs any local reduction in energy disorder brought about on earth by biological processes, whether evolutionary or otherwise. It is possible, of course, to ask questions from the standpoint of Information Theory itself as to the likelihood that enough information (in the technical sense) could have been generated in a few hundred million years of random trial-and-error to specify the marvellously intricate structures of living organisms. This, however, is a separate issue from the thermodynamic one, and is still hotly debated.[11]

The second area of debate concerns the so-called 'heat death of the universe'. The Second Law predicts that any *closed* system will tend finally towards an equilibrium in which all parts will have the same (probably very low) temperature. Apply this to the whole universe, and you have a prediction of the end of the world, not in either a bang or a whimper, but in icy nothingness. Many fine sagas have been written by scientific journalists on this theme, which undeniably stirs the imagination.

But is it science? What the myth-makers have to assume here is that in the technical sense of the Second Law the universe is a *closed system*. Unfortunately this seems an unprovable assumption. Scientific theories of 'continuous creation' come and go, and no existing evidence (some would say no conceivable evidence) can rule out speculations that the orderliness of the universe is continuously replenished, or even oscillates up and down over some long time scale.[12]

The basic point here is that all talk of 'probability' is *relative*. The probability of an event depends on the evidence available to the knower. If I offer to read out to you the sequence of digits down the right-hand column of our local telephone directory, the probability-for-you that the last digit (or any digit) will be 9 may be 1 in 10. But for the people at the exchange every digit is fully specified, and talk of 'probability' would be pointless. (Incidentally, this example illustrates nicely the fallacy of confusing the two senses of 'randomness' (p. 200). The sequence of digits is quite random in sense 2. As a numerical sequence it has no discernible order. But anyone who on these grounds were to describe it as 'meaningless' or 'purposeless', or 'random' in sense 1, would be simply missing the point. It is in fact so highly ordered that not a single misprint could be tolerated.)

To speak of the entropy of the whole universe brings up a similar problem. Entropy is defined in terms of probabilities. The definition presupposes that the detailed state of the system is not fully specified. If we take seriously the concept of a sovereign Creator, however, any talk of 'probability' for him must be beside the point. He knows all. There can be no rational grounds for holding that he is bound or limited by the Second Law.

In short, the data of science leave entirely open the future course of the cosmic drama. The Second Law of Thermodynamics can do no more than assure us that a gradual winding down of the universe is one of the possible Last Acts. If the drama is actually held in being by a divine author, of course, the Last Act may be different from our wildest imaginings.

6. Conclusion

We have pursued the theme of 'chance' in its scientific sense from the sub-microscopic level of atomic events to the cosmic level at which men contemplate the future of the universe. Our analysis has, I hope, made it clear that for science as such the term has a strictly defined and theologically innocent function. It denotes simply *what defies determination on the basis of precedent*. It is the scientist's name for the unforeseeable, not the meaningless. As such it implies no resistance whatsoever to the biblical doctrine that even in the case of the most scientifically inscrutable event, 'the whole disposing thereof is of the Lord'. For the biblical writers it is unquestionable that the Holder-in-being of this strange drama in which we find ourselves has ultimate sovereignty, no less over its unforeseen twists and turns than over its scientifically predictable stretches.

Superficially, it may seem meaningful to ask of a particular event whether it was due to the agency of God or to chance. But if the God we are talking about is the God whom Christians worship as Creator and Sustainer of the universe, this is strictly a *non-question*. To speak of 'leaving something to chance', if it means anything more than just 'leaving something to happen', must mean simply 'leaving it to the will of the Creator'. It is meaningful to ask whether or not a particular event followed from precedent; and it is also meaningful (though not a scientific question) to ask whether this event betokened in a special way God's personal concern with the situation, or whether it should be accepted simply as part of his normal 'care and maintenance'. These are real questions, not easily answered. But the question of 'God or chance' is a theological howler.

The Blind Watchmaker – a review[1]

Richard Dawkins describes himself as a 'passionate advocate' of Darwinism who is out 'to persuade and even . . . to inspire (p. x.) He evidently feels that this confession absolves him from the duty to be objectively fair in summarizing the evidence for and against the theory he favours, and cheerfully warns the reader accordingly. He sees himself as arrayed in battle for popular support against the well-known teleological arguments of William Paley, and seems to think that the case for theistic belief in the createdness of our world hangs on the possibility of disproving Darwinian explanations of the origin of species. In thinking this of course he shares some presuppositions of those (mainly Californian) opponents who wave the banner of 'scientific creationism'; but Dawkins clearly feels that he is on the winning side. With a disarmingly juvenile chortle, he assures us on p. 5 that Paley's argument, for all his 'passionate sincerity' and 'biological scholarship', is 'wrong, gloriously and utterly wrong'.

In assessing the merits of the book it is important to distinguish between two questions that Dawkins constantly (and apparently willingly) confuses. One is whether the technical theory of self-organizing systems, from which he borrows his key ideas, predicts that random mutation plus natural selection can meet *quantitatively* the constraints set by geological data, especially on the time available for 'trial-and-error' on the Darwinian model. The other is how far the case for theistic belief would be strengthened if Darwinian theory failed.

On the first score, Dawkins makes a case that many will find persuasive, and devotes much skill and patience to an exposition of the principles behind it. An able and imaginative teacher, he exposes clearly the fallacies in general arguments that 'order could not arise from chaos' and in misapplications of the Second Law of Thermodynamics. The issue he fails to address quantitatively is whether in fact the accumulation of small genetic changes (with retention and favoured reproduction of advantageous ones) could have bridged *quickly* enough the gaps between species lacking complex structures such as the mammalian auditory or visual system, and those enjoying their advantages. For evolution to work smoothly and rapidly, the selective advantage must be a fairly continuous function of location in genetic space, such that the exploratory process can be expected on average to 'roll downhill' automatically towards the outcome that needs explanation. In general, however, the theory of self-organizing systems has had to recognize what is called the 'mesa problem'. Instead of a continuous function with a well-defined downward gradient at any point, the selective advantage may sometimes form a surface with relatively flat regions (no appreciable gradient) separated by discontinuities (like the canyons between mesas) in which the exploratory process can easily get trapped, since the only effect of small displacements there are disadvantageous. Whether and where such problems may arise is a quantitative empirical question; and it is hardly good enough for Dawkins to wave it aside on p. 78 with the trite remark that 'geological time is awfully long'. 'My feeling is that, provided the difference between neighbouring intermediates in our series leading to the eye is *sufficiently small*, the necessary mutations are almost bound to be forthcoming' (p. 79). Well, well, maybe. But it is not the work of a careful scientist to advance any theory as dogmatically as Dawkins does on the basis of such inadequately supported 'feelings'. Somebody, some day, had better do the sums; and until then, honesty demands that the intellectual gap be recognized.

A related technical point is fluffed on p. 232, where Dawkins rightly argues that the probability of improvement resulting from a random genetic adjustment will be closer to one half, the smaller the adjustment. What he fails to bring into his calculation is the fact that the selective advantage of a vanishingly small unit change will generally also be vanishingly small, so that the 'improved' variant will take correspondingly longer to get established so as to provide a jumping-off point for further mutations in the 'right' direction. What needs to be calculated is not just the size of unit change that will equalize probabilities of improvement and the reverse, but the size of change that will *optimize* the compromise-relationship between the *chance* that the change will be advantageous and the *magnitude* of the selective advantage if it does turn out to be advantageous. In general this will *not* require the change to be as small as possible, as Dawkins suggests on p. 232, where his aim is to discredit 'saltationist' theories that postulate large 'macro-mutations' to bridge gaps in evolutionary development.

The other question – how far the case for theistic belief would be strengthened if Darwinian theory failed – surfaces only by implication from time to time, and is never adequately faced. Hugh Montefiore gets a good deal of stick for expressing doubts about the adequacy of Darwinian theory, as well as for 'smuggling God in by the back door' as a supervisor of the evolutionary process (p. 316). Such beliefs, we are told, are superfluous, and '*assume* the existence of the main thing we want to *explain*, namely organized complexity'. Deities have (for Dawkins) far too much organized complexity to be postulated as 'given'.

The theological muddle thus created is the worst feature of an otherwise enjoyable and informative book. Dawkins seems quite unaware that from the standpoint of biblical theism, as distinct from classical deism, the case for belief in the createdness of our world – its *ontological* origin in God's creative word – would not be strengthened by any conceivable failure on our part to trace the *chronological* origin of its present structure. When we say that a novel has an author, we do not imply that there are inexplicable discontinuities in the past of the world he has created; nor would the discovery of such things strengthen our belief in his authorship. The divine authorship of our world, according to theism, is what accounts for there being 'something rather than nothing' – regardless of its complexity. That our world is in fact complex may set us all kinds of chronological puzzles of the sort that Dawkins seeks to solve; but he – and we – would be grossly mistaken to imagine that the solving of such puzzles could remove any need to believe in the God of theism. Whether *that* concept is superfluous depends on whether, as a matter of fact, there is God to be reckoned with. And for evidence on that score, the Scriptures would direct our attention elsewhere.

18

Christian priorities in science[1]

Introduction

I expect you know the story of the wife who gave her husband two ties and when he came down for breakfast wearing one of them, she said, 'So you didn't like the other one.' I was reminded of that story when I tried to decide what things to leave out of this little paper and I hope that if I don't attempt to make all the points you won't think it is because I never liked some of them.

The start of the paper is a familiar one. We have the image of the scientist as a map-maker, mapping not only objects but also events and relationships between events, and I make first the point that our basic duty is that of an honest craftsman. You don't have to be a Christian scientist, you just have to be a good scientist to be that. 'What does it mean to be a good scientist?' is all we need to ask, given that the Scriptures, of course, provide us with our criterion of what it means to be good, and I begin by implicitly trying to dispose of the, to my mind, confused and silly argument over whether there is such a thing as value-free knowledge in science. It is a confusion because I think there are three different questions:

1. Is scientific knowledge value-free in the sense that whatever your values you have to reckon with it, whether you like it or not? And the answer to that I believe is clearly and biblically, yes. We have to take the world as it is, map it obediently whether we value it or not, and for whatever purpose we value it.

2. The second question, which is nearly always confused with this

in argumentation, is whether scientific knowledge has value, and the answer to that is quite obviously, yes. Common sense.

3. There is a third question which is the one that brings us to our topic now. Need a scientist have values (or can he function simply as a calculating machine)? To this, most obviously, the answer is again, yes.

Confronted with a scientific map which is reliable, we have lost the innocence of ignorance and we can be held morally accountable for the expectations we entertain. We can be asked by God ultimately, and by our fellows, 'but didn't you know that if you add this to that you get an explosive mixture?' And it is no good our rolling our eyes piously and talking about epistemology and how uncertain all scientific knowledge is. God will clip us on the side of the head and say, stuff and nonsense! There are certain facts about my world which are robust facts, that you are not only entitled to say you know, you are obligated to recognize that you know. That is, I think, the core of the aim of the Christian who is a scientist, to try and get this as clearly outlined as possible so that in the end we cannot excuse ourselves for responsibility to reckon with these solid data.

Now in the second paragraph on evaluation and science, I have listed just a sample dozen areas and I will put it in the form of questions. A map-maker has obligations; do you accept these obligations? What will you choose to map? In what categories do you think it worthwhile to draw the map: geological, agricultural, or whatever? What are the relative costs and benefits and in relation to what needs? How do you judge those needs? What financial support will you think it proper to seek and/or proper to accept? Are the research methods that seem to be necessary ethically and morally acceptable? What hypotheses would seem to you to be worth testing? If you find data adverse to your chosen hypothesis, are you going to be as rigorous and merciless to yourself as your colleagues certainly will be to you in due course? What kinds of application of your scientific discoveries will you encourage, or discourage? If given applications raise new scientific problems, will you accept these as priorities for you? And what picture will you give to the general public as to the implications of your map-making and that map which is gradually unfolding?

Now, as I say, this is not meant to be an exhaustive list, but I think some list like this is a useful check-list in terms of which to bring down to earth and common sense the implications of our discussion of Christian aims. I hope it is clear that I am not just admitting, but insisting that the practice of science cannot be value-free, but is shot through with questions of value and valuation of quite different sorts as we have seen. That, however, doesn't, of course, in the least introduce elements of arbitrariness or subjectivity into the object of our enterprise, which is the making of a map as accurate as possible of some aspects of the way our Creator has said, 'let there be this world and not another'.

Now the key priority, as I see it, is making love the ruling spirit of our enterprise and this is not the least a soft criterion. This, I think, is the toughest of all our criteria in terms of which the others have to be evaluated. Love to him as our master and redeemer, a master who Christ reminded us is not to be fooled with, and love to our neighbour which must never fall short of the love we have, or ought to have, for ourselves. Among the implications of this spirit of love to our master and maker are not merely diligence, but initiative. There is particularly among non-scientific Christian critics of our age a tendency to suggest that it would be more pleasing to God that we should sit back and wait to be pushed, as it were, into developing something new on the basis of scientific knowledge. One author recently has recommended the wisdom of discovering the wholeness of perfection of nature as God created it. Now, of course, that kind of doctrine would sound perfectly rational in the Garden of Eden, but ours is quite specifically and emphatically in Scripture a fallen world, and we have our Lord's own example before us in urging us to seek with initiative to remedy what we can of the deplorable conditions that issue from the fallenness of our world. Having said that though, I emphasize in section 3 that in a Christian with biblical priorities science is meant to be fun as well as labour. Even though, as I say, in a fallen and needy world we must be prepared for claims of compassion to compete sometimes and to crowd out those of curiosity.

I have a section which stresses the point that the Christian is in total contrast with the pagan in his attitude to nature, he is not a nervous interloper waiting to be pounced on by the owner of the garden. He is a son of the house, a servant son who is at home in his father's creation, he belongs there and the Bible encourages him to roam in the domain of the natural world in responsible freedom, showing all the respect that is due to his father's creation, but none of it the superstitious reverence that would deny its status as a created thing, like himself. I commend the quotation from

Professor Hooykaas at the foot of page 224 as an admirable summing-up of this point.

1. The scientist as map-maker

The scientist is by profession a map-maker; and like other map-makers he is pledged to allow his own particular values to distort as little as possible the representation he makes of the state of affairs. 'Whether I like it or not, or you like it or not, that's the way it is as far as I can see.' In this sense, he strives to make scientific knowledge 'value-free'. His maps are meant to be reliable guides to other people, of whose values he can know nothing; so 'scientific detachment' and 'depersonalization', far from being arbitrary eccentricities of the trade, are all part of his duty as an honest craftsman.[2]

The world mapped by the scientist is a world of events as well as entities – a world where one thing *causes* another. His maps are not merely of observables but of *correlations* between observables and (in due course) of interacting causal factors. Thus, unlike a map of the continents or even a motoring route-map, his maps offer *explanations* and *predictions* as well as descriptions. His 'laws' are *prescriptive*, not in the sense that they make things happen, but in the sense that they tell us what in given circumstances we ought to expect on the basis of precedent. Confronted with a reliable (and comprehensible) scientific map, we have lost the innocence of ignorance and can be held morally accountable for the expectations we entertain in the relevant domain. Scientific laws (as mere codifications of precedent) do not of course assure us that the unprecedented cannot occur; but they impose an obligation on us to justify any contrary expectations.

This emphasis on value-free objective knowledge might be taken to suggest that evaluation, as distinct from meticulous observation, plays little or no part in the practice of science, and that there should be little need for a whole paper on 'Christian Priorities in Science'; but let us see.

2. Evaluation in science

Once we think of science as a human enterprise, questions of value crowd thick and fast upon us. To list just a few examples, science demands of us evaluation, explicit or implicit,

(i) In accepting the obligations, both ethical and social, of map-making;
(ii) In choosing what to map;
(iii) In choosing the categories in terms of which to map (*e.g.* geological, agricultural *etc*);
(iv) In assessing relative costs and benefits in relation to identified 'needs';
(v) In deciding where and in what terms to apply for financial support;
(vi) In assessing the ethical/moral acceptability of research methods;
(vii) In the creative process of inventing hypotheses to test;
(viii) In noticing and reporting data adverse to a chosen hypothesis;
(ix) In selecting *what* to publish, and *when* and *where;*
(x) In encouraging/discouraging specific applications of scientific discoveries;
(xi) In accepting/rejecting new scientific problems that may be raised by given applications;
(xii) In presenting to the general public, including any fellow-Christians who have to make pronouncements in the name of the church, the implications (practical, theoretical, philosophical, religious if any) of scientific discoveries.

This list is not meant to be exhaustive, and it would make a dull paper indeed to run down it with the Bible in hand to identify relevant Christian priorities in each case, but I hope it may serve as a useful check-list in terms of which to test the implications of what follows.

3. Christian priorities

'Man's chief end is to glorify God and to enjoy him forever.' So the Shorter Catechism sums up the rubric under which the Christian must practise his science. Not only must he seek to live to that end, but in all his efforts to serve his fellow men he must aim to further, and not to hinder, their own prospects of doing the same. This already constitutes quite a severe filter, as a glance at our twelve examples of evaluation will show. We glorify God first and foremost by establishing love (in its strongest sense) as the ruling spirit of our whole enterprise – love to him as our Master and Redeemer, and as the giver of being to all our data and all our powers; and love to our neighbour which must never fall short of the love we have, or ought to have, for ourselves.

Love of God involves grateful and obedient service with all our heart (enthusiastic commitment), mind (scrupulous acceptance of the rational implications of God's data) and strength (diligence in action). Though God can be glorified by mere admiring contemplation of his works (*e.g.* Psalms 8, 104), full obedience, especially for the scientist, demands precisely those emphases on accuracy, objectivity and rationality that (in most disciplines claiming the name of 'science') are recognized as professionally essential. Our service being that of stewards, our Master sets a high priority on *initiative* as well as diligence.[3] We are meant to use our gifts of imagination as pioneers in areas where no specific biblical instructions may have been given, and in which we can be guided, or at least limited, only by general biblical principles. This is so not only in exploring new territory for the benefit of our fellow men, but also in cases where we may see no immediate practical relevance (*e.g.* in cosmology or some branches of pure mathematics). In these fields too, our Master is glorified by imaginative enterprise and let down by lack of it. We cannot remind ourselves too often that 'God has given us richly all things *to enjoy*',[4] and that the works of the Lord are meant to be 'sought out by those who *take pleasure* in them'.[5] For the Christian with biblical priorities, science is meant to be fun as well as labour, even though in a fallen and needy world he must be prepared for claims of compassion to compete sometimes with those of curiosity, however highly motivated.

4. Biblical or pagan?

Already we see a strong contrast between the biblical concepts of nature and man and a variety of pagan ideas. Many people in our day, as in previous ages, suppose the typically 'religious' attitude toward natural science to be that embodied in the ancient Greek legend of Prometheus, who stole the sacred fire. Nature is thought of as semi-divine; she has her secrets. The gods would like to keep some of these to themselves, and jealously resent any advances in man's knowledge of them. Science is thus thought of as an irreverent and dangerous pursuit in which sinful man aspires unto the place of God. If disaster results from attempts to apply man's scientific knowledge, this is considered to be what he deserves for prying into the sacred mysteries of the Creator.

Now it cannot be denied that if your idea of God (or the gods) were that of the ancient Greeks, indeed of almost any pagan religion, all this would make good sense. To some people it might seem to represent the proper humility of man before the majesty of his Maker. But is it in fact biblical? I think not. The Bible has no time for human pride; but its teaching about the natural world is precisely the reverse of the pagan's at crucial points.

The Bible sets man in perspective as a creature of God, a part of the vast created order that owes its continuance in being to the divine upholding power. Unlike the rest of the natural world known to us, however, human beings have powers of foresight, planning and action that make us especially responsible in the eyes of our Creator. With these powers, according to the Bible, goes a special obligation toward the Creator. Men are commanded, not merely permitted, to 'subdue the earth' (Genesis 1:28). This is to be done not, indeed, in a spirit of arrogant independence, but as the stewards of God's creation. Human beings are answerable to him for the effectiveness with which they have fulfilled his mandate.

The Christian ethos is thus in complete contrast to the pagan caricature with which it is so often confused. In place of the craven fear that haunts the unwelcome interloper, we are meant to enjoy the peaceful confidence of a servant-son at home in his Father's creation. We know that we are on our Father's business no less when investigating his handiwork than when engaged in formal acts of worship. In place of jealously secretive gods we have One whose very nature is truth and light, himself the Giver of all that is true, who rejoices when any of his truth is brought to the light and obeyed in humility (*e.g.* 1 John, *passim*).

The Bible encourages man to roam the domain of the natural world in responsible freedom, showing all of it the respect due to his Father's creation, but none of it the superstitious reverence that would deny its status as a created thing like himself. As Professor Hooykaas has put it.

> The Bible knows nothing of "Nature" but knows only "creatures" who are absolutely dependent for their origin and existence on the will of God. Consequently, the natural world is admired as God's work and as evidence of its creator, but it is never adored. Nature can arouse in man a feeling of awe, but this is conquered by the knowledge that man is God's fellow-worker who shares with Him the rule of the fellow-creatures,

the dominion over the fish of the sea, and over the fowl of the air, and over the cattle, and over all the earth . . . Thus, in total contradiction to pagan religion, nature is not a deity to be feared and worshipped, but a work of God to be admired, studied and managed. In the Bible God and nature are no longer both opposed to man, but God and man together confront nature.[6]

5. God's fellow-worker

The biblical concept of man as God's fellow-worker is not without its logical difficulties. If God is almighty, why does he need our help? If he has willed things thus and so, how can any action of ours improve upon his presumably perfect will? The answer sometimes offered is that God voluntarily sets limits to his power, and leaves us room to supplement his action. According to this model God does so much, and man's part is to do the rest. I will not go into the further theological difficulties that are raised by such an answer. All I would say now is that it is emphatically not the answer offered in the Bible itself.

For the biblical writers there is no question of any such partition of action between God and man. 'Work out your own salvation with fear and trembling, for it is God who is at work in you to will and to do of his good purpose' (Philippians 2:12–13). This injunction was given to New Testament Christians. The Old Testament is just as clear that in one sense at least all men, whether they love God or hate him, are giving expression to the creative purposes of God by their choices and actions. 'You thought evil against me,' says Joseph to his brothers, 'but God meant it unto good . . .' (Genesis 50:20). God is the immediate giver of being to all that is and all that moves, the wicked as well as the good. In a profound sense the whole drama of creation unfolds according to his 'determinate counsel and foreknowledge' (Acts 2:23).

It would thus be a logical blunder to interpret human responsibility in the Bible as something that takes over where God leaves off. The Bible clearly represents us as both wholly dependent on God for every event of our existence, and wholly answerable to him for the responses we make. The slogan: 'Work as though all depended on you; pray as though all depended on God' may be somewhat oversimplified, but it comes far closer to expressing the spirit of biblical realism than any attempt to parcel out zones of responsibility between God and man.

This is not the place to spell out the logical fallacy in attempts to make a contradiction out of these complementary emphases.[7] Suffice it here to say that if we pay attention to the differences in logical standpoint between talk about a creator (any creator) and talk about his creatures, it becomes clear that the agency of the creator is not an alternative to, but a necessary condition of, the agency of his creatures. This does not make the creator morally answerable for the actions of his creatures (it would make no sense to hold Shakespeare guilty as an accessory to the murder committed by Macbeth!). Nor does it abolish the moral responsibility of the creatures for the exercise of their created capacities. But if, as the Bible declares, our Creator is One to whom it makes sense to pray, then it makes abundantly realistic sense for us to acknowledge in prayer our total dependence on him. Simultaneously, as agents within his created drama, we recognize also our full responsibility for our action or inaction, and the logical absurdity of shrugging any of it off on to him.

To put it in another way, it is essential to distinguish between two quite distinct meanings of the will of God. One, denoting what we might call his creative will, is what is expressed in the Genesis phrase, 'Let there be . . . ' . Any idea of our going contrary to God's creative will is strictly meaningless, since apart from his creative word nothing happens. 'He upholds [gives continued being to] all things by the word of his power' (Hebrews 1:3).

The other concept we might term God's normative will. This is what is expressed, for example, in the Ten Commandments or the Sermon on the Mount, in the words 'Thou shalt . . . ' . The idea of our going contrary to God's normative will is, alas, far from meaningless, however wrong and unrealistic it may be. Without God's help, according to the Bible we will lack both the ability to recognize his normative will and the desire and strength to carry it through. The gift of vision and strength to do God's normative will is what the Christian knows as *grace*. It is mediated through God's creative will. It is the daily experience of living in dependence on the grace of God that unifies the complementary doctrines of divine sovereignty and human responsibility.

6. Technology in biblical perspective

The contrast between biblical and pagan theologies of nature is at no point more decisive than where science comes to inspire technology. 'What right has man to improve upon nature; aren't we beginning to usurp the prerogatives of the Creator?' Such questions are often asked rhetorically, backed by observations of the kind parodied by Flanders and Swann: 'If God had meant men to fly, he would never have given us the railways.'

There is of course a sober warning for all ages in the story of the Tower of Babel, where men sought to build 'a tower whose top may reach unto heaven' (Genesis 11:4). What the context makes clear, however, is that their sin consisted not in the building but in the motivation for it – an arrogant desire to be independent of God. Nowhere in the Bible is technological achievement disapproved, except where it expressed human pride and vainglory. More relevant is the reiterated biblical teaching that 'He that knoweth to do good and doeth it not, to him it is sin' (James 4:17). From the biblical standpoint whatever needs to be done to alleviate the lot of our fellow men is a duty from which we can excuse ourselves only for good cause.

The contrary pagan notion that it is both impossible and illicit for man to compete with or improve upon nature has had a long and fascinating history from ancient times. The Greek concept of the Golden Age, when men were supposed to have lived healthy and contented lives without technological aids, coloured much classical and medieval thinking. The supposed divinity of nature was taken to imply that man would be claiming divine prerogatives if he attempted to copy or improve upon it. The general belief of the Middle Ages was that feats of nature could be surpassed only by magic.

The most powerful biblical arguments against this pessimistic view were advanced by Francis Bacon:

> If there be any humility towards the Creator, if there be any reverence for or disposition to magnify His works, if there be any charity for man, (we should) dismiss those preposterous philosophies which have led experience captive, and approach with humility and veneration to unroll the volume of creation.

As Hooykaas puts it, Bacon:

> blew the trumpet in the war against the sins of laziness, despair, pride, and ignorance; and he urged his contemporaries, for the

> sake of God and their neighbours, to re-assume the rights that God had given them and to restore that dominion over nature which God had allotted to man. His ideal was a science in the service of man, as the result of restoration of the rule of man over nature. This to him was not a purely human but a divinely inspired work: "The beginning is from God . . . the Father of lights."

It is worth noting that traces of the Graeco-medieval tradition lingered even in such a champion of biblical Christianity as C. S. Lewis, who justified his anti-technological bias by identifying human dominion over nature with *hubris*, commending instead the (Stoic) 'wisdom' of 'conforming the soul to reality'. Significantly, perhaps, he did not adduce biblical support for this attitude! As Hooykaas comments:

> It is true that results of our dominion over nature have been unhealthy in many cases; the powerful river of modern science and technology has often caused disastrous inundations. But by comparison the contemplative, almost medieval, vision that is offered as an alternative would be a stagnant pool.

7. Materialism

Here, if not before, I can imagine some fellow-Christians becoming restive. 'Your science-based technology,' they say, 'is all part of the quest of Western man to free himself from the necessities imposed upon him by religion, society and nature. Science has been drawn in, perhaps without its knowledge, to become the engine of an essentially godless project of human self-mastery. Its most notable effect is the all-pervasive materialism of which our culture is spiritually dying.'

That a culture hell-bent on 'freedom' from its Creator's demands will distort its scientific priorities accordingly has proved tragically true in many parts of our contemporary world, and I would say nothing to diminish the biblical content of such prophetic warnings. What worries me, however, is the confused and confusing tangle (as I see it) of extra-biblical presuppositions behind much currently fashionable 'science-bashing', and the damage that can be done to the Christian concept of science and its priorities when fellow-Christians climb on this particular bandwagon. I have discussed this elsewhere,[8] and I want here only to draw one or two distinctions that seem essential if Christians are to make sense (let alone command respect) in this connection. First, the spiritually rebellious and damaging 'materialism' that the Bible condemns was clearly as rampant in the pre-scientific days of the prophets and of Jesus Christ as it is today. Even the first man who built a shelter from the rain could have seen it as 'freeing him from the necessities imposed by God and nature'. He could have – but he need not. He could equally have seen it as a God-given improvement to be enjoyed with thanksgiving. Without belabouring the point, it is surely obvious that what is wrong in 'materialism' in the anti-Christian sense is the *lack of filial love to God* in its self-gratifying enterprises, rather than any resulting 'freedom from necessities'.

Secondly, the fact that (classical) physical science is built upon the concept of 'matter' and its 'properties', and is thus 'materialistic' in a technical sense, is totally irrelevant to this issue. If TV sets and washing machines can one day be designed effectively using a new physics that discards the concept of 'matter', they will present no less, and no more, temptation to the 'materialism' that biblical preachers rightly deplore. A physics based on 'matter' may offer more scope for some forms of reductionist 'nothing-buttery', but that is in any case logically fallacious.[9]

Thirdly, whatever a few godless scientific popularists may have suggested, the whole idea of human 'self-mastery' by scientific means is so manifestly incoherent in strictly philosophical terms that it is misleading to the Christian public if we preach against it as if it were conceptually a live option. 'He that sits in the heavens shall laugh at them'[10] – and if there are good analytic reasons for our doing the same without invoking the authority of divine revelation, it is surely these that we should first urge. There is no merit, and grave risk of confusion, in urging fellow-Christians to give such nonsense the dignity of requiring specifically theological rebuttal.

8. 'Fashioning the future'?

Some Christians express particular unhappiness with the idea that our scientific knowledge should be applied to what they call 'fashioning the future' as distinct from simply 'acting together'. This, they argue, would deny or take the place of faith in divine providence. *Actions*, they say, are all right. An action has a beginning and an end; and when one completes what one is doing, what happens to it is out of one's own control. To act well, then, requires faith in divine providence, because one must hope (without the possibility of calculative proof) that what one has done will be used for the service of others rather than their hurt. To 'fashion the future', however, (they would say) is to refuse to let one's act go. It is to strive to extend one's control even to directing the stream of history. It is to assume a '*totalistic*' responsibility for what will happen.[11]

Now we must agree that a God-defying spirit like that of the builders of Babel, snatching at *total* responsibility for our future, would invert Christian priorities. But who in his right mind, one wonders, ever imagined that technology *could* give anyone such total control of the future? The radical incoherence of the very notion has been well demonstrated by people like Sir Karl Popper[12] who have no religious axe to grind. Here again, utopian talk in these terms can be dismissed merely on technical grounds. To try to oppose it by contrasting 'acting together' and 'fashioning the future' is to fasten on the wrong distinction. Consider, for example, the actions of a Christian driver in steering a car-load of people to work. Is he morally or spiritually wrong to 'refuse to let his act go' by applying continual feedback, so as to direct the stream of his local history in accordance with the norms of good stewardship and compassion for his passengers and other road users? If so, by what biblical criterion? As accident statistics show only too well, his control does not eliminate the need for faith in divine providence; but he would rightly reject as immoral and frivolous any suggestion that there would be merit in 'letting go' his efforts to shape his future course as precisely as possible. The same applies to larger-scale operations in which the health, wealth and happiness of a whole community may depend upon continuous exercise of foresight and regulative power which it would be a mere dereliction of God-given duty to 'let go', yet in the course of which faith in divine providence is even more necessary.

The danger in objections on the lines I have cited is that they fasten on the wrong distinction. They suggest that any attempt to change or control the shape of the future, however partially, must either be of the 'act and let go' kind, or else fall into the 'totalistic' category. This neglects a huge class of everyday actions of the sort that an engineer would term 'closed-loop'. Only a special class (termed 'open-loop') conforms to the 'act and let go' description.

No, the morally significant contrast that we must hold on to as Christians is not between open-loop and closed-loop efforts, nor between efforts to exercise our stewardship on a small scale and on a large scale (whether in space or time). It is between efforts in obedient love, and efforts in rebellious defiance, towards the Master who has given us that stewardship.

It is arguments in the other spirit, I fear, that make a professed unbeliever like Sir Peter Medawar[13] so angry with what he calls 'postural anti-scientism'. He cites an historic comment by *The Times* on Edwin Chadwick's (fortunately successful) efforts to promote the Public Health Act of 1848: 'We prefer to take our chance of cholera and the rest than to be bullied into health. England wants to be clean, but not cleaned by Chadwick' (Medawar, p. 20); and he complains savagely of the 'unquestioning, unthinking, almost reflexly contemptuous relegation to the devil of science and all its works and the attribution to it of all evils, especially those that are in reality due to political incompetence or commercial greed'. Of course few Christian writers, however anti-scientific, would qualify for Medawar's description. What I would ask, however, given the solid biblical basis for both science and its uses for human benefit, is why Christian writers are not more unanimous and vocal in dismissing as unbiblical the irrational science-bashing of our day.

It can rightly be argued that if ever we had the technical means to reshape human society at large, we should still as fallen sinners have little or no assurance that our choice of ends would be for our good, or that of posterity. 'Learning what to want', as Sir Geoffrey Vickers[14] has pointed out, is even more difficult, most of the time, than learning how to achieve what we want. But the Christian who depends in humility on God for his standards of 'the good' can still sympathize with Medawar when he observes that 'to make the world a better place to live in is an ambition not falsified or diminished by the propensity of those who seek the reputation of finely critical minds to say knowingly, "Ah, but what do you mean by better?"!'

9. How things can go wrong

As a would-be servant of his Creator, man suffers from two limitations that we must take care not to confuse. The first is his sinfulness. We are by fallen nature headstrong, rebellious, reluctant to accept wholeheartedly the 'kingly rule of God'. The second we may term simply his finiteness. At his best, and with the best will in the world, a man can take only a limited number of factors into account when planning to do what he believes to be God's normative will. Because both his knowledge and his foresight are limited, things can go painfully wrong in ways that it would be superficial and cruel to attribute simply to human sinfulness.

This is not to deny that our sinfulness makes things worse, but to point out that the best of motives afford no automatic exemption from the unforeseeable risks of experimentation. It is both unnecessary and misleading, for example, to write down the development of the American dust bowls simply to human greed. The most selfless humanitarians, eager to increase the supply of food for the starving of the world, might have fallen into the same ecological trap as the hapless Mid-Western farmers. Again, the most conscientious steward of God's creation, totally devoid of any greed, might have been forgiven for thinking that DDT spraying was the responsible thing to do on a large scale in subduing the earth for the benefit of mankind. The temptation to ferret around for some ingredient of 'sin' to blame when these things turn out disastrously must be resisted if Christians are to think biblically and realistically about their wider responsibilities. Selfish unheeding of foreseeable costs and risks is indeed inexcusable; but man at his best is only, as Pascal called him, a 'thinking reed'. What hindsight allows the rest of us to condemn as short-sightedness is sometimes an inescapable aspect of our being human. 'Let him that thinketh he standeth take heed lest he fall' (1 Corinthians 10:12).

So when we turn to consider the possibilities for good in the large-scale application of scientific discoveries, it is important not to imagine that the Bible's one prerequisite for success is the elimination of sinful motives and the adoption of worthy goals. We are feeling our way to the controls of a world whose mechanism is more complex and delicately balanced than we are ever likely to comprehend. What the proverbial bull could do in a china shop is as nothing compared with the havoc we could wreak by a single well-intentioned error. The biblical moral is not that we should leave well alone. All is far from well, and it may be our responsibility in God's sight to do something about it. The moral is that if we are not to make matters disastrously worse by our meddling, we shall need a wisdom infinitely greater than our own. If our Creator is willing to give this wisdom to those who ask in humility and sincerity, desiring only to be used by him for good, then nothing could be more realistic than to beg it from him 'who giveth to all men liberally, and upbraideth not' (James 1:5). We are likely to need the reassurance of those last three words!

10. Compassion – individual and communal

We have noted several times the Christian priority of 'compassion'; but as we all know, judging what is the compassionate thing to do, especially in face of competing claims and much confusion between real 'needs' and mere 'wants', can involve layer upon layer of value-judgments with few if any simple biblical maxims to short-circuit the process. As shown by the example of David's action in feeding his hungry men on the sacred bread,[15] which had Christ's apparent approval,[16] not even general divine prohibitions can always be used safely to exclude options in an emergency.

While all this is well-trodden ground, there is one aspect of the problem of compassion that may particularly trouble the scientist and those he advises, which I feel needs urgent attention from Christians. This is the conflict that can arise between compassionate assessments in terms of the interests of the individual, and of those of a whole population. To begin with a simple example, if a child catches a dangerously contagious disease, it may seem cruelly lacking in compassion to prohibit its mother from nursing it among the family at home; but at the community level the reverse may be true. The claims of 'individual' and 'communal' compassion here pull in opposite directions. Again, most Christians regard it as something of a scandal that more people die annually of starvation around the world today than a century ago; yet in demographic terms this fact can be traced directly to the success of last century's efforts (largely motivated by Christian compassion) to reduce global infant mortality, without any corresponding efforts towards control of population growth.

As anyone who knows the difference between arithmetic and geometric progression can see, attempts to deflect this point by recommending agricultural improvements are hopelessly shortsighted. Food supplies ought, of course, to be augmented as a short-term remedy; but as long as vast tribes of fertile people continue to double the world's population every few decades as a matter of family or national pride and principle, it is far from obvious what is the most compassionate way to divide scarce resources among the competing demands for the preservation of infant life, the development of food supplies and the control of fertility. I have actually seen Christians recommend in print that all we need do is to 'feed the hungry' and trust God for the rest. This may sound pious; but it is hard to defend as responsible stewardship. It is precisely in such situations that the confusion pointed out in section 8 above can be disastrous, and the distinction between rebellious and biblically-responsible efforts to 'shape the future' needs to be recognized. It is vital that when Christian stewards are trying to find the biblically and communally compassionate course in such situations, they are not discouraged by bogus theological objections from working out and steering by the foreseeable implications of their alternatives. Now that more and more policies are settled at the global level, there is an urgent need for theologians to work out the actually relevant biblical principles that should govern and inspire attempts to integrate individual and communal compassion.

11. Retrospect

We have uncovered no startling novel priorities for Christian in science or technology, though I have tried at one or two points to give our well-known priorities a new thrust where it might be easy to neglect them. Think of what it means biblically to be a loving son in his Father's house, a compassionate steward with specific talents, a rescued sinner in a fallen world, still plagued by the misperceptions natural to a fallen race, yet vassal to the one great God of truth and love. Take time to consider prayerfully the workings-out of these images in each of the twelve headings we reviewed at the beginning (listed in section 2), and you should discover the difference it ought to make for a scientist to have Christian priorities. It is obvious that to most of our practical questions, even of the evaluative kind, the Bible contains no ready-made answers; but it does, I believe, enunciate principles sufficiently clear to allow us – indeed to encourage us – to go on enthusiastically with our scientific map-making, in that biblical 'fear and trembling' which does nothing to abate the joy of it.

Notes on chapters

Chapter 1 – Persons and things

1. Originally appeared in *Science and Faith Today* (Lutterworth, 1953).

Chapter 2 – A scientist in God's world

1. Originally printed in *Science, Chance and Providence* (Oxford University Press, 1978).
2. Donald M. MacKay, *The Clockwork Image* (IVP, 1974), ch. 6.
3. Arnold J. Toynbee, 'The Genesis Pollution', *Horizon* 15, No. 3, Summer 1973.
4. M. B. Foster, 'The Christian Doctrine of Creation and the Rise of Modern Natural Science', *Mind* 43 (1934), pp. 446–468.
5. To quote Michael Foster again: 'The voluntary activity of the Creator (*i.e.* that in his activity which exceeds determination by reason) terminates on the *contingent* being of the creature (*i.e.* on that element of its being which eludes determination by form, namely its matter and the characteristics which it possesses *qua* material). If such voluntary activity is essential to God, it follows that the element of contingency is essential to what He creates' (*loc. cit.*, p. 464).
6. R. Hooykaas, *Religion and the Rise of Modern Science* (Scottish Academic Press and Chatto & Windus, 1972).
7. R. Hooykaas, *The Christian Approach in Teaching Science* (Tyndale Press, London, 1960), p. 10.
8. John Donne, *Eighty Sermons*, no. 22, 1640. Cited in R. Hooykaas, *The Principle of Uniformity in Geology, Biology and Theology* (Brill, Leiden, 1963), p. 225.
9. A variety of views of this kind are surveyed and criticized in *Reason and Commitment* by Roger Trigg (Cambridge University Press, 1973). See also *Objective Knowledge*, ed. Paul Helm (IVP, 1987).

Chapter 3 – Looking for connections

1. Originally appeared in *Where Science and Faith Meet* (IVP, 1953).

Chapter 4 – What makes a contradictiion?

1. Offprinted from *Faith and Thought: The Journal of the Victoria Institute*, Vol. 97, No. 1, Spring 1968

Chapter 5 – Man as a mechanism

1. An edited version of a paper which originally appeared in *Faith and Thought* 91 (1960), and was revised in *Christianity in a Mechanistic Universe* (IVP, 1965).

2. The big difficulty with the charioteer model is that, whereas the earlier scientists who sometimes used it thought that there were plenty of loose ends in the brain on which, as it were, the soul in its chariot could pull and push to control the way the machine moves, recent discoveries, fragmentary though they are, seem to indicate that all the really important control links form closed loops, so that there may be no 'loose ends' of the sort that would be wanted for this kind of job.

Chapter 6 – What determines my choice?

1. Originally appeared in *Cerebral Correlates of Conscious Experience*, eds. P. H. Buser and A. Rougeul-Buser (North Holland Publishing Co., Amsterdam, 1978).
2. D. M. MacKay, *Zygon* 9 (1974), pp. 225–244.
3. D. M. Mackay, *Mind* 69, (1960), pp. 31–40.
4. D. M. Mackay, *Freedom of Action in a Mechanistic Universe* (Eddington Lecture, Cambridge University Press, London and New York, 1967). Reprinted in *Good Readings in Psychology*, ed. M. S. Gazzaniga and E. P. Lovejoy (Prentice Hall, 1971), pp. 121–138.
5. D. M. MacKay, in *The Proper Study*, ed. G. N. A. Vesey (Royal Institute of Philosophy Lectures, Macmillan, London, 1971), Vol. 4, pp. 48–63.
6. D. M. Mackay, *Brit. J. Phil. Sci.* 24 (1973), pp. 405–408.
7. K. R. Popper, *Brit. J. Phil. Sci.* 1 (1950), pp. 117–133.
8. J. C. Eccles, *The neurophysiological basis of mind* (Oxford, Clarendon Press, 1 1953), pp. 278–279.
9. J. C. Eccles, *Facing Reality* (Springer-Verlag, New York/Heidelberg/Berlin, 1970), pp. 123–126.
10. D. M. MacKay, *Brit. J. Phil. Sci.* 2 (1951), pp. 105–121, especially 118.
11. A. Gierer, *Ratio* 12 (1970), pp. 47–64.
12. D. M. MacKay, *The Clockwork Image: A Christian Perspective on Science*, London, 1974).

Chapter 7 – Brain research and human responsibility

1. Originally appeared in *Horizons in Science*, ed. Carl Henry (Harper & Row, New York, 1978).
2. A detailed survey of the biblical evidence is given by G. C. Berkouwer in *Man: The Image of God* (Eerdmans and IVP, 1962).
3. See for example his *Facing Reality* (Longman and Springer-Verlag, 1970).
4. D. M. MacKay, 'A Mind's-Eye View of the Brain', in *Cybernetics of the Nervous System*, ed. Norbert Wiener and J. P. Schade, *Progress in Brain Research* 17 (Elsevier, 1965), pp. 321–332.
5. D. M. MacKay, 'The Use of Behavioural Language to Refer to Mechanical Processes', *Brit J. Phil. of Sci.* 13 (1962), pp. 89–103; also in *Human & Artificial Intelligence*, ed. F. J. Crosson (Appleton-Century-Crofts, 1971).
6. B. T. Gardner and R. A. Gardner, 'Two-way communication with an infant chimpanzee', in A. M. Schrier & F. Stollnitz (eds.), *Behaviour of Non-human Primates* (New York: Academic Press, 1971).
7. D. M. MacKay, 'From Mechanism to Mind', *Trans. Vict. Inst.* 85 (1953), pp. 17–32; also *In Brain and Mind*, ed. J. R. Smythies (Routledge and Kegan Paul, 1965), pp. 163–200, and comments on pages 129–131. See also 'Artificial Intelligence – a Christian appraisal' in this volume.
8. D. M. MacKay, 'Brain and Will', *The Listener*, 9 and 16 May 1957; also (revised) *Faith and Thought* 90, (1958), pp. 193–215; also in *The Art of Philosophy*, ed. F. A. Westphal (Prentice-Hall, 1972), pp. 162–167.
9. D. M. MacKay, 'On the Logical Indeterminacy of a Free Choice', *Mind* 69 (1960), pp. 31–40.
10. D. M. MacKay, 'Information and Prediction in Human Sciences', in *Information and Prediction in Science*, ed. S. Dockx and P. Bernays (*Symp. of Int. Acad for Phil. of Sci.*, 1962 Academic Press, New York, 1965), pp. 255–269.
11. D. M. MacKay, *Freedom of Action in a Mechanistic Universe* (Eddington Lecture; Cam-

bridge Univ. Press, London and New York, 1967). Reprinted in *Good Readings in Psychology*, ed. M. S. Gazzaniga and E. P. Lovejoy (Prentice Hall, 1971), pp. 121–138.
12. D. M. MacKay, 'The Logical Indeterminateness of Human Choices', *Brit. J. Phil. Sci.* 24 (1973), pp. 405–408.
13. D. M. MacKay, *The Clockwork Image: A Christian Perspective on Science* (IVP, 1974), especially Chapter 8 and Appendix.
14. D. S. Borguonkar and S. A. Shah, 'The XYY chromosome male – or syndrome?' in *Progress in Medical Genetics*, Vol. X; also E. B. Hook, 'Behavioural Implications of the human XYY genotype', *Science* 179 (1973), pp. 139–150.
15. This has occasionally been done in an attempt to mitigate epileptic seizures.
16. H. L. Teuber, 'The riddle of frontal-lobe function in man', in *The Frontal Granular Cortex and Behaviour*, ed. J. M. Warren and K. Akert (New York: McGraw-Hill, 1964), pp. 410–444; also H. L. Teuber 'Unity and diversity of frontal lobe functions', *Acta Neurobiol. Exp.* 32 (1972), pp. 615–656.
17. M. S. Gazzaniga, *The Bisected Brain* (Appleton-Century-Crofts, New York, 1970). See also Chapter 1 of *The Neurosciences* (ref. 19).
18. R. Hooykaas, *Religion and the Rise of Modern Science* (Scottish Academic Press and Chatto & Windus, 1972).
19. R. J. Wurtman and J. D. Fernstrom, 'Nutrition and the brain', in *The Neurosciences, Third Study Program*, ed. F. O. Schmitt *et. al* (MIT Press, Cambridge, Mass.' 1974).
20. See the chapter by Prof. M. A. Jeeves in *Free to be Different*, ed. John Stott (Marshalls, 1984).
21. *Man and his Future*, ed. G. Wolstenholme (Churchill, 1963).
22. A. E. Bergin and S. L. Garfield (eds.), *The Handbook of Psychotherapy & Behavior Change* (Wiley, New York, 1971).

Chapter 8 – Biblical perspectives on human engineering

1. Originally published in *The Journal of the Institute for Reformational Studies* 219 (1986).
2. This first point is expanded later on pages 222–233.
3. In *Religion and the Rise of Modern Science* (1972).
4. Quoted by R. Hooykaas in *Christian Faith and the Freedom of Science* (Tyndale Press, 1957), p. 18.
5. In what follows I have made use of extracts from my paper on *Information Technology and the Manipulability of Man*, which was published in German in *Zeitschrift für Evangelischer Ethik, X11/3* (1968); and in English in *Study Encounter V/I*, (1969), pp. 17–25.
6. Deterministic theories of behaviour thus offer no excuse from responsibility, since the foregoing argument requires no assumptions to be made as to the existence or non-existence of physical or psychological causes of our actions.
7. There is however one interesting condition in which even an isolated manipulator can be indefinitely embarrassed by his victims, namely if they can equip themselves with an equivalent observing and calculating system, so that they are able to see the outcome of his calculations as fast as he does, and so are in a position to upset the basis of any predictions he might otherwise have made.
8. Four current views can usefully be distinguished: (a) Personal identity depends on *bodily* identity (especially of brain); (b) Personal identity is carried by *memory and character*; (c) Personal identity is only evidenced by, but not *constituted* by, either of these; (d) Personal identity is a matter of *degree.* I am indebted to my colleague Professor R. G. Swinburne for the following references illustrative of each of these views: (a) B. Williams, 'Personal Identity and Individuation', reprinted in his *Problems of the Self* (Cambridge University Press, 1973); B. Williams, 'The Self and the Future', *Phil. Rev.* 79 (1970), pp. 161–180; D. Wiggins, *Identity and Spatio-Temporal Continuity* Pt. IV (Blackwells, 1967). (b) A. Quinton, 'The Soul', *J. Philosophy* 59 (1962), pp. 393–409. (c) R. G. Swinburne, 'Personal Identity', *Proc. Aristot. Soc.* (1973/74), pp.231–248; R. M. Chisholm, 'The Loose and Popular and the Strict and Philosophical Senses of Identity', in N. S. Pear and R. H. Grimm (eds.), *Perception and Personal Identity* (Cleveland, 1969). (d) D. Parfit, 'Personal Identity': *Phil. Rev.* 80 (1971), pp. 3–27.

9. D. M. MacKay, 'Man as a Mechanism', in *Christianity in a Mechanistic Universe* (D. M. MacKay, ed., IVF, 1965).
10. D. M. MacKay, *The Clockwork Image* (IVP, 1974), chapters 4, 7 and 8.
11. D. M. MacKay, *The Clockwork Image* (IVP, 1974), chapters 4, 7 and 8.
12. For example, of the kind popularized recently by Teilhard de Chardin.
13. On this theme see G. Vickers, *The Art of Judgment* (Chapman & Hall, 1965); *Freedom in a Rocking Boat* (Allan Lane, 1970).

Chapter 9 – Artificial intelligence? – a Christian appraisal

1. Previously unpublished.
2. D. M. MacKay, 'The Use of Behavioural Language to Refer to Mechanical Processes', *Brit. J. Phil. of Sci.* 13 (1962), pp. 89–103. Also in F. J. Crosson (ed.), *Human and Artificial Intelligence* (New York, 1971).
3. This section is based on a paper given to the Annual Conference of the British Society for the Philosophy of Science, Oxford, 22–24 September 1961 (see note 2).
4. It should be noted that only the two 'mechanical' (or the two 'personal') columns offer analogues of one another. Personal activity and mechanical activity (on either side) are not analogues but correlates.
5. D. M. MacKay, 'Mindlike Behaviour in Artefacts', *Brit. J. Phil. of Sci.* Vol. 2 (1951), pp. 105–121. Also Vol. 3 (1953), pp. 352–353. 'Mentality in Machines', *Proc. Aristot. Soc. Suppt.* Vol. 26 (1952), pp. 61–86.
6. J. R. Lucas, 'Minds, Machines and Gödel', *Philosophy* 36 (1961), pp. 112–127.
7. Lest this account seems altogether too remote from the 'objective' 'physical' definition of entropy-change as $\Delta Q/T$, it should be remembered that the power to extract work from such a molecular assemblage depends directly on the extent to which its energy-configuration can be ascertained. This explains why what may seem a highly subjective concept turns out to be of crucial importance in the theory of engines.
8. Underspecified, not in the sense of leaving any parts unaccounted for, but in the sense of being compatible with more than one state of the parts.
9. D. M. MacKay, 'On the Logical Indeterminacy of a Free Choice', *Proc. XIIth Int. Congress of Philosophy* Vol. 3 (1958), pp. 249–256; and expanded version in *Mind.* Vol. 69 (1960), pp. 31–40. *Freedom of Action in a Mechanistic Universe* (Eddington Lecture), (London/New York, 1967), reprinted in M. S. Gazzaniga and E. P. Lovejoy (eds.), *Good Readings in Psychology* (New York, 1971), pp. 121–138. 'What Determines My Choice?' in P. A. Buser and A. Rougeul-Buser (eds.), *Cerebral Correlates of Conscious Experience* (Amsterdam/New York/Oxford, 1978), pp. 335–346.
10. See for example *Cerebral Correlates of Conscious Experience*, ed. P. A. Buser and A. Rougeul-Buser (Amsterdam: Elsevier, 1978).
11. I used this illustration in my unpublished Fremantle Lectures given at Balliol College, Oxford in 1975.
12. For example, see J. C. Eccles, *The Human Psyche* (Berlin/Heidelberg/New York: Springer International, 1980).
13. D. M. MacKay, 'Operational Aspects of Some Fundamental Concepts of Communication', *Synthese* 9 (1954), pp. 182–198; 'Towards an Information-Flow Model of Human Behaviour', *Brit. J. Psychol.* 47 (1956), pp. 30–43; 'Information and Learning', in *Learning Automata*, ed. H. Billing (Munich: Oldenbourg, 1961), pp. 40–49; 'Mind Talk and Brain Talk', in *Handbook of Cognitive Neuroscience*, ed. M. S. Gazzaniga (New York: Plenum, 1983), pp. 293–317.
14. See Eccles, *loc. cit.*, especially Chapter 7.
15. See for example W. Penfield, *The Mystery of the Mind* (Princeton N.J.: Princeton University Press, 1975) and references therein.
16. D. M. MacKay, 'Mindlike Behaviour in Artefacts', *Brit. J. Phil. of Sci.* 2 (1951), pp. 105–121. Also III (1953), pp. 352–353; 'Cerebral Organization and the Conscious Control of Action', in *Brain and Conscious Experience*, ed. J. C. Eccles (New York: Springer-Verlag, 1966), pp. 422–445; 'Conscious Agency with Unsplit and Split

Brains', in *Consciousness and the Physical World*, eds. B. D. Josephson and V. S. Ramachandran (Oxford: Pergamon, 1980), pp. 95–113; 'Neural Basis of Cognitive Experience', in *Neural Communication and Control*, eds. G. Szekely, E. Labos and S. Damjanovich (Oxford: Pergamon and Budapest: Akademiai Kiado, 1981), pp. 315–332.

17. W. Penfield, in *Brain & Conscious Experience*, ed. J. C. Eccles (New York: Springer-Verlag, 1966), pp. 253–254.
18. D. M. MacKay, 'The Beginnings of Personal Life', *In The Service of Medicine* 30 (1984), pp. 9–13.
19. D. M. MacKay and V. MacKay, 'Explicit Dialogue Between Left and Right Half Systems of Split Brains', *Nature* 295 (1982), pp. 690–691.
20. D. M. MacKay, 'Information and Prediction in Human Sciences', in *Information and Prediction in Science*, eds. S. Dockx and P. Bernays (New York: Academic Press, 1965), pp. 255–269; 'Scientific Beliefs about Oneself', in *The Proper Study*, ed. G. N. A. Vesey (London: Macmillan, 1971), pp. 48–63.
21. D. M. MacKay, 'Mind Talk and Brain Talk', in M. S. Gazziniga (ed.), *Handbook of Cognitive Neuroscience* (New York, 1983), pp. 293–317.
22. D. M. MacKay, 'Complementarity II', *Aristotelian Soc. Suppt.* Vol. 32 (1958), pp. 105–122; 'Complementarity in Scientific and Theological Thinking', *Zygon* Vol. 9 (1974), pp. 225–244.
23. R. W. Sperry, *Science and Moral Priority* (Oxford, 1983).
24. While accepting that at the physical level 'the laws of causation are nowhere broken or open (excepting perhaps in quantum-level indeterminacy which is here irrelevant)', Sperry still claims to 'counter and refute . . . the classic physicalist assumption of a purely physical determinacy of the central nervous system' (Sperry (1983) pp. 81, 89). If by 'purely' here he only means 'exclusively', I would agree (see notes 2, 4, 5); but the confusion that can be caused by Sperry's choice of terms is brought out if we imagine a parallel argument in the case of our digital computer.
25. A. M. Turing, 'Computing Machinery and Intelligence', *Mind* Vol. 59 (1960), pp. 433–460. Note that in this context the term 'personality' has an unfortunate ambiguity. (a) We speak of the 'personality' of a character in a play or a novel, meaning (roughly) the dispositional features that distinguish that character psychologically, without any implication that he exists as a person. But when we ask whether we can rightly attribute 'personality' to a robot, we may be raising (b) the ontological question whether the robot *is* a person (a centre of conscious awareness), as distinct from merely behaving *like* a person.

    I must plead guilty to some inconsistency in past uses of the term. In 'The use of behavioural language to refer to mechanical processes' (note 2) I argued that a suitable artefact might have a personality in sense (a). In 'A mind's eye view of the brain' (note 36) I used the term in sense (b) and denied that behavioural criteria were sufficient to settle the *ontological* question of personality. In each case I would still affirm what I meant, which I hope was clear from the context.
26. D. M. MacKay, 'In Search of Basic Symbols', in H. von Foerster (ed.), *Proc. 8th Conf. on Cybernetics* (New York, 1951), pp. 181–122; 'From Mechanism to Mind', *Trans. Vict. Inst.* Vol. 85 (1953), pp. 17–32; 'Operational Aspects of Some Fundamental Concepts of Human Communication', *Synthese* Vol. 9 (1954), pp. 182–198; 'Operational Aspects of Intellect', *Mechanization of Thought Processes* (Her Majesty's Stationery Office, 1959), pp. 37–52; 'Digits and Analogues', in H. E. von Gierke, W. D. Keidel and H. L. Ostreicher (eds.), *Principles and Practice of Bionics* (London, 1970), pp. 457–466; see also note 21.
27. D. H. Ackley, G. E. Hinton and T. J. Sejnowski, 'A Learning Algorithm for Boltzmann Machines', in *Cognitive Science* Vol. 9 (1985), pp. 147–167.
28. See for example Derek Parfit, *Reasons and Persons* (Oxford, 1984).
29. D. M. MacKay, 'Ourselves and our Brains: Duality without Dualism', *Psychoneuroendocrinology* Vol. 7 (1982), pp. 285–294. See also MacKay (1980), note 36.

30. John R. Searle, 'Minds, Brains and Programs', *The Behavioral and Brain Sciences* Vol. 3 (1980), pp. 417–458.
31. L. Wittgenstein, *Tractatus Logico – Philosophicus* 6.432: 'There are indeed things that cannot be put into words. They *make themselves manifest.*'
32. M. Polanyi, *The Tacit Dimension* (London, 1967).
33. D. M. MacKay, 'The Mechanics of Tacit Knowing', *I.E.E.E. Trans. on Systems, Man and Cybernetics* SMC-4 No. 1 (1974), pp. 94–95.
34. Witness Wittgenstein's comment in a letter of 9 April 1917 to Engelmann: 'The poem by Uhland is really magnificent. And this is how it is: if only you do not try to utter what is unutterable then *nothing* gets lost. But the unutterable will be – unutterably – *contained* in what has been uttered!' See P. Engelmann, *Letters from Ludwig Wittgenstein* (Oxford, 1967), p. 7.
35. K. R. Popper 'Indeterminism in Quantum Physics and in Classical Physics', *Brit. J. Phil. Sci.* 1 (1950), pp. 117–133 and 173–195.
36. D. M. MacKay, 'On Comparing the Brain with Machines', *The Advancement of Science* Vol. 40 (1954), pp. 402–406. Also *American Scientist* Vol. 42 (1954), pp. 261–268; and 'A Mind's Eye View of the Brain', in Norbert Wiener and J. P. Schadé (eds.), *Cybernetics of the Nervous System, Progress in Brain Research* Vol. 17 (1965), pp. 321–332; 'Selves and Brains', *Neuroscience* Vol. 3 (1978), pp. 599–606. Also D. M. MacKay, *Human Science and Human Dignity* (London/Downers Grove, Illinois, 1979); *Brains, Machines and Persons* (London/Grand Rapids, 1980).
37. D. M. MacKay, 'Man as Observer – Predictor', in *Man in his Relationships*, ed. H. Westmann (London: Routledge, 1955), pp. 15–28.
38. D. M. MacKay, 'Seeing the Wood and the Trees', in *Thinking: The Expanding Frontier*, ed. W. Maxwell (Philadelphia: Franklin Institute Press, 1983), pp. 5–12.
39. D. M. MacKay, 'From Mechanism to Mind', *Trans. Vict. Inst.* 85 (1953), pp. 17–32.
40. M. Buber, *I and Thou* (Edinburgh: T. & T. Clark, 1937).
41. In *Brains, Machines and Persons* (London: Collins, and Grand Rapids: Eerdmans, 1980), pp. 100–102; 'Selves and Brains', *Neuroscience* 3 (1978), pp. 599–606.

Chapter 10 – Value-free knowledge: myth or norm?

1. This is a slightly abbreviated form of an article which first appeared in *Faith and Thought* Vol. 107, No. 3.
2. See R. Hooykaas, *Religion and the Rise of Modern Science* (Scottish Academic Press, 1972); also Charles Webster, *The Great Instauration (1975)*. By the time that the *social* sciences reached self-consciousness, of course, the religious climate had changed; but the same theological principle is equally applicable to them.
3. Thomas Kuhn, *The Structure of Scientific Revolutions* (Chicago, 1961).
4. See for example the review of my book *Human Science and Human Dignity* by N. Isbister and D. Lyon in *Faith & Thought* 106. (1979), pp. 178–183.
5. Our present theoretical picture of the structure of matter, for example, embodies concepts such as 'the electron' whose status is much open to dispute, however reliable the predictions we have learned to base upon it.
6. (a) H. A. Simon, '"Bandwagon" and "Underdog" Effects', *Public Opinion Quarterly* (1954), pp. 245–253. (b) D. M. MacKay, *Man as Observer-Predictor*, in H. Westmann (ed.) *Man in his Relationships* (Routledge, London, 1955), pp. 15–28.
7. I have explored the implications of this point at greater length in (a) 'Machines and Societies' in G. Wolstenholme (ed.), *Man and His Future* (Churchill, 1963), pp. 153–167. (b) 'Scientific Beliefs about Oneself' in G. N. A. Vesey (ed.), *The Proper Study*, Royal Institute of Philosophy Lectures, Vol. 4. (Macmillan, London, 1971), pp. 48–63. (c) *Information Technology and the Manipulability of Man, Study Encounter, V*, No. 1, pp. 17–25, 1969. (d) Chapter 3 of *Human Science and Human Dignity* (Hodder & Stoughton, 1979).
8. A specially illuminating treatment of this theme is given by Sir Geoffrey Vickers in *The Art of Judgment* (Chapman & Hall, 1965).

9. A. W. Gouldner, *For Sociology* (Pelican, 1975), p. 66. It is important not to confuse the question of objectivity in science with that of the *ethical neutrality of scientists*, which Gouldner also addresses. 'If technical competence provides no warrant for making value judgments', he asks on p. 5, 'then what does?' A Christian would answer that technical competence is not enough; but that the more we (objectively) know, the more accountable we are for the use we make of that knowledge in our judgments of value. Objectivity is not an *alternative* to an ethical attitude on the part of the scientists, but rather one of its preconditions.
10. Note that this does *not* necessarily mean that *what God knows* is what either the scientist or Joe would be correct to believe if only they knew it; for one of the things God knows is that they do not know it!
11. D. M. MacKay, (a) *Science, Chance & Providence* (Oxford, 1978), Chapter III; (b) *Brains, Machines & Persons* (Collins, 1980), pp. 86–97.

Chapter 11 – The open mind – an evangelical approach to the Bible

1. R. Hooykaas, *Christian Faith and the Freedom of Science* (Tyndale Press, 1957).

Chapter 12 – Science and the Bible

1. Originally appeared in *Essential Christianity* (1961).
2. See chapter 15.

Chapter 13 – Apologetics today

1. *Science* 177 (1972), p.1155; 179, (1973) p.953; *Nature* 239 (1972), p.420.
2. R. P. Aulie, 'The Doctrine of Special Creation', *The American Biology Teacher* (April and May 1972), pp. 191, 261.
3. The 'ontological argument', first put forward by Anselm in the eleventh century, is generally regarded as an attempt to demonstrate the *existence* to God, from the very *idea* of God as 'that which nothing greater can be thought'. It was also used by later philosphers such as Aquinas and Descartes. (Ed.).
4. 'The argument from design' received its popular and influential presentation from William Paley in the eighteenth century, although it is present in Aquinas' thought. Sometimes called the 'teleological argument', an attempt is made to argue for the existence of an ultimate designer from the datum of the apparent order of the world and the apparent 'design' of its component parts, each to fulfil one or more 'purposes' within the overall order. (Ed.).
5. See *What makes a contradiction?*, p. 38 and *Man as a mechanism*, p. 45.
6. *A scientist in God's world*, p. 20 and *The sovereignty of God in the natural world*, p. 184.
7. See *The mythology of chance*, p. 197.
8. See *Language, meaning and God*, p. 165.
9. 'Positivism' was an approach associated with a group called the 'Vienna Circle' and became influential in Britain through A. J. Ayer. The position was held that statements which were not either meaningful by definition (*e.g.* All batchelors are male) or capable of empirical investigation were 'meaningless'. This method was called 'the verification principle'. (Ed.).
10. See R. Hooykaas, *Religion and the Rise of Modern Science* (Scottish Academic Press, 1972).

Chapter 14 – Language, meaning and God

1. Originally appeared in *Philosophy: The Journal of the Royal Institute of Philosophy* 47, No. 179, 1–18 (Cambridge University Press, 1972).
2. D. M. MacKay, *Information, Mechanism and Meaning* (MIT Press, 1969), chapter 9. See also discussions in F. S. C. Northrop and H. Livingston (eds.), *Cross-Cultural Understanding: Epistemology in Anthropology* (Harper and Row, 1964).
3. Note that according to this criterion, *symptoms* (such as spots on the face indicating measles) can be said to have meaning, but do not constitute a communication in the same sense, since no question of *intention* arises.

4. More detailed discussions of this topic will be found in my *Information, Mechanism and Meaning* (see note 2). Dr. S. C. Brown (personal communication) has suggested that I should mention a further distinction of importance here, between utterances that make *claims* (assessable as true-false, or reasonable-unreasonable), and those that make only *affirmations* or *avowals*. The briefest way to do so in the present terms might be to say that affirmations and avowals have as their primary target the recipient's internal representation of the *originator-as-agent*, whereas the targets of claims are representations of *that-which-stands-to-be-reckoned-with-by* the originator as agent (and, usually, others).
5. Note that this concept of reality does not restrict us to spatially locatable objects.
6. The ability to say what would falsify a statement does not however guarantee that the statement as a *whole* is meaningful. We may agree that 'John played bzrk in London yesterday' would be falsified by evidence that John was in Paris all day; but its meaning might still escape us.
7. It should perhaps be pointed out that disparity between two repertoires can exist without one being necessarily inferior in scope to the other, if they embody mutually exclusive principles of organization (see notes 2 and 18).
8. Note that this may mean developing new patterns of behaviour as well as new skills of thought. Linguistic expressions can indeed become meaningful as a result of behavioural learning processes, without the user's necessarily *understanding* what they denote.
9. A. G. N. Flew, in *New Essays in Philosophical Theology* (SCM 1956), pp. 107–108.
10. P. Van Buren, *The Secular Meaning of the Gospel* (SCM 1963).
11. Including what he does in transforming the Christian's own attitudes and capacities, as well as in historical acts of self-revelation and redemption.
12. I ought perhaps to make clear that the point of this example is to bring out the role of event-language in explicating talk about existents, not to suggest that the concept of personal agency or the concept of God should be explicated by close analogy with the concept of electricity!
13. R. B. Braithwaite, *An Empiricist's View of the Nature of Religious Belief* (Cambridge University Press, 1955).
14. Note that we are *not* here saying what Ronald Hepburn[19] accuses the Barthian of alleging, that 'doubt is never honest'. The biblical response to the sceptic who 'honestly can't see it' is not to accuse him of insincerity, but to invite him to make an experiment: to consider soberly how far he would be ready to follow up the consequences in obedience if he did 'see it'. This will be no matter of a snap answer, but a searching experience in the course of which his 'conditional readinesses' will be challenged at ever deeper levels. The promise of Christ is that the man who perseveres in facing these challenges will find himself given as much as he asks of the grace he will need to meet them adequately; and in that discovery, he will begin to know what it means to reckon with God.
15. In *Do Religious Assertions make Sense?* (SCM, 1969), S. C. Brown also argues strongly that with respect to certain kinds of statements, belief and understanding are inseparable.
16. Italics mine.
17. On this see M. A. Jeeves, *The Scientific Enterprise and Christian Faith* (IVP, 1969); D. M. MacKay, *Science and Christian Faith Today* (Falcon Booklet, 1960).
18. D. M. MacKay, 'Complementarity II': *Aristotelian Soc. Suppt.* 32 (1958), pp. 105–122.
19. R. W. Hepburn, *Christianity and Paradox* (Watts, 1958).

Chapter 15 – The sovereignty of God in the natural world

1. Paper read at International Conference of Research Scientists' Christian Fellowship, Oxford, 1965. Subsequently published in *Scottish Journal of Theology*, 21, 13–26 (Scottish Academic Press, 1968).
2. On this see the following writings by Donald MacKay: 'Brain and Will', *The Listener*, 9 and 16 May 1957; also (revised) in *Body & Mind*, ed. G. N. A. Vesey (Allen & Unwin,

1964), pp. 392–402; Part I in *A Modern Introduction to Philosophy*, revised edition, ed. Edwards and Pap (The Free Press, New York, 1965), pp. 38–42; 'On the Logical Indeterminacy of a Free Choice', *Mind* lxix (1960), pp. 31–40; 'Freewill and Causal Prediction', in *Cross-Cultural Understanding: Epistemology in Anthropology*, ed. F. S. C. Northrop and Helen Livingston (Harper and Row, 1964), pp. 162–179; 'Information and Prediction in Human Sciences', in *Information and Prediction in Science*, ed. S. Dockx and P. Bernays (*Symp. of Int. Acad. for Phil. of Science, 1962*, Academic Press, New York, 1965); *Freedom of Action in a Mechanistic Universe* (Cambridge University Press, 1967).
3. Dorothy Sayers, *The Mind of the Maker* (Methuen, 1941).
4. *E.g.* in Colossians 1:16–17; Hebrews 1:3.
5. D. M. MacKay, *op. cit.*; K. R. Popper, 'Indeterminism in Classical and Quantum Physics', *Brit. J. Phil. Sci.* 1 (1950), pp. 117–133 and 173–195.
6. A further distinction is of course necessary in biblical theology between God-manifest-in-time in Jesus Christ, and in the Holy Spirit. My intention is not – Heaven forbid! – to present a *theory* of the nature of God, but only to point out that the need to recognize more than one 'person' in the Godhead is logically implicit in the notion of God as a Creator who interacts with his creation.

Chapter 16 – The mythology of chance
1. Originally appeared in *Science, Chance and Providence* (Oxford University Press, 1978).
2. Pierre Simon Laplace, *A Philosophical Essay on Probabilities*, 6th edn., trans. F. W. Truscott and F. L. Emory (Dover, New York, 1961), p. 4.
3. A. Einstein, Letter in *The Born-Einstein Letters*, translated by Irene Born (Macmillan, New York, 1971), p. 149.
4. *Ibid.*, p. 82.
5. This is well expressed by R. J. Spilsbury in *Providence Lost: A critique of Darwinism* (Oxford University Press, London, 1974), p. 115n.: 'Creative ideas are unpredictable, but are not the fruit of an aimed-at unpredictability.'
6. Jacques Monod, *Chance and Necessity* (Collins, London, 1972), pp. 110, 136, 137, 167.
7. For a penetrating analysis of the contrasts between biblical and Greek concepts of creation, see M. B. Foster, 'The Christian Doctrine of Creation and the Rise of Modern Science', *Mind*, 43 (1934), pp. 439–466.
8. Lewis Carroll, *Alice through the Looking Glass*, chapter vii.
9. G. G. Simpson, *The Meaning of Evolution* (Yale University Press, New Haven, 1949), p. 344.
10. C. E. Shannon and W. Weaver, *The Mathematical Theory of Communication* (University of Illinois Press), 1949; D. M. MacKay, *Information, Mechanism and Meaning* (MIT Press, Cambridge, Mass., 1969).
11. L. M. Spetner, 'Natural Selection: An Information-Transmission Mechanism for Evolution', *J. Theoret Biol.* 7 (1964), pp. 412–419; 'A New Look at the Theory of Evolution', in *Challenge: Torah Views on Science and its Problems*, ed. A. Carmell and C. Domb, (Feldheim Publishers, Jerusalem–New York, 1976); P. S. Moorhead and M. M. Kaplan (eds), *Mathematical Challenges to the Neo-Darwinian Interpretation of Evolution*, Wister Inst. Monog. No. 5 (Philadelphia, 1967).
12. See, for example, W. J. Kaufmann III, *Relativity and Cosmology* (2nd edn.) (Harper & Row, New York, 1977).

Chapter 17 – The Blind Watchmaker – a review
1. A review of the book by Richard Dawkins in *Faith and Thought*, Vol. 113, No. 2 (1987).

Chapter 18 – Christian priorities in science
1. Paper presented at the conference 'Christian Faith and Science in Society', a joint meeting of the American Scientific Affiliation, Canadian Scientific and Christian Affiliation and the Research Scientists Christian Fellowship (1985) in Oxford.
2. D. M. MacKay, '"Value-Free Knowledge" – Myth or Norm?', *Faith and Thought*, 107 (1980), pp. 202–209.

3. James 4:17; Ecclesiastes 9:10.
4. 1 Timothy 6:17.
5. Psalm 111:2.
6. R. Hooykaas, *Religion and the Rise of Modern Science* (Scottish Academic Press, 1972).
7. D. M. MacKay, 'The Sovereignty of God in the Natural World', *Scottish Journal of Theology* 21 (1968), pp. 13–26.
8. D. M. MacKay, *Science and the Quest for Meaning* (Eerdmans, Grand Rapids, 1982).
9. D. M. MacKay, *The Clockwork Image: A Christian Perspective on Science* (IVP, 1974).
10. Psalm 2:4.
11. Oliver O'Donovan, *Begotten or Made?* (Oxford University Press, 1984).
12. K. R. Popper, *The Open Universe* (Hutchinson, 1982).
13. Peter Medawar, *The Limits of Science* (Oxford, 1984).
14. Geoffrey Vickers, *The Art of Judgment* (Chapman & Hall, 1965); *Freedom in a Rocking Boat* (Allen Lane, 1970).
15. 1 Samuel 21:6.
16. Mark 2:25–26.

Index